"I am delighted to see the work on the ICNALE corpus coming to fruition. In this volume the scale and importance of the corpus are made clear both by a careful description of its contents, but also by a good survey of the research context that ICNALE contributes to. The research possibilities opened up by ICNALE are shown in a host of fascinating studies of learner language. These cover topics as diverse as vocabulary, pragmatics and paralinguistic features. Ishikawa has produced a book which all researchers interested in learner language, especially in East Asian contexts, must read."

Tony McEnery, Lancaster University

"This book by Shin Ishikawa is the culmination of years of work with one of the best learner corpus resources available – the ICNALE. This practical introduction to learner corpus studies of written and spoken L2 registers is a goldmine for teachers and researchers of L2 vocabulary, grammar and pragmatics, while also covering lesser-explored areas of gesture and assessment through Shin's wonderful ICNALE resource. As a regular user of the ICNALE, this guide is essential reading for both experts and newcomers to the field of LCR, and stands to make an amazing contribution to language teaching and learning."

Peter Crosthwaite, University of Queensland

"This is the first comprehensive introduction to the ICNALE project directed by Shin Ishikawa. The ICNALE is arguably one of the most ambitious and well-designed corpus projects for its international scope, unique design criteria, and rich metadata. This book will provide an overview of the project as well as major findings from the corpus, which will serve as an invaluable resource for anyone interested in researching the use of the English language by Asian learners or users and how their usage or use will be affected by various learner and environmental factors."

Yukio Tono, Tokyo University of Foreign Studies

THE ICNALE GUIDE

This book provides a practical and extensive guide for the International Corpus Network of Asian Learners of English (ICNALE), a unique dataset including more than 15,000 samples of Asian learners' L2 English speeches and essays. It also offers approachable introductions to a variety of corpus studies on the aspects of Asian learners' L2 English.

Key topics discussed in the book include:

- background, aims, and methods of learner corpus research,
- principles, designs, and applications of the ICNALE,
- vocabulary, grammar, and pragmatics in Asian learners' L2 English, and
- individual differences of Asian learners and assessments of their speeches and essays.

With many case studies and hands-on guides to utilise ICNALE data to the fullest extent, *The ICNALE Guide* is a unique resource for students, teachers, and researchers who are interested in a corpus-based analysis of L2 acquisition.

Shin'ichiro Ishikawa is Professor of Applied Linguistics at the School of Languages & Communication, Kobe University, Japan. His research interests cover corpus linguistics, statistical linguistics, TESOL, and SLA. He has been a leader of the ICNALE learner corpus project.

THE ICNALE GUIDE

An Introduction to a Learner Corpus Study on Asian Learners' L2 English

Shin'ichiro Ishikawa

Routledge
Taylor & Francis Group
LONDON AND NEW YORK

Designed cover image: © Getty Images

First published 2023
by Routledge
4 Park Square, Milton Park, Abingdon, Oxon OX14 4RN

and by Routledge
605 Third Avenue, New York, NY 10158

Routledge is an imprint of the Taylor & Francis Group, an informa business

British Library Cataloguing-in-Publication Data
A catalogue record for this book is available from the British Library

ISBN: 978-1-032-17259-0 (hbk)
ISBN: 978-1-032-18025-0 (pbk)
ISBN: 978-1-003-25252-8 (ebk)

DOI: 10.4324/9781003252528

Typeset in Bembo
by SPi Technologies India Pvt Ltd (Straive)

CONTENTS

PART II
Aspects of Asian Learners' L2 English Use 71

FIGURES

TABLES

ACKNOWLEDGEMENTS

First of all, my warmest thanks go to all who contributed to the ICNALE project, including the college students from China, Hong Kong, Indonesia, Japan, Korea, Malaysia, Pakistan, the Philippines, Singapore, Taiwan, and Thai, who provided their spoken and written L2 output samples, the international collaborating researchers, who were in charge of collecting data from local students, and many other professionals such as transcribers, software developers, and web designers. In addition, I would like to thank Sylviane Granger, Andrew Hardie, Chiaki Iwai, Andy Kirkpatrick, Rie Koizumi, Tony McEnery, Masumi Narita, Vincent Ooi, Kumiko Sakoda, and Yukio Tono, who joined the ICNALE symposia held in Japan as keynote speakers and gave many valuable comments for the project. My thanks also go to colleagues at Routledge, especially Katie Peace, Payal Bharti, Khin Thazin, Yassar Arafat, and Ting Baker who helped me complete this publication. I also deeply thank the Japan Society for the Promotion of Science for their continuing support. ICNALE has been developed on the basis of the support of the MEXT/JSPS KAKENHI Grant (19720135, 22320104, 24652120, 25284104, 15K12909, 17H02360, 20H01282). Finally, I am grateful to Yuka Ishikawa for her continuous encouragements and devoted supports.

ABBREVIATIONS

CEFR	Common European Framework of Reference for Languages
CHN	China/Chinese
CIA	contrastive interlanguage analysis
CL	corpus linguistics
EFL	English as a foreign language
ELF	English as a lingua franca
ENS	L1 English native speaker(s)
ESL	English as a second language
HKG	Hong Kong
ICLE	International Corpus of Learner English
ICNALE	International Corpus Network of Asian Learners of English
IDN	Indonesia/Indonesian
JPN	Japan/Japanese
KOR	Korea/Korean
LC	learner corpus/corpora
LCR	learner corpus research
LINDSEI	Louvain Interlanguage Database of Spoken English Interlanguage
MYS	Malaysia/Malaysian
PAK	Pakistan/Pakistani
PHL	The Philippines/Philippine
PTJ	a part-time job for college students (a topic in the ICNALE)
SIN	Singapore/Singaporean
SMK	non-smoking at restaurants (a topic in the ICNALE)
THA	Thailand/Thai
TWN	Taiwan/Taiwanese

PART I

Introduction to the Learner Corpus Research

1

LEARNER CORPUS RESEARCH

An Overview

1.1 Background

Corpus refers to a wide range of "collection of naturally occurring language text, chosen to characterise a state or variety of language" (Sinclair, 1991, p. 171). As one of its subtypes, learner corpus (LC) is defined as a "computer textual database, of the language produced by foreign language learners" (Leech, 1998) or "electronic collections of writing or speech produced by foreign or second language learners" (Gilquin & Granger, 2015, p. 418). LC-based studies are often called learner corpus research (LCR).

The history of corpus linguistics (CL) is said to date back to the 1960s, when Brown Corpus, a one-million-word collection of written texts published in the US, was compiled. Meanwhile, it is unclear when LCR began in the history of linguistics. McEnery and Hardie (2012) mention Dulay and Burt (1973) and Krashen et al. (1978) as examples of "work based on what might very broadly be termed learner corpus data" (p. 82). The former collected English oral outputs from 151 Spanish-speaking children, and the latter collected English writing samples from 70 adult students with different first-language (L1) backgrounds. These datasets were used to test the natural order hypothesis that children who learn English as a second language (L2) acquire a set of grammatical morphemes in a predetermined "natural" order, despite the differences in their backgrounds. The data they had collected might be called an LC archetype, but it was prepared mainly for the verification of a particular acquisition theory, and there was neither enough data nor was it representative of the target population.

Since the 1980s, thanks to the spread of computers, many large-sized L1 English corpora have been compiled, and a set of corpus analytical techniques such as KWIC (keyword-in-context) search, frequency-list generation, collocation

DOI: 10.4324/9781003252528-2

search, and statistical keyword identification has been introduced. Such a drastic change in linguistics influenced the researchers who were interested in the descriptive analysis of learners' L2 outputs. Granger et al. (2015) note that a new research strand of LCR "emerged in the late 1980s as an offshoot of corpus linguistics, a field which had shown great potential in investigating a wide range of native language varieties (diachronic, stylistic, regional) but had neglected the non-native varieties" (p. 1).

Problematising such underrepresentation of a "foreign learner variety of English," Sylviane Granger and her team at Université catholique de Louvain in Belgium decided to compile a new dataset with a "focus on the L2 output itself" (Granger, 1993). Then, they collaborated with researchers mainly in Europe and began collecting academic essays written by advanced college students. The team collected more than 3,600 essays, whose size amounts to 2.5 million words. They were released under the name of the International Corpus of Learner English (ICLE) in 2002 (Granger et al., 2002). ICLE contributed a great deal to the establishment of LCR as a new research field integrating CL, foreign language teaching, linguistic theory, and second language acquisition (SLA) (Granger, 2009). It also enabled researchers to discuss the aspects of learners' interlanguage, a linguistic system independent from their native and target languages (Selinker, 1972), from a new empirical viewpoint. Granger (1998) showcases a variety of research based on the data collected during the early stage of the ICLE project. As McEnery and Hardie (2012) emphasise, there is "little doubt that Granger's work on learner corpora has stimulated a whole new field" of research, in that it has developed a new "link between two previously disparate fields of corpus linguistics and foreign/second language research" (Granger, 2002).

Availability of ICLE and other sizable LC means that three critical principles of CL as a science—replicability, total accountability, and falsifiability (McEnery and Hardie, 2012, pp. 14–16)— have also been fulfilled in LCR. A publicly accessible LC guarantees the replicability of a research finding: anyone can check and recheck a reported finding by reanalysing the same dataset. It also requires a researcher to account for the whole of the data rather than a few examples fitting a theory that one wishes to support. This leads to falsifiability (Popper, 1934). If a researcher intentionally chooses a set of samples supporting their claim, it could never be invalidated. In this sense, using "the entire corpus—and all relevant evidence emerging from analysis of the corpus" is a necessary process when testing a hypothesis in a scientific manner.

LCR has developed into a rich melting pot of varied research fields, including linguistics, SLA, foreign and second language teaching, natural language processing (NLP), and more. It has also come to discuss a variety of L2 learners, including learners of Spanish (Czerwionka & Olson, 2020), German (Belz et al., 2017), French (Deshors, 2018), Finnish (Kekki & Ivaska, 2022), Chinese (Zhang, 2014), Korean (Shin & Jung, 2021), and Japanese (Ishikawa, 2017). This book focuses on the LCR of L2 English learners, especially in Asia.

1.2 Learner Corpora

1.2.1 ICLE and LINDSEI

Sylviane Granger's team released two ground-breaking LC: the International Corpus of Learner English (ICLE) and the Louvain International Database of Spoken English Interlanguage (LINDSEI) (Gilquin et al., 2010). Both of them are used most widely in LCR, and they have become a model for many other LC.

First, we would like to have a brief look at ICLE. As mentioned above, its first version (ICLE1) was released in 2002 (Granger et al., 2002). It included 3,640 essays (2.5 million words) produced by European learners, which were subdivided into 11 national subcorpora. The team continued their efforts in data collection, which led to the release of the second version (ICLE2) in 2009 (Granger et al., 2009). It included 6,085 essays (3.7 million words) by a greater variety of learners, which were subdivided into 16 subcorpora. Then, the third version (ICLE3) appeared in 2020 (Granger et al., 2020). It includes 9,529 essays (5.7 million words) by international learners, which are subdivided into 25 subcorpora covering Europe (Bulgarian, Czech, Dutch, Finnish, French, German, Greek, Hungarian, Italian, Lithuanian, Macedonian, Norwegian, Polish, Russian, Serbian, Spanish, and Swedish), Asia (Chinese, Japanese, Korean, and Pakistani), the Middle East (Iranian and Turkish), and the other areas (Tswana and Brazilian).

ICLE collects its data from university undergraduates in English, mostly in their third or fourth year. Seen from the external criterion of a school year, they are all regarded as advanced learners. However, a small verification study, in which the ICLE team made 500 sample essays assessed by raters, shows that around 40% of the participants may be at B2 or lower level (Granger et al., 2020, pp. 11–12) on the proficiency scale of the Common European Framework of Reference for Languages (CEFR) (Council of Europe, 2001). Regarding gender, approximately 77% of the participants are reported to be female (p. 6).

Around 94% of the collected samples are argumentative essays, and the remaining are literary essays and others (Granger et al., 2020, pp. 13–14). They cover a wide range of topics: the total number of topics in ICLE1 was 922 (Granger et al., 2002, p. 18). The top three most popular topics are "Some people say that in our modern world, dominated by science, technology and industrialization, there is no longer a place for dreaming and imagination. What is your opinion?" "Most university degrees are theoretical and do not prepare us/students for the real world/life," and "Marx once said that religion was the opium of the masses. If he was alive at the beginning of the 21st century, he would replace religion with television" (Granger et al., 2020, pp. 15–16). The average essay length is 605 words (p. 15); 35% of the essays are timed (p. 17), 28% are written under the exam condition (p. 17), and 44% are written with the help of reference tools (p. 18).

All the ICLE data is lemmatised and part-of-speech (POS) tagged with the Constituent Likelihood Automatic Word-tagging System (CLAWS) C7 tagset (pp. 20–22). In addition, some data are error-tagged (Granger et al., 2009, pp. 43–44). Details of the tagging procedures are introduced in the project's tagging manual (Dagneaux et al., 2008), which has been recently updated (Granger et al., 2022). Error tags help corpus users to conduct a computer-aided error analysis (CAE). Granger (2003) also suggests a possible "synergy" of error-tagged LC and computer-aided language learning (CALL).

ICLE does not include the comparable essays of L1 English native speakers (ENS), but users are recommended to refer to the Louvain Corpus of Native English Essays (LOCNESS) (Granger, 2005), a 320,000-word collection of British pupils' A-level essays, British university students' essays, and American university students' essays.

Next, we will survey major aspects of LINDSEI. LINDSEI, which was released in 2010, is the first full-scale dataset of learner speeches. It includes around 790,000-word speeches collected from 554 learners, which are subdivided into 11 national subcorpora covering Europe (Bulgarian, Dutch, French, German, Greek, Italian, Polish, Spanish, and Swedish) and Asia (Chinese and Japanese).

As in the case of ICLE, the participants are university undergraduates in English in their third or fourth year, and they are regarded as advanced learners. However, a verification study based on the assessments of 50 sample speeches suggests that 64% of the participants may be at B2 or lower level. Corpus developers, therefore, conclude that "the proficiency level in LINDSEI is best described as ranging from higher intermediate to advanced" (Gilquin et al., 2010, pp. 10–11). Then, regarding gender, approximately 79% of the participants are reported to be female (p. 33).

Speech data is collected from interviews, which consist of three tasks: set topic, free discussion, and picture description. First, participants are presented with three topics (an experience that has taught them an important lesson, a country that has impressed them, and a film/play that was good or bad for them), and after a few minutes of preparation, they are told to talk about one of them for three to five minutes. Next, participants answer the questions given by an interviewer, some of which concern the chosen topic. Finally, they are presented with four pictures and told to make up a story and describe what they saw (p. 8). The mean duration of an interview is around 14 minutes (p. 31), and the mean number of tokens uttered by a participant is 1,430 words (p. 25)—44% in a set topic, 40% in a free discussion, and 16% in a picture description—(p. 29).

LINDSEI adopts various types of speech tags to show how learners actually spoke in the interviews, which cover pauses, filled pauses, unclear passages, truncation, overlapping, laughing, coughing, and so on (pp. 13–18).

Comparable ENS speeches are not included, but users can refer to the Louvain Corpus of Native English Conversation (LOCNEC) (De Cock, 1995), which includes 120,000-word interview speeches taken from 50 British university students.

Although LINDSEI is usually classified as a learner speech corpus, the developers carefully use the term "database" rather than "corpus." This is because they think the collected speeches may not be entirely natural in that they were "not produced for real communicative purposes" (pp. 5–6), and therefore they may not meet a prerequisite of a corpus as a "collection of naturally occurring language text" (Sinclair, 1991, p. 171).

1.2.2 Recently Developed LC

Releases of ICLE and LINDSEI have given an impetus to the development of a great variety of LC in the world. Here we like to have a brief look at some of the recently developed LC. Most of them aim to cover up the weakness in the first-generation LC by focusing on (i) young learner data, (ii) longitudinal data, (iii) phonological data, (iv) multi-lingual data, and (v) data quantity.

First, the International Corpus of Crosslinguistic Interlanguage (ICCI) collects more than 530,000-word essays from young learners of English in Grade 3–12 in Austria, China, Hong Kong, Israel, Poland, Spain, and Taiwan (Tono, 2012; Tono & Díez-Bedmar, 2014). This dataset is comparable to the JEFLL Corpus (Tono, 2007), a 670,000-word collection of essays written by secondary school students in Japan.

Second, the University of Pittsburgh English Language Institute Corpus (PELIC) includes 4.2-million-word essays written by more than 1,100 students joining an intensive English program offered at the university. The data is collected several times during a semester or a few semesters (Naismith et al., 2022). Then, the Longitudinal Learner Corpus in Italiano, Deutsch, English (LEONIDE) includes 240,000-word essays that 163 lower secondary school students wrote in their L1 (Italian and German), L2 (German and Italian), and L3 (English). The data is collected over the span of three consecutive years (Glaznieks et al., 2022). These datasets, which are usually called longitudinal or developmental LC (see Section 1.2.4), enable researchers to analyse individual learners' progress in L2 in a direct manner.

Third, the Interphonology of Contemporary English Corpus (IPCE-IPAC) includes the phoneme-level pronunciation data collected in a variety of word/sentence/text-level read-aloud tasks. The data are collected in France, Italy, Spain, and China (Herry-Bénit et al., 2021). Such a dataset promotes the study of learners' acquisition of segmental and suprasegmental features in L2.

Fourth, the Diapix Foreign Language (DiapixFL) Corpus includes the bilingual speeches of L1 English learners of Spanish and L1 Spanish learners of English, who converse to solve a picture-based "spot-the-difference" task in their L1 and L2 (Lecumberri et al., 2017). Also, as mentioned above, LEONIDE includes learners' trilingual output data.

Finally, several LC aim to collect a larger amount of L2 output samples from existing data sources. For example, the Trinity Lancaster Corpus (TLC) includes more than four million-word speeches of over 2,000 learners with different L1 and cultural backgrounds and at different proficiency levels. The data is all from the Graded Examinations in Spoken English (GESE) administered by Trinity College London (Gablasova et al., 2019). The ETS Corpus of Non-Native Written English includes 12,000 essays that learners with 11 L1 backgrounds wrote during the Test of English as a Foreign Language (TOEFL) (Blanchard et al., 2014). Then, the EF-Cambridge Open Language Database (EFCAMDAT) includes 83-million-word essays written by more than 170,000 learners with varied L1 backgrounds and at varied CEFR levels in the world. These essays, which were originally submitted to an online language school administered by EF Education First, are processed by NLP techniques (Alexopoulou et al., 2005). Thus, the corpus now includes the data of dependency parsing (Huang et al., 2018). The details of the recent update and modification of the corpus (EFCAMDAT2) are reported in Shatz (2020).

As briefly surveyed above, a variety of LC have been compiled to date. There is much to be learned from the experience of developing a corpus. Kwon et al. (2018) introduce the process of compiling their "local" corpus, which includes essays written by first-year international students at a US university. They report that the collaborative experience of corpus compilation has led to the significant growth of faculty members and graduate students as writing instructors.

1.2.3 LC and Asian Learner Data

Then, to what extent do existing LC cover the L2 English outputs of Asian learners? Among major international LC introduced above, ICLE3 includes essays of Chinese, Japanese, Korean, and Pakistani learners, and LINDSEI collects speech data from Chinese and Japanese learners. Also, JEFLL/ICCI include essays of young learners in China, Hong Kong, Japan, and Taiwan; TLC includes speeches of test-takers from China, India, and Sri Lanka; and ETS Corpus includes essays of test-takers with L1 Chinese, Hindi, Japanese, Korean, and Telugu backgrounds. As another example, the UCLan Speaking Test Corpus (USTC) (Jones et al., 2018) collects interview speeches of test-takers from China, Japan, and Korea.

In addition, there exists a variety of local LC, a part of which is listed in "Learner Corpora around the World," an online LC directory maintained at Université catholique de Louvain. Table 1.1 shows some of the locally compiled LC that collect more than 500,000-word data from a particular L1 group in Asia.

When combining large-scaled international LC with several locally compiled LC shown above, it seems that we already have access to a sufficient amount of L2 English output samples from Asian learners. However, there still remain several problems.

First, L1 or regional coverage is not necessarily enough. Most of the existing LC collect data from learners in China, Japan, and Korea, and sometimes from learners in India, Pakistan, and Malaysia. It is clear that a greater variety of Asian learners should be covered as the number of English learners is booming in every corner of the region.

Second, as different corpora adopt different data collection schemes, we cannot directly compare the findings obtained from them. What matters is to collect comparable data.

Third, the quantity of speech data is still scant in comparison to that of essay data, though this can be a problem common to LC and native corpora (De Cock, 2010, p. 123).

Fourth, some of the existing LC do not seem to offer detailed metadata about learners' backgrounds. Gilquin (2015) emphasises that "many of the variables that affect the nature of interlanguage concern the learners themselves," which include

TABLE 1.1 Major locally compiled LC including Asian learner data

L1	*Major locally compiled LC (size)*
Chinese	[S] College Learners' Spoken English Corpus (COLSEC), 0.7M
	[W] Chinese Learner English Corpus (CLEC), 1M
	[W] Ten Thousand English Compositions of Chinese Learners (TECCL), 1.8M
	[W] Hong Kong University of Science & Technology (HKUST) Learner Corpus, 25M
	[W] Taiwanese Corpus of Learner English (TLCE), 2M
	[SW] Bilingual Corpus of Chinese English Learners (BICCEL), 2M
	[SW] Spoken and Written English Corpus of Chinese Learners (SWECCL), 2M
	[SW] TELEC Secondary Learner Corpus (TSLC), 2M
Japanese	[S] NICT Japanese Learner English Corpus (NICT-JLE), 2M
	[W] Japanese EFL Learner Corpus (JEFLL), 0.7M
	[W] SILS Learner Corpus of English, 3.2M
Korean	[W] Seoul National University Korean-speaking English Learner Corpus (SKELC), 0.9M
	[W] Yonsei English Learner Corpus (YELC), 1M
	[W] Gachon Learner Corpus, 2.5M
	[SW] Neungyule Interlanguage Corpus of Korean Learners of English (NICKLE), 1M
Malay	[W] English of Malaysian School Students Corpus (EMAS), 0.5M
	[W] Malaysian Corpus of Students' Argumentative Writing (MCSAW), 0.5M

Notes: [S] and [W] represent spoken and written corpora. [SW] refers to corpora including both spoken and written data. Some LC (e.g., SILS, Gachon, MCSAW) also include a small amount of data taken from the other L1 speakers.

age, gender, country/area (region), mother tongue, proficiency level, exposure to the target language inside or outside the classroom, knowledge of other foreign languages, L2 learning motivation, and so on (p. 17). If these metadata are not appropriately recorded and made public, corpus users just have "nothing but disconnected words of unknowable provenance or authenticity" (Burnard, 2005, p. 31).

Finally, and most importantly, many of the local LC listed above do not seem to be (readily) available at the time of writing this book. Examining the availability of major LC developed in Korea, Yoon (2020) concludes that most of them have become publicly unavailable. McEnery and Hardie (2012) emphasise that corpus builders need to make sure that "the data they hold remains intact and available" and ensure that "the data they produce is made available to analysts in the future" because "a key goal of corpus linguistics is to aim for replicability of results" (p. 66), but it is not easy for an individual researcher and even for an institute to assure the access to the collected data for many decades with regularly maintaining its content. These backgrounds explain why the author of this volume has decided to compile the International Corpus Network of Asian Learners of English (ICNALE).

1.2.4 Typology of LC Data

As introduced in Section 1.1, LC are usually defined as "electronic collections of writing or speech produced by foreign or second language learners" (Gilquin & Granger, 2015, p. 418). Though this definition is balanced and reasonable, in reality, there is a great diversity in the types of LC data.

LC researchers, therefore, are required to carefully consider (i) how "foreign or second language learners" are defined, (ii) what type of "writing" or "speech" data is included, and (iii) how data "collections" are made in each of the available LC and choose the one most suitable for their research purposes. Table 1.2 illustrates a part of the possible LC data diversity.

We would like to begin by discussing three learner-related categories. First, regarding the age or school year, many of the existing LC collect data from learners within a specific age range. For example, the participants of JEFLL are secondary school students, those of Yonsei Corpus are pre-university students (high-school graduates), and those of ICLE/LINDSEI are college students in their third or fourth year.

Second, regarding the learner proficiency, most LC collect data from learners at a narrow proficiency level. JEFLL/ICCI collect data from beginner and novice learners, and ICLE/LINDSEI collect data from advanced (or at least expected-to-be-advanced) learners. It should be noted that different LC may adopt different approaches to estimate learner proficiency and define the range of learners in a different manner. Learner proficiency is estimated in terms of a school year in ICLE/LINDSEI, an external test score in ICNALE (see Section 2.2.4.2), and an output

TABLE 1.2 LC data types

	Category	*Major subcategories*
(i)	Age/School Year	Children
		Secondary school students
		College students
		Adult speakers
	Proficiency	Beginner (pre-A1) and Novice (A1–A2)
		Intermediate (B1–B2)
		Advanced (C1–C2)
		Professional (English as a lingua franca: ELF)
	Area	Local/domestic
		International
(ii)	Production Mode	Written (academic essays, business letters, research papers)
		Spoken (monologue, dialogue, interview)
(iii)	Data Modality	Mono-modal (text only)
		Multi-modal (text + audio/video)
	Period	Cross-sectional (data collected at one time)
		Longitudinal (data collected over time)
	Annotation	Unannotated
		Annotated (POS/error/speech feature)

assessment by raters in ICCI, TLC, and NICT-JLE, for example. Also, there exist varied standpoints as regards whether professional L2 speakers should be regarded as learners. For example, the Michigan Corpus of Academic Spoken English (MICASE) includes the outputs of non-ENS US college students (Simpson-Vlach & Leicher, 2006), and the Vienna-Oxford International Corpus of English (VOICE) includes the outputs of speakers of English as a lingua franca (ELF), a specific type of English used mainly for professional communication between non-native speakers with different L1 backgrounds (Seidlhofer, 2012; Jenkins, 2009). Though these datasets are usually distinguished from LC, Friginal (2018) regards both as "spoken learner corpora" (pp. 93 –97).

Third, different LC have different regional targets. Some LC collect data from one L1/regional group. For example, COLSEC collects data only from China. Other LC collect data from several countries in a particular area, such as Europe (ICLE1) and Asia (ICNALE). Also, some larger LC—ICLE3, TLC, EFCAMDAT, for example—aim to collect data globally.

Next, we would like to consider the L2 production modes. A great majority of existing LC include written outputs only, though they may collect different types of written outputs. For example, ICLE collects argumentative and literary essays, ICNALE collects argumentative essays only, and JEFLL/ICCI collect argumentative and narrative essays. Meanwhile, spoken outputs have been collected less extensively, which is because speech collection usually takes more time and cost. Spoken corpus developers are usually required to prepare recording devices, recruit the participants, design a speech elicitation task, record their oral outputs, establish a transcription protocol, which determines how fillers (e.g., "ah," "ahh," "uh," etc.), pauses, mispronunciations (e.g., "I *sink"), and false starts (e.g., "I, I …, no, you …") should be transcribed into texts, transcribe each of the collected speeches, and carefully check or double-check the final transcripts. Speeches can be collected by using various elicitation tasks: monologue data is collected from sentence reading and story description tasks, while dialogue data is usually taken from oral proficiency interviews (OPI) (Yoon, 2020). It should be noted that there exist a few LC that collect both speeches and essays—the Longitudinal Database of Learner English (LONGDALE) (Meunier, 2015b; see below), SWECCL, and ICNALE, for example.

Finally, we will discuss three factors related to data collection. First, regarding speech data modality, almost all of the existing spoken LC are monomodal in that they include transcribed texts only. However, discussing the aspects of learner speeches only with the transcripts would be extremely difficult. For example, researchers cannot decide how "yes" in the transcript is actually pronounced by a learner. They may have simply shown agreement, or instead, they may have tried to show disagreement by pronouncing it with a rising intonation. However, with sound data, researchers can analyse the phonological elements of learner speeches, including pronunciation and intonation. They can also look into learners' use of pauses and various non-lexical fillers. In addition, with video data, they can also scrutinise the learners' use of eye contact and body language during their speeches, and even their emotions represented in their facial expressions. Although the number of multimodal spoken

LC that include audio and/or video in addition to transcripts is still quite small, one exception is ICNALE (see Section 2.2.5). A combined analysis of speech transcripts, audio, and video would expand the scope of LCR.

Second, regarding the data collection period, Whong and Wright (2013) suggest that most LC include cross-sectional data obtained at a single point in time from a large number of learners “placed in low, intermediate and advanced proficiency groups,” while very few include longitudinal data obtained by following “the same set of learners over a certain length of time (usually at least six months) in order to document the development of individual interlanguage grammars.” When using the cross-sectional LC, researchers often compare the data of novice and advanced learners to “indirectly” discuss L2 development, which is sometimes called a quasi-longitudinal analysis. Meanwhile, when using the longitudinal data, they can discuss learners’ L2 development in a more direct manner. As easily expected, collecting longitudinal data is much more challenging than collecting cross-sectional data because of the “practical reason of time—both in terms of commitment by the researcher and the continued participation by the learners”. As one of the few longitudinal LC, LONGDALE follows the same students for three to four years and regularly collects their spoken and written outputs (Meunier, 2015b).

Third, many of the LC offer raw (i.e., unannotated) texts and part-of-speech (POS) tagged texts. Processed with Constituent Likelihood Automatic Word-tagging System (CLAWS) C5 tagset, a sentence of “There were three apples on the table” is annotated as “There_EX0 were_VBD three_CRD apples_NN2 on_PRP the_AT0 table_NN1.” These tags, such as EX (existential *there*), VBD (past form of *be*-verb), CRD (cardinal), NN (noun), PRP (preposition), and AT (article), would enable researchers to discuss the linguistic features of learner texts in greater detail. It should be noted, however, that different LC often adopt different tagsets or different automatic tagging systems, which leads to incomparability of the tag data from different LC. In addition to the POS tags, some LC offer error tags: NICT-JLE Corpus, for example, annotates a sentence of “Usually, museum open on Saturday and Sunday” as “Usually, <at crr=“the“></at> museum <v_agr crr=“opens“>open</v_agr> on <n_num crr=“Saturdays“>Saturday</n_num> and <n_num crr=“Sundays”>Sunday</n_num>,” which suggests that “museum” should be corrected to “the museum” (at/article error), “open” to “opens” (v_agr/verb agreement error), “Saturday” and “Sunday” to “Saturdays” and “Sundays” (n_mum/noun number errors). Also, some spoken LC offer speech features tags to represent how each word is actually pronounced: LINDSEI, for example, adopts a set of tags such as <overlapping>, <…> (long pause), <coughs>, and <starts laughing>.

1.3 Method and Scope

1.3.1 Techniques and Approaches

As in the case of LC in general, there exist various data analytical techniques and approaches that can be adopted in LCR.

First, regarding techniques, LC researchers can utilise almost all of the techniques that have been proposed in CL. For example, they examine how learners use a particular word or phrase in the context (concordance analysis or keyword-in-context [KWIC] analysis), how they use a word in a particular collocation pattern (collocation analysis), and how often learners use various sets of vocabulary (frequency analysis), and they also compare the outputs of learners and ENS or those of learners with different backgrounds to identify keywords, that is, a set of the words characteristically overused or underused by the target learner group (statistical keyword analysis). Keyness is usually measured by statistical values such as chi-squared values and log-likelihood ratios (LLR or G^2).

Second, regarding approaches to corpus data and a theory, LC researchers, just like CL researchers, choose their orientation between the two ends: "corpus-as-theory" and "corpus-as-method" approaches or, more simply, "corpus-driven" and "corpus-informed" approaches. As McEnery and Hardie (2012) illustrate (pp. 147–152), at the early stage of the development of CL, the "corpus-as-theory" approach, which refuses to bring existing theories into corpus analysis and aims to create new theories from corpus data itself, attracted much attention. Sinclair (2004) insisted on the need to "trust the text" rather than a theory, and Tognini-Bonelli (2001) mentioned the need for CL to "define its own sets of rules and pieces of knowledge" without "accepting certain facts as *given*" (p. 1). Though such a view may seem novel and catchy, it would be almost impossible to analyse learner data in a meaningful way without any knowledge about language and language learning. Criticising that such an attitude may eventually lead to an irrational rejection of effective CL practices such as text sampling and corpus annotation, McEnery and Hardie (2012) conclude that it is only the "corpus-as-method" approach that stimulates theoretical innovations (p. 163).

1.3.2 Contrastive Interlanguage Analysis

Many of the LC-based studies adopt an analytical method called contrastive interlanguage analysis (CIA). CIA is a practical technique to effectively analyse the features of learner outputs, but at the same time, it is a kind of theoretical framework to discuss L2 acquisition, especially the effect of L1 transfer in it.

CIA was proposed in Granger (1996) and then revised in Granger (2015), which we call CIA1 and CIA2, respectively. The outlines of these two models are shown in Table 1.3.

TABLE 1.3 Original and revised CIA models

CIA1 (Granger, 1996)	*CIA2 (Granger, 2015)*
[NL vs. IL] | [IL vs. IL]	[RLV vs. RLV vs. RLV] vs. [ILV vs. ILV vs. ILV vs. ILV]

Notes: NL and IL represent native language and interlanguage. RLV and ILV represent reference language varieties and interlanguage varieties.

CIA1 consists of a comparison between a native language (NL) and an interlanguage (IL) and an additional comparison between different interlanguages. The former helps researchers identify the divergence seen in the interlanguage of the target learner group. The latter helps them decide whether the divergence is specific to that group, which means that the problem is caused by an L1 transfer, or it is common to a variety of learner groups, which suggests that the problem should be attributed to a general L2 acquisition pattern. For example, by comparing the essays of Chinese learners of English to those of ENS as a yardstick, we can identify the divergent features of Chinese learners' L2 English. Then, by comparing the essays of Chinese learners to those of Japanese or Korean learners, we can investigate whether the features observed in the first comparison are unique to Chinese learners or not, in other words, whether they are the results of the transfer from L1 Chinese or not.

These comparisons are usually conducted with a keyword identification function incorporated in major corpus analytical tools such as AntConc (Anthony, 2022) and Wordsmith Tools (Scott, 2020). These tools automatically count the frequency of all the words appearing in a target text and a reference text and identify the words occurring significantly more or less in the target text, which are interpreted as "overuse" or "underuse" by a target group.

CIA1, which was a simple but powerful analytical technique, spread widely in LCR, but its use of ENS outputs as a yardstick of comparison was severely criticised (see Section 2.2.6). Thus, CIA2 (Granger, 2015) replaces the term "native language" with "reference language" and emphasises its diatypic (i.e., register-related) and dialectal (i.e., dialect-related) variability. Also, it suggests the possible task and learner variabilities in interlanguage. CIA2 reflects a shift from "one norm to rule them all" toward diversified "corpus-derived rules" (Gilquin, 2022) in LCR, and it has come to be "more in line with the current state of foreign language theory and practice" (Callies, 2015, p. 40).

In the history of applied linguistics, CIA can be connected to three analytical frameworks proposed in the early days (see Thomas, 2013): contrastive analysis (CA) (Fries, 1945; Lado, 1957), which aimed to clarify the structural differences between L1 and L2 as a possible source of difficulties in L2 learning, error analysis (Corder, 1967), which aimed to probe the status of interlanguage by analysing learners' L2 errors, and interlanguage analysis (Selinker, 1972), which aimed to examine the whole of interlanguage as an independent linguistic system in its own right. Granger (1996) explicitly mentions the link between CA and CIA by noting that CA "went through a period of disfavour" after the 1960s, but it is re-emerging and reviving "as a major approach in translation and interlanguage studies" thanks to "the new age of computerized bilingual and learner corpora." Thus, she proposes a new "integrated CA/CIA contrastive model" to discuss L1 transfer as an SLA fact (Selinker, 1992, p. 171), which involves "constant to-ing and fro-ing between CA and CIA." CA formulates prediction about what transfer occurs in interlanguage, and then it is empirically tested with CIA, which serves as a diagnostic test of CA. The importance of such integration of CA and CIA is also illustrated in Gilquin (2000).

In addition, CIA contributes to the redefinition of error analysis and interlanguage analysis because it enables researchers to analyse misuse (errors), overuse, and underuse seen in learners' interlanguage in a combinatory way. Though identifying misuse is more challenging than identifying over/underuse, it could be facilitated by the use of error-tagged LC and software developed for computer-aided error analysis (CAE) (Dagneaux et al., 2008).

A CIA-based analysis is "a real eye-opener" in LCR (Gilquin, 2020, p. 291). As such, CIA is expected to continue to be used as a primary analytical framework of LCR.

1.3.3 Statistical Methods

Statistics have contributed much to CL in general. Recent volumes on statistics for CL (e.g., Wallis, 2021; Brezina, 2018) showcase a variety of statistical methods that we can use when analysing corpus data. Also, one of the recently published CL handbooks (Paquot & Gries, 2020) assigns nine of the 27 chapters to explanation of statistical methods, which cover (i) descriptive statistics (mean, median, interquartile range, standard deviation, coefficients of correlation, bar plots, mosaic plots, histograms, cumulative frequency plots, boxplots), (ii) cluster analysis (hierarchical clustering, k-means clustering), (iii) multivariate exploratory approaches (correspondence analysis, principal component analysis, exploratory factor analysis), (iv) monofactorial tests (null-hypothesis significance testing, parametric and non-parametric tests, chi-squared test, *t*-test, ANOVA, Mann-Whitney U test, Kruskal-Wallis test, Pearson's correlation, effect size, and confidence interval), (v) fixed-effects regression modelling ([multiple] linear regression, binary logistic regression), (vi) mixed-effects regression modelling (random effects model, hierarchical or multilevel modelling), (vii) generalised additive mixed models (generalised linear model, generalised additive model), (viii) bootstrapping techniques (bootstrap, random forest analysis), and (ix) conditional inference trees and random forests (CIT and CRF algorithm).

In comparison to CL and SLA as the two adjacent research fields, LCR utilised a narrower range of statistical methods. Paquot and Plonsky (2017) overview the statistical methods adopted in 1,276 journal papers in the LCR field and point out four common problems: relying too much on hypothesis testing, reporting mean values without standard deviations, reporting significance levels without effect sizes, and avoiding the use of multivariate analyses. Among these, a multivariate or multifactorial analysis seems to be a particularly useful method for LCR because LC data, which is usually collected from plural L1 groups, plural L2 proficiency bands, plural individuals, and plural elicitation conditions, is essentially multiple. Also, in the framework of a complex dynamic systems theory (CDST), which emphasises the importance of seeing an L2 output not as a single stable unit but as an ever-changing dynamic system, in other words, a set of numberless time-scale data pieces (see Section 7.1.1.4), LC data can be all the more manifold. In this sense, statistical techniques such as multivariate/multivariable regression analysis, cluster analysis, and correspondence analysis would help LC researchers to deal with L2 output data more appropriately.

LCR is currently "undergoing methodological reform" (Paquot & Plonsky, 2017) to catch up with the recent development in statistics, and it has begun to explore a greater variety of sophisticated statistical methods, some of which are showcased in Le Bruyn and Paquot (2021a).

1.3.4 Expanding Scopes

The scope of LCR more or less overlaps with that of CL in general. However, there are several topics discussed intensively in LCR, which has traditionally dealt with research questions related to over/underused linguistic features, native language transfer, and language areas where learners find a learning difficulty, use avoidance strategy, and cannot achieve native-like performance (Leech, 1998, p. xiv).

One of the recently published LCR handbooks (Granger et al., 2015) covers such topics as corpus design (data collection, grammar/speech/error annotation), analysis of interlanguage (lexis, phraseology, grammar, discourse, pragmatics), LC-based SLA studies (transfer, developmental patterns, learning context), language teaching (English for academic purposes, English for specific purposes [ESP], material design, language testing), and NLP (automatic grammar/spelling checks, automated scoring, native language identification)—which exemplifies a widening scope of the recent LCR. Among these, LCR's potential to reform and redesign foreign language teaching has attracted much attention since its birth, but "up-and-running pedagogical resources that make full use of learner corpus data are still relatively rare" (Gilquin & Granger, 2015, pp. 420–421).

LCR, which is essentially "exploratory or descriptive" (Gilquin & Granger, 2015, pp. 420–421), is usually regarded as opposite to SLA, which is more theory-oriented. However, more and more researchers have come to pay attention to the integration of LCR and SLA. Le Bruyn and Paquot (2021b) touch upon "how SLA theory can be used today to inform learner corpus analyses, and how learner corpus findings can be used to inform SLA theory" and conclude that this "cross-fertilization" is the result of the broadening of learner data collected in LCR (p. 3). Collaboration between the two fields, whose importance is also suggested from the viewpoint of methodological triangulation in Egbert and Baker (2020), is clearly a promising path to go, but several gaps remain in their orientations. Inheriting much from CL, LCR tends to use large-sized "all-purpose" cross-sectional datasets, focus on written data, depend on quantitative analysis, and avoid discussion of L2 development from a theoretical viewpoint, while SLA tends to use small-sized "purpose-built" longitudinal datasets, focus on spoken data, depend on qualitative analysis, and aim to discuss L2 development directly (Granger, 2021). How to fill these gaps for the realisation of cross-fertilisation is a big challenge for LCR.

2

ICNALE

Major Features

2.1 Background

As discussed in the overview in Section 1.2.3, many researchers have already tried to collect L2 outputs of Asian learners of English. However, there still remain several limitations, including limited coverage of L1 and regional diversity in Asia, incomparability of plural datasets, lack of Asian learners' speech data, insufficiency in learners' metadata survey (especially L2 proficiency), and limited data access.

Considering these backgrounds, the author of this volume began the development of a new international learner corpus focusing on L2 English learners in Asia. The project began in 2007, and the International Corpus Network of Asian Learners of English (ICNALE) team has collected more than 14,000 samples of speeches and essays produced by approximately 4,000 learners in 10 countries and regions in Asia, as well as L1 English native speakers (ENS). The collected data has been released as different modules of the ICNALE.

ICNALE currently comprises three core modules: Written Essays, Spoken Monologues, and Spoken Dialogues, and two additional modules: Edited Essays and Global Rating Archives. It has become one of the largest learner corpora (LC) focusing on Asian learners of English.

2.2 Features

There are many features in ICNALE. In the following subsections, we touch upon the seven key features: (i) covering a variety of Asian learners and ENS (participant diversity), (ii) collecting various types of outputs and additional data (output diversity), (iii) controlling the condition for speaking and writing (condition control), (iv) investigating learner proficiency and other metadata (metadata survey),

DOI: 10.4324/9781003252528-3

(v) distributing audios and videos (multimodality), (vi) taking needed countermeasures against ENS centrism (opposing ENS centrism), and (vii) distributing the data in two ways (data distribution).

2.2.1 Participant Diversity

Many of the existing LC have paid relatively limited attention to the potential diversity in target learners, as well as ENS as a yardstick for comparison. The ICNALE team, therefore, has decided to collect learner data from college students in ten countries and regions in Asia and ENS data from college students, teachers, and business persons in more than five countries in the world.

First, regarding learner diversity, we need to realise that there exist two types of learners in Asia: learners in the Outer Circle, where English has been used as a second language with official status as a result of "extended periods of colonization," and learners in the Expanding Circle, where English is introduced as a foreign language (Kachru, 1985, pp. 12–13; Kachru, 1992, pp. 356–357). In the Asian context, it is crucial for us to survey both English as a second language (ESL) used in the Outer Circle and English as a foreign language (EFL) used in the Expanding Circle.

In the literature, ESL is often regarded as a linguistic innovation or a linguistic nativisation contributing to identity construction, while EFL is seen merely as deviation, misuse, and errors, but the difference between these two English varieties is unclear. Some LC researchers mention the gaps (Gries & Deshors, 2005; Rosen, 2016; Koch et al., 2016; Horch, 2016), but others emphasise the similarity and suggest that EFL may need to be redefined from a new perspective (Edwards & Lange, 2016; Rautionaho & Deshors, 2018; Callies, 2016; Schneider & Gilquin, 2016; Deshors et al., 2016; Leuckert, 2018). Deshors et al. (2016), for example, note that, as drawing a line between an innovation and an error is extremely difficult, there will be "a significant change in the way EFL speakers are perceived; that is, as creative language users instead of 'defective native speakers.'"

Thus, the ICNALE core modules collect L2 output data from four ESL regions (Hong Kong, Pakistan, the Philippines, and Singapore/Malaysia) as well as six EFL regions (China, Indonesia, Japan, Korea, Thailand, and Taiwan). Regarding Chinese speakers, ICNALE collects the data from mainland China, Taiwan, and Hong Kong, which enables researchers to distinguish the influences of an L1, a region, and the ESL/EFL type, and analyse each of them. It is true that there still remain many uncovered regions, but when compared to the previous LC, ICNALE includes the data of a much wider range of learners in Asia. Thus, ICNALE can also be regarded as a source of the studies of World Englishes (Lange & Leuckert, 2020, pp. 173–176).

Next, regarding ENS diversity, Granger (2015) suggests the importance of paying attention to dialectal, in other words, regional variabilities in her revised contrastive interlanguage analysis (CIA2) model (see Section 1.3.2). What should be noted here is that, in Asia, different countries adopt different English models. For example, a British English model is adopted in (many parts of) mainland China, while American English is regarded as a primary learning model in Japan. LC researchers, therefore, need to carefully consider the background of the learners to be analysed and choose appropriate ENS samples for CIA. As regards this point, Chen (2013) presents an interesting report that Chinese learners underuse phrasal verbs when compared to an American norm but not so when compared to a British norm. Citing Chen's study, Gilquin (2022) recommends that "the best advice is probably to opt for the [ENS regional] variety that the learners represented in the corpus are most likely to have been exposed to." Thus, ICNALE collects ENS data not only from one country but from more than five countries in the world.

Another thing to be considered is occupational variety of ENS. ENS college students, a direct counterpart of Asian college students, may not be the best yardstick for CIA because the quality of their L1 outputs, especially in speeches, is not necessarily guaranteed (Leech, 1998; see Section 2.2.6). Callies (2015) mentions that the "choice of control corpus has significant implications for learner corpus analysis and the interpretation of findings," and it raises the question of whether researchers should "compare learner data to L1 peers, e.g., novice writers of similar academic standing (students), or expert writers (professionals)," which Callies regards as a "serious but yet unresolved issue in CIA" (p. 40). ICNALE, therefore, collects L1 English outputs from ENS students (ENS_1: a peer reference), ENS teachers (ENS_2: a pedagogical reference), and ENS business persons (ENS_3: a business reference). ICNALE users can choose the yardstick most suitable for their research purposes.

Thus, the ICNALE Written Essays includes 400 essays written by 200 ENS participants from Australia (17), Canada (28), the UK (28), New Zealand (13), and the US (114). Among them, 100 are college students, 44 are teachers, and 56 are business persons. The ICNALE Spoken Monologues includes 600 speeches produced by 150 ENS participants from Australia (16), Canada (10), the UK (25), Nigeria (1), New Zealand (1), and the US (97). Among them, 50 are college students, 75 are teachers, and 25 are business persons. Then, the ICNALE Spoken Dialogues includes 200 speech clips produced by 20 ENS participants from Australia (1), Canada (2), the UK (3), Ireland (1), New Zealand (1), the Philippines (2), and the US (10). With this module, all the data are taken from teachers.

Although ICNALE includes a much wider range of ENS output data in comparison to existing LC, the ICNALE users can also utilise the assessment data offered in the ICNALE Global Rating Archives to adopt a set of high-quality L2 learner outputs as an alternative or additional reference for CIA (see Section 8.4).

2.2.2 Output Diversity

Learners' L2 performance should be discussed ideally from the integrative analysis of their spoken and written outputs. In this sense, we need learner data taken from "different media and text types" (Nesselhauf, 2004, p. 132). However, this has not been easy because the quantity of learners' L2 speech data available to the researchers has been very scarce. As noted in Section 1.2.3, the number of LC collecting

Asian learners' L2 speech is quite small, and most of them are not currently available. This is also the case with LC in general. Ballier and Martin (2015) report that among more than 140 entries in the "Learner Corpora around the World" directory (see Section 1.2.3), only 38 correspond to spoken data and conclude that "[s]poken learner corpora are still rare today" (p. 107). In addition, most of the spoken LC that we can utilise are developed independently, and therefore they cannot be directly compared to the existing written LC.

Therefore, the ICNALE team has decided to collect not only Asian learners' essays but also their speeches. As the same topics are given (see Section 2.2.3), speeches and essays collected in the project are comparable to a large extent. The three ICNALE core modules include 4,400 monologues, 425 interview speeches, which are subdivided into 4,250 task-based speeches, and 5,600 essays. Sizable speech and essay data included in ICNALE makes it possible for researchers to examine Asian learners' L2 use in a more balanced manner.

Regarding speeches, we need to note that there exist two production modes: monologues and dialogues. Introducing the Survey of English Usage Corpus (see Crystal & Quirk, 1964), Crystal (1995) explains that speeches can be divided into monologues and dialogues in terms of "participation," and the former is further subdivided into spontaneous speeches and prepared speeches (to be spoken or to be written), while the latter is subdivided into conversation (face-to-face or telephone) and public discussion. In order to cover these two sides of speeches, the ICNALE Spoken Monologues collects learners' topic-based monologue speeches recorded on the answering phone system, and the ICNALE Spoken Dialogues collects their spoken outputs in the oral proficiency interviews. As the interviews consist of three types of speaking tasks such as picture descriptions, roleplays, and related Q&A sessions, ICNALE as a whole includes a more comprehensive range of learner speeches, which differ in terms of task type, participation, content, speech situation, preparation, time, and formality level (Table 2.1).

Thus, the ICNALE users can conduct a comparative analysis of different types of learner speeches, as well as a comparison of learner speeches and essays.

TABLE 2.1 Speech subtypes collected in ICNALE

Modules	*Spoken Monologues*	*Spoken Dialogues*		
Task	*Topic speech*	*Picture description*	*Conversation*	*Persuasion*
Participation	Monologue w/o a listener	Monologue to a listener	Dialogue	Dialogue
Content	Talk about the given topics	Describe the pictures	Answer the questions	Do roleplays
Situation	On the phone	Face-to-face	Face-to-face	Face-to-face
Preparation	With prep time	With prep time	W/o prep time	W/o prep time
Time	Timed (60 sec)	Not-timed	Not-timed	Not-timed
Formality	Formal	Casual	Casual	Formal

In addition to speeches and essays, ICNALE also collects edit and assessment data. The ICNALE Edited Essays is a collection of the fully edited versions of learners' original essays sampled from the ICNALE Written Essays. Though the ICNALE data is not error-tagged, one can quickly identify learners' errors and inappropriate use of words, phrases, and constructions by comparing original and edited essays. Then, the ICNALE Global Rating Archives is a collection of assessments of learner speeches sampled from the ICNALE Spoken Dialogues and learner essays sampled from the ICNALE Written Essays. This unique dataset collects the learners' output assessments by more than 100 raters with varied L1 and occupational backgrounds in Asia. These two additional modules will enhance the value of the learners' diverse output data collected in the core modules.

2.2.3 Condition Control

Learners' L2 speeches and essays can be easily influenced by a variety of task-related variables. Gilquin (2015) lists three speech-related variables (preparation time, written support such as a memo, and recording device [invasive or not]), four essay-related variables (time constraints, reference tools such as dictionaries, intertextuality [access to secondary sources], and computerisation [hand-writing or keyboard input]), and two variables common to both (an exam condition [as a part of the exam or not] and topic) (pp. 16–17).

LC developers often face a dilemma between collecting a greater variety of output samples without strictly controlling the task variables versus collecting a limited variety of samples while strictly controlling the variables. The former approach allows learners to use various words, phrases, and constructions, which enables an analysis of a broader range of lexical and grammatical features in learners' L2 use. However, it may decrease the reliability of comparative analyses. The latter approach, on the other hand, elicits more homogenous outputs from learners and naturally enhances the reliability of comparative analyses. However, it may not offer sufficient examples of the lexical or grammatical items that researchers like to study. These two approaches are often trade-offs, and which is better depends on the research purposes. For example, the International Corpus of Learner English (ICLE) allows a great variety of topics and writing conditions, though they are all appropriately recorded as metadata. The ICLE team admits that "[a] large degree of freedom was left to the national coordinators as regards the topic and other task variables such as timing, exam conditions and use of reference tools" (Granger et al., 2020, p. 13). Meanwhile, the Louvain Interlanguage Database of Spoken English Interlanguage (LINDSEI) adopts a structured interview platform (Gilquin et al., 2010), which helps to elicit homogenous data.

Though having many merits, the former approach sometimes leads to confusion in data interpretation. Comparing the Swedish subcorpus of ICLE with LOCNESS as an ENS reference dataset, Altenberg (1997) reported that Swedish learners prefer an overly involved and personal style in writing, which she interpreted as a result of their limited awareness of a text genre. However, the follow-up study by Ädel (2008), who reanalysed the data while considering the possible effect of related variables, proved that the observed divergence should be attributed to two task-related variables: time for writing and access to secondary sources. This suggests that comparing datasets collected under different conditions may cause misinterpretation. As Ädel (2008) emphasises, differences found between groups may be simply "due to the corpora under comparison not being comparable." More recently, Caines and Buttery (2018) analysed the data from the Cambridge Learner Corpus, a huge collection of essays by the student sitting Cambridge English examinations, and they report that the difference in topic (prompt) types leads to the significant differences in essay length, accuracy in predicting the topic types from lexical clues, part-of-speech distribution, and the use of subcategorisation frames (i.e., the relation between verbs and arguments). They strongly advise LC researchers "to control for variables such as document length, task, topic and first language as far as possible," and they also add that "by attempting to control such factors, or at least being aware of them, researchers can avoid making inappropriate inferences over highly heterogeneous data."

Bearing this in mind, the ICNALE team has decided to control various task-related variables that may (or may not) influence the outputs as strictly as possible, even if it leads to collecting a narrower range of learner outputs. First, the team has decided to limit the number of prompts for essays and monologues only to two: "It is important for college students to have a part-time job" (a part-time job) and "Smoking should be completely banned at all the restaurants in the country" (non-smoking). All the participants, including both learners and ENS, are required to write and speak about these two topics.

In comparison to essays, collecting speeches under controlled conditions is much more difficult. Therefore, when collecting the monologue speeches, the team developed an automatic monologue speech collection system. The system was installed on a server, and it was connected to the international telephone network. All participants made a phone call to the system, listened to the instructions, and made their monologue speeches on the phone. The system gave the same instructions in the same order and at the same timing to all the participants despite where they were. Also, the speech recording automatically stopped after the pre-set time, meaning that the same time was given to all participants. Then, when collecting the dialogue speeches, the team prepared a detailed interview protocol and gave enough training sessions to the interviewers. They were required to do a trial interview. The team scrutinised it and gave advice for improvement. Only those who had passed this test were allowed to begin data collection. These efforts seem to have enhanced the comparability of the collected speech data.

As Gilquin (2015) notes, there are many variables that potentially influence learner outputs. In the ICNALE data collection, in addition to the topics, many variables are controlled as well (Table 2.2).

Among the variables listed in Gilquin (2015), the team did not explicitly regulate the use of written support and a secondary source, though they seem to be hardly used by the participants.

TABLE 2.2 Variable control in the ICNALE core modules

	Written Essays	*Spoken Monologues*	*Spoken Dialogues*
Time for preparation	Included in the time for writing	20 sec for 1st-time speech 10 sec for 2nd-time speech	No prep time (Excluding picture descriptions)
Time for a task	20–40 min for one essay	60 sec for one speech	20–50 min for a whole interview
Length	200–300 words		
Reference use	No	No	No
Data collection method	Written on MS Word	Recorded	Videotaped (camera was not hidden)
Exam condition	No	No	No

2.2.4 Metadata Survey

In the previous section, we discussed how task-related variables were controlled in the ICNALE project. However, there is another set of variables to be considered: learner-related variables. They usually include basic attributes (age, gender, country/area, mother tongue), language attributes (native language, the parents' native languages, the language(s) spoken at home, knowledge of other foreign languages), L2 proficiency (different measures of the learner's proficiency), L2 exposure (number of years spent learning the target language, pedagogical materials used, contact with the target language in everyday life, stays in target-language countries), and L2 learning motivation (Gilquin 2015, p. 17). Also, they might include additional variables such as attitude toward the target language, self-attributed importance to particular types of L2 competence, experience/ability in the language-related fields (Gut, 2012), personality, and L1 aptitude (Meunier, 2015a, p. 385).

Ideally, all these variables (or more) should be surveyed, but it does not seem to be always possible. Thus, LC developers choose a set of learner-related variables to be surveyed and recorded as metadata, reflecting their research purposes. Considering the variety of ESL and EFL learners in Asia, the ICNALE team has focused on collecting the metadata about four major variables: basic attributes, L2 learning history, motivation, and proficiency. All the collected metadata is included in the ICNALE Learner Background Survey Sheet.

2.2.4.1 Basic Attitudes, Motivation, and Learning History

First, regarding basic attributes, the team examined gender, L1, country/region, age, school year (freshman, sophomore, junior, senior, or graduate levels), academic major (law, economics, linguistics, computer sciences, nursing, etc.), academic fields (humanities, social sciences, science and technology, and life science), experiences of staying overseas, and so on. For ENS participants, the team also examined educational and occupational backgrounds.

TABLE 2.3 L2 learning history survey

L2 Learning in primary school	*L2 Learning in secondary school*
When I was a primary school student … (1) I often used English in class. (2) I often used English outside class.	When I was a secondary school student … (3) I listened to English a lot in class. (4) I read English a lot in class. (5) I spoke English a lot in class. (6) I wrote English a lot in class. (7) I listened to English a lot outside class. (8) I read English a lot outside class. (9) I spoke English a lot outside class. (10) I wrote English a lot outside class.
L2 Learning in College	*Additional learning experiences*
Now at college … (11) I listen to English a lot in class. (12) I read English a lot in class. (13) I speak English a lot in class. (14) I write English a lot in class. (15) I listen to English a lot outside class. (16) I read English a lot outside class. (17) I speak English a lot outside class. (18) I write English a lot outside class.	So far … (19) I have been taught by English native speakers. (20) I have been taught English pronunciation. (21) I have been taught speaking or presentation. (22) I have been taught essay writing.

Second, regarding L2 learning history, the team presented the participants with a questionnaire that included the 22 statements (Table 2.3) and required them to self-judge to what extent they agreed with each of the statements, from 1 (strongly disagree) to 6 (strongly agree). These statements examine how learners have studied and used L2 at different stages of education and whether they have had experiences in specific types of L2 learning.

The purpose of this survey is to clarify the aspects of learners' previous L2 learning with a focus on the L2 learning stages, L2 skill types (listening, reading, speaking, and writing), and the situations in which they use L2 (inside or outside classrooms).

By averaging the learners' responses to a set of related statements, the team calculated the mean values for 13 kinds of learning history indices, including five indices related to the quantity of L2 learning in different situations (primary schools, secondary schools, colleges, inside classrooms, outside classrooms), four indices related to the quantity of four-skill learning (listening, reading, speaking, writing), and four indices related to additional learning experiences (ENS teachers, pronunciation, speech presentation, and essay writing).

Third, regarding L2 learning motivation, we presented a questionnaire that included the 12 statements (Table 2.4) to the participants and required them to self-judge to what extent they agreed with each of the statements ranging from 1 (strongly disagree) to 6 (strongly agree).

TABLE 2.4 L2 learning motivation survey

I study English because ...	
(1) I find pleasure when I understand the content sufficiently.	(7) I want to achieve a good mark on the tests.
(2) I want to get a better job in the future.	(8) I am interested in the content, even if it is difficult.
(3) Learning content is more important than being awarded high grades.	(9) Learning something new is fun, even if it is difficult.
(4) I want to be socially acknowledged.	(10) I find pleasure in discovering something new.
(5) Being awarded high grades is important for me.	(11) I want to get a better grade than others.
(6) Learning English is what we have to do anyway.	(12) Increasing English knowledge is fun.

These statements reflect two sub-types of motivation: an instrumental motivation of learning L2 from a "practical need to communicate in the second language," such as passing a test or obtaining a good grade, and an integrative motivation of learning L2 from "an interest in the second language and its culture" as well as "the intention to become part of the culture" (Gardner & Lambert, 1972; see Section 7.1.1.4). They are also operationalised as extrinsic (i.e., caused by something outside of a learner) and intrinsic (i.e., caused by something inside a learner) motivations (Deci & Ryan, 1985). Previous studies suggest that an instrumental (extrinsic) motivation and an integrative (intrinsic) motivation concern short-term success and long-term success, respectively (Gardner & MacIntyre, 1991). Though we find a few exceptions (e.g., Hilton et al., 2008), surveying learner motivation as metadata has not been very common in LCR. However, motivation seems to play a crucial role for Asian L2 English learners, especially in the Expanding Circle, where we can easily find the students who receive good scores in English tests but speak and write very poorly.

Statements 2, 4, 5, 6, 7, and 11 concern an instrumental motivation, while statements 1, 3, 8, 9, 10, and 12 concern an integrative motivation. By averaging the learners' responses to a set of related statements, we calculated the mean values for four kinds of motivation indices: strengths of instrumental, integrative, and overall motivations, as well as the difference between the strengths of instrumental and integrative motivations.

2.2.4.2 Proficiency

Here we introduce the ICNALE approach to deal with learner proficiency. As Carlsen (2012) suggests, proficiency is "a fuzzy variable" in LCR, and therefore many researchers have tried to operationalise it mainly from two viewpoints: the learner-centred measurement (school year, teacher opinion, external test scores) and the text-centred measurement (output-based test scores, teacher opinion, rater group assessment). Regarding the latter, learners' self-rating may be added (Lozano & Mendikoetxea, 2010).

Among these, many LC estimate learners' proficiency simply in terms of their school years, which, however, may not guarantee their actual L2 performance levels. As mentioned in Section 1.2.1, the assessment of sample outputs in ICLE and LINDSEI showed a considerably large gap even in a group of learners in the same school years. Also, Leńko-Szymańska (2015) analyses the linguistic/lexical quality of young student essays and reports that "school grade is an inadequate yardstick of a learner's level" (p. 134).

Therefore, ICNALE collects four kinds of learner- and text-centred proficiency measurement data: (i) school years, (ii) external test scores, (iii) learners' self-ratings, and (iv) raters' output assessments.

First, learners' school years were examined by questionnaires. In the case of the ICNALE Written Essays, 44% of the learners were in the first year (freshmen), and 34% were in the second year (sophomores). Unlike in ICLE and LINDSEI, the ratio of the students in the third and fourth years was rather small.

Second, the team examined learners' external test scores and estimated their CEFR levels based on them. When recruiting the participants, the team required them to report their scores in internationally acknowledged English proficiency tests such as TOEFL, TOEIC, and IELTS. However, as some of the participants had not taken these high-stakes tests before, the team also required all the participants to take an English monolingual version of the Vocabulary Size Test (VST) (Nation & Beglar, 2007). The original VST consists of either 14 or 20 levels (1,000-word level to a 14,000 or 20,000-word level), but our test covered only the top five levels (1,000-word level to 5,000-word level) because a range of 5,000 words is usually regarded as an appropriate ceiling when observing non-native speakers' vocabulary size (Meara & Milton, 2003; Milton, 2010). As there were 10 vocabulary-matching questions for each level, the participants answered 50 questions in total (Table 2.5).

As regards the participants who did not report their scores in the high-stakes tests, the team aligned their VST scores with the scores in the TOEIC L/R, which was taken by many participants, especially in Japan and Korea. Choosing the data of 268 participants who took both tests, the team conducted linear regression modelling

TABLE 2.5 Vocabulary size test (sample questions from Levels 1, 3, and 5)

Level	*Question items*
1	SEE: They *saw* it. (a) cut, (b) waited for, (c) looked at, (d) started
3	SOLDIER: He is a *soldier.* (a) person in a business, (b) student, (c) person who uses metal, (d) person in the army
5	DEFICIT: The company had a large *deficit.* (a) spent a lot more money than it earned, (b) went down a lot in value, (c) had a plan for its spending that used a lot of money, (d) had a lot of money in the bank

TABLE 2.6 Score conversion table

Lev.	*TOEIC L/R*	*TOEFL PBT*	*TOEFL iBT*	*IELTS*	*VST*
A2	−545	−486	−56	3+	−24
B1_1	550+	487+	57+	4+	25+
B1_2	670+	527+	72+	4+	36+
B2+	785+	567+	87+	5 (5.5) +	47+

Notes: (1) The thresholds for B1_2 were determined from the threshold scores for B1 and B2. (2) The thresholds regarding the two versions of TOEFL were based on the official score guide distributed by ETS around 2010. ETS, however, released a new report, which regards 42 in iBT (≈ 440 in PBT) as B1, and 72 (≈ 533) as B2. To maintain consistency in score conversions, the team has continued using the old conversion guideline. (4) Meara and Milton (2003) analyse the vocabulary sizes of Greek and Hungarian EFL learners and suggest that B1, B2, C1, and C2 levels are roughly equivalent to the knowledge of 2,500, 3,250, 3,750, and 4,500 words, respectively. However, this conversion seems to overestimate Asian learners' proficiency levels.

and converted the VST scores to the TOEIC score by applying an obtained regression formula (10.495 * VST Score + 289 = TOEIC L/R Score [r^2 =.21]).

Next, the team examined the official score guide issued by each of the test agencies and decided on the score conversion table (Table 2.6). Then, based on the scores in the high-stakes test or in the VST, all non-native-speaker participants were classified into four proficiency bands linked to the scale of the Common European Framework of Reference for Languages (CEFR): A2 (Waystage), B1 Lower (B1_1) (Threshold Lower), B1 Upper (B1_2) (Threshold Upper), and B2+ (Vantage or higher).

Classification of learner proficiency based on the external test scores is one of the assets of ICNALE. It would enable researchers to examine the relationship between learners' L2 skills and their actual L2 use more reliably than when classifying them only in terms of their school years. However, we need to admit that several limitations exist in our proficiency data management. First, there remains room for improvement in the method of mapping the VST scores on the CEFR levels. Second, the team did not consider the difference in major high-stakes tests. TOEIC L/R, TOEFL PBT, and VST are receptive skills tests, while TOEFL iBT and IELTS include direct assessments of productive skills such as speaking and writing. Though the number of participants who took the latter type of test was quite small, we need to carefully reconsider how to deal with the score data obtained from different tests.

Third, learners' self-rating data were collected for the ICNALE Spoken Monologues and the ICNALE Spoken Dialogues. Regarding the former, at the end of the speech tasks, all the participants were told to self-evaluate the quality of their own monologue speeches with 0–3 point. Then, regarding the latter, at the end of the interviews, the interviewers asked the participants how they felt about the overall quality of their own oral performance.

Finally, output assessment data were collected for the ICNALE Edited Essays and the ICNALE Global Rating Archives. Regarding the former, the team asked a proofreader to edit a learner's original text and also to rate it based on the five-category rubric. Then, as regards the latter, the team hired more than 100 raters with varied backgrounds and asked them to assess 140 essays and the same number of dialogue speeches, which were taken from the persuasion roleplays, based on the ten-category rubric.

2.2.5 Multimodality

As mentioned above, the number of spoken LC is relatively small. Moreover, "[o]f the few spoken learner corpora that are available, most do not come with audio files, but simply consist of transcripts" (Ballier & Martin, 2015, p. 107). Transcription, however, is a kind of "filtering process" (Ochs, 1979, p. 44), and it does not completely represent "phenomena like false starts, repetitions, hesitations and overlapping utterances." Therefore, "spokenness" or "the very nature of spoken discourse" may be fundamentally altered there (De Cock, 2010, p. 124). With only transcripts, which Bailler and Martin call "mute spoken data," it would be difficult to analyse learner speeches from the viewpoints of pronunciation, intonation, and phonetics, to say nothing of gesture use.

This exemplifies the need to collect and distribute the audio-visual data together with the transcripts. Regarding the recent research trends in corpus linguistics (CL) in general, McEnery and Hardie (2012) say that "[c]orpora which include gesture, either as the primary channel for language (as in sign language corpora) or as a means of communication parallel to speech, are relatively new" in CL but "[t]he integration of video analysis with textual analysis is clearly crucial for the development and use of such corpora" (p.5). Of course, there have been several LC that attempted to collect multimodal data. As "newcomers to the field" of LCR, Gilquin (2015) introduces several corpora (p. 12), which include the Multimedia Adult ESL Learner Corpus (Reder et al., 2003) and the Multimedia Learner Corpus of Basic Presentation (Hashimoto & Takeuchi, 2012). However, neither of them seem to be publicly accessible. Meanwhile, the ICNALE Spoken Monologues and the ICNALE Spoken Dialogues collect and distribute the audios and the videos in addition to the transcripts.

When collecting the audio-visual data from learners, what matters is to protect their privacy and anonymity. If a speaker can be easily identified, it might cause various problems that one cannot expect beforehand. Regarding the speech data collection for the British National Corpus, McEnery and Hardie (2012) point out that the respondents and their collocutors might have "sacrificed their privacy" (p. 61). Therefore, after confirming that there was no major privacy leakage in learner speeches, the ICNALE team took two additional measures to protect the privacy and anonymity of the participants. First, all of the monologue speeches were artificially morphed by changing a pitch, which maintained the original utterances' phonetic features but drastically changed their auditory images. The parameter for morphing was kept secret. Second, when collecting the dialogue speeches, the team required all non-native-speaker participants to wear a mask for anonymity, though

ENS participants, all of whom were language teachers, chose not to wear one. Also, the interviewers confirmed that the participants did not say anything inappropriate during the interviews.

Registered users can download all the sound and video files and analyse them with various types of software according to their research interests. For instance, users can analyse the phonetic features of learner speeches with software such as Praat (Figure 2.1). They can also analyse the speakers' body language on platforms like YouTube (Figure 2.2), whose automatic captioning may help users to examine learners' language and body language in alignment (see Section 6.4). In addition, they can analyse the body motion of a speaker in greater detail with software like Kinovea (Figure 2.3).

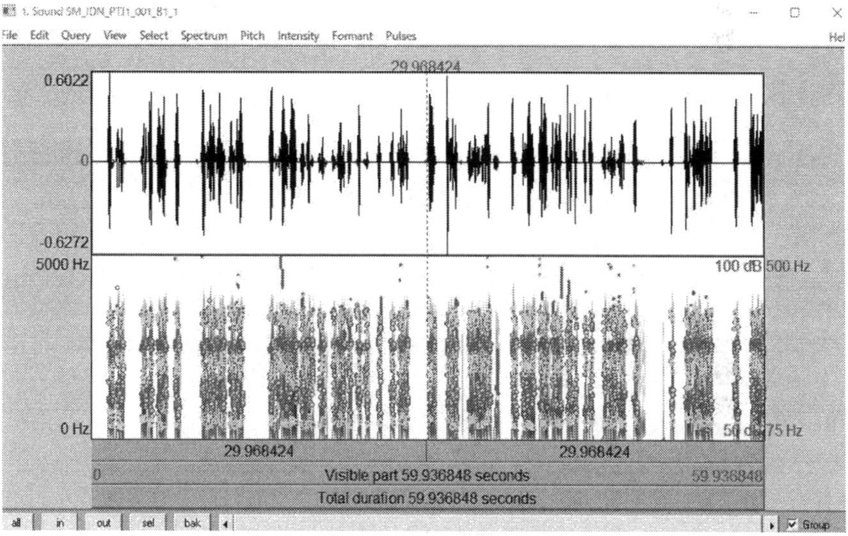

FIGURE 2.1 Phonetic analysis of a learner's monologue speech (IDN_001)

FIGURE 2.2 Alignment analysis of a learner's utterance and body language (CHN_016)

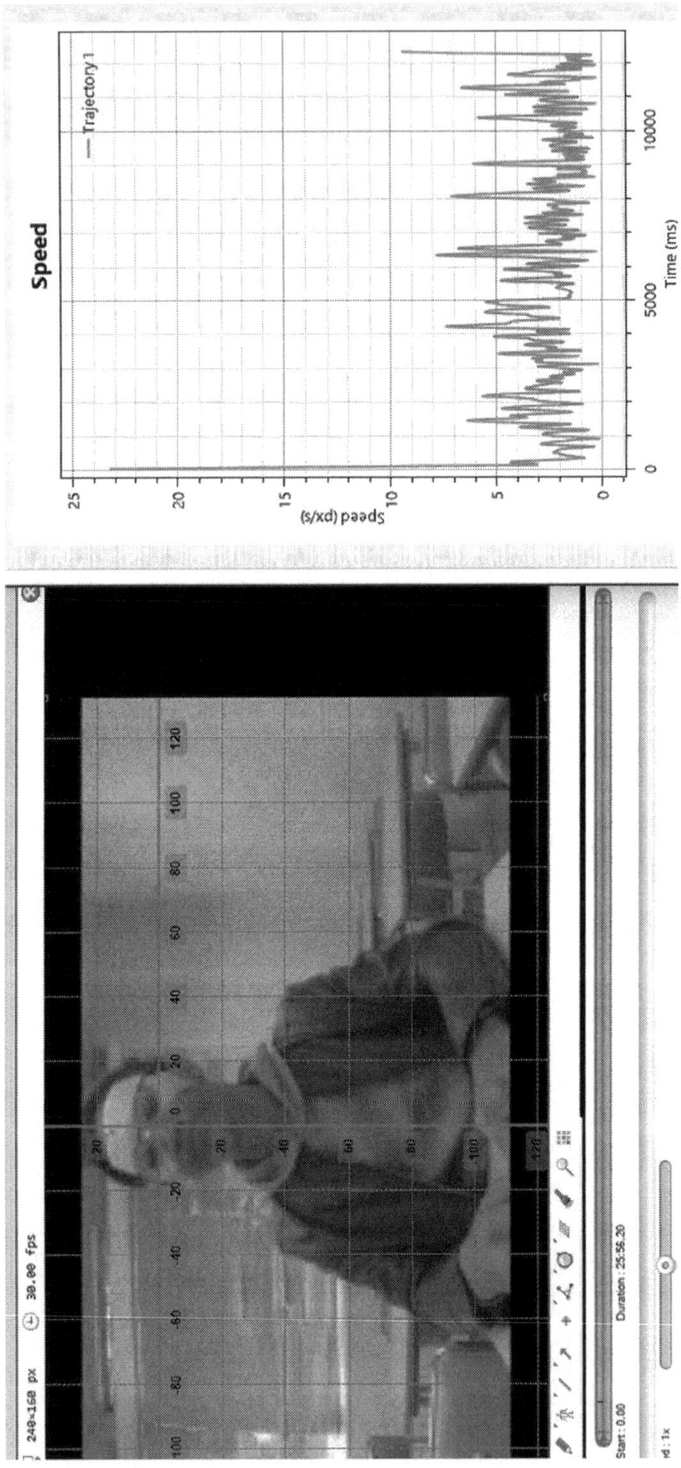

FIGURE 2.3 Analysis of a learner's head motion (HKG_014)

These multimodal analyses of learner speeches would bridge LCR and SLA and open up new possibilities in LCR.

2.2.6 Opposing ENS Centrism

As mentioned in Section 1.3.2, CIA has been a staple analytical framework for LCR. Surveying 57 representative LC studies, Gilquin (2022) reports that 56% of them involve direct comparisons of learner and ENS data, and 26% of them refer to ENS norms in some manner. However, some applied linguists problematise a CIA approach because it may slight learners' interlanguage data, regard a small amount of, and a narrow range of ENS samples as an absolute reference, and impose a false idea of ENS centrism on learners, teachers, and researchers. Granger (2015) also admits that "[o]ver the years, CIA has been subjected to a range of criticism, most targeted at the L1/L2 branch.".

Here we would like to survey the backgrounds of three types of criticisms. First, when comparing learner outputs with something else, LC researchers naturally see the former indirectly and with decreased attention. In one sense, the comparison makes learners and their outputs marginalised, which Bley-Vroman (1983) calls comparative fallacy. He emphasises that as the linguistic system of a learner or an interlanguage grammar is an independent system, comparisons between interlanguage grammar and other systems are not legitimate under any circumstances. He concludes, "work on the linguistic description of learners' languages can be seriously hindered or sidetracked by a concern with the target language" as an external reference. Selinker (2014) also suggests that "interlanguages must be described in their own terms" rather than in comparison to an external reference. A similar viewpoint is suggested by many researchers of English as a lingua franca (ELF). Emphasising the situationality, creativity, and variability in the ELF interactions, Pitzl-Hagin (2022) notes, "Why do we need to compare? Why should ELF use always be 'judged' and analysed through the lens of one or more reference norms?"

Next, when conducting an L1/L2 comparison, LC researchers often rely on a relatively limited number of ENS output samples, which may not be regarded as a good model to follow and may not reflect the possible variety of English language in the contemporary world. Regarding the former, Leech (1998) suggests that native-speaking "students do not necessarily provide models that everyone would want to imitate", especially in speeches. Then, regarding the latter, Leech adds, "Yet which native speakers? American, Australian, British, or Caribbean? Highly educated or less so? Old or young?" (p. xix). It should also be noted that most of the CIA researchers have not paid due attention to World Englishes and ELF interactions. Prodromou (1998) ironically mentions that what is real for ENS may also be real for the learners studying in Britain, but it may be unreal for EFL learners in Greece and surreal for ESL learners in Calcutta (p. 266). Then, Timmis (2013) notes, "[i]f the majority of communication in English takes place between nonnative speakers, and that preponderance is highly likely to rise, why encumber learners with the 'luxury' items of native speaker spoken language?" (p. 84). Thus, LC researchers often have a dilemma in choosing the reference. For example, Callies (2015) suggests that researchers always face the questions such as:

> Should this [a yardstick of comparison] be only corpora representing the language of (monolingual) native speakers? And if so, what variety should serve as the comparative basis? And should researchers compare learner data to L1 peers, e.g., novice writers of similar academic standing (students), or expert writers (professionals)?
>
> *(p. 40)*

Last, when identifying learners' overuse, underuse, and misuse from the comparison with the ENS outputs as a reference, LC researchers may unconsciously accept and even strengthen a set of biased views that (i) ENS are superior and learners are inferior, (ii) learners need to get closer to ENS, (iii) English is a sole referential language in the world, (iv) English should be taught only by ENS teachers, and (v) learners need to accept an ENS' or Western identity. First, Cook (1997) showcases how SLA researchers have accepted and reproduced a view that "L2 learners are failures compared to native speakers." Larsen-Freeman (2014) comments that "[b]y continuing to equate identity with idealized native speaker production as a definition of success, it is difficult to avoid seeing the learner's IL [interlanguage] as anything but deficient" (p. 217). Second, Leech (1998) explicitly casts doubt on the view that "the goal of foreign language learning is to approximate closer and closer to the performance of native speakers" (p. xix). Third, Phillipson (1992) regards "the dominance of English worldwide, and efforts to promote the language" as English linguistic imperialism, which he notes "permeates all the other types of imperialism, since language is the means used to mediate and express them" (p. 65). Phillipson (2018) adds that linguistic imperialism entails "exploitation, injustice, inequality, and hierarchy that privileges those able to use the dominant language." Fourth, Holliday (2006) points out that there exists "the belief that 'native-speaker' teachers represent a 'Western culture' from which spring the ideals both of the English language and of English language teaching methodology," which he calls native speakerism. Such an attitude undoubtedly marginalises and stigmatises non-native English teachers. Holliday also adds that "the 'native speaker' ideal plays a widespread and complex iconic role outside as well as inside the English-speaking West." Prodromou (2008) points out that such a bias may be inherent in CL itself, which he says has continuously advocated a dogma of "real English" in foreign language teaching (pp. 5–7), and the link between authenticity and native speakerism is also mentioned in Lowe and Pinner (2016). Fifth, Timmis (2013) warns that teaching the features of ENS' authentic outputs would inevitably involve "imposing a false identity on the learners" (p. 84).

Among these, the criticism of comparative fallacy may be somewhat extreme in that such a position finally leads to the abolition of any type of comparison in scientific research, which very few would support (Granger, 2015). However, the remaining two criticisms are convincing. Therefore, the ICNALE team has decided to take several precautionary measures so that the corpus keeps a distance from dogmatic ENS centrism, and the ICNALE-based studies do not help such a biased view spread over English language teaching and learning in Asia.

First, the team paid sufficient attention to the possible occupational and regional variability of ENS and collected the output data from college students, English teachers, and business persons from various regions. This would enable corpus users to appropriately choose an ENS reference suitable for their research purposes (e.g., student essays or expert essays) (Callies, 2015, p. 40). Second, the team intentionally appointed local non-native English teachers, not ENS teachers, as a narrator for the ICNALE Spoken Monologues and interviewers for the ICNALE Spoken Dialogues, which could be a countermeasure against native speakerism. Third, when compiling the ICNALE Global Rating Archives, the team recruited more than 90% of raters from a variety of non-native ELF speakers mainly in Asia, all of whom use English regularly for their professional purposes. This unique assessment dataset could be utilised for the identification of a set of learner outputs whose quality is guaranteed by the majority of raters, which will be a good alternative or addition to a conventional ENS reference. Thus, the ICNALE users can choose a reference not only from a variety of ENS outputs but also from a variety of high-quality learner outputs. Though it may not be a perfect answer to the criticisms hurled against CIA, the team hopes that a flexible corpus design of ICNALE may neutralise, at least to some extent, the ENS centrism deeply rooted in CL, LCR, and English language teaching. Details of these measures will be introduced in detail in Chapter 3.

2.2.7 Data Distribution

LC developers are responsible for making their datasets accessible for a long time because they are expected to uphold the FAIR data principles—the research data should be findable, accessible, interoperable, and reusable—(Wilkinson et al., 2016), and the data accessibility is also a prerequisite for replicability, total accountability, and falsifiability of CL (McEnery and Hardie, 2012, pp. 14–16; see Section 1.1).

The ICNALE team, therefore, has decided to distribute the whole of the collected data, including audio and videos, in two ways—as a download version and an online version.

First, registered users can download the whole data and freely analyse it on their own computers. It enables them to tag the raw texts with their favourite part-of-speech (POS) taggers and syntactic parsers and to analyse them on appropriate concordancers, such as AntConc (Anthony, 2022) and WordSmith Tools (Scott, 2020).

Second, users can also access an online data query platform called the ICNALE *Online*. It offers five kinds of retrieval options (Table 2.7).

Surveying the development of corpus analytical tools in CL, McEnery and Hardie (2012) call web-based corpus query systems "the fourth-generation concordancers," which they say solve three technical problems of "the limited power

TABLE 2.7 Data query functions of the ICNALE *Online*

Query	*Functions*
KWIC	Show a word (word-form or lemma) or a phrase in its context. A part-of-speech (POS) search is also possible.
Wordlist	Generate a word (word-form or lemma) frequency list. A list is downloadable in CSV format.
Collocation	Generate a positional collocation table, which lists the high-frequency collocates occurring at each of L5 (the fifth word on the left of the node) to R5 (the fifth word on the right) positions. Users can choose a statistic from raw frequency, t-score, log-likelihood ratios, and mutual information score.
Keywords	Compare the target and reference subcorpora and identify the words significantly overused or underused in the target subcorpus. Users can choose a statistic from chi-squared values and log-likelihood ratios.
Frequency Graph	Generate a bar graph showing how the frequency of a target word changes across different learner groups (inter-regional comparison) or across different proficiency levels in a particular learner group (domestic comparison). This function is offered only for the essay analysis.

of desktop PCs, problems arising from non-compatible PC operating systems, and legal restrictions on the distribution of corpora" (p. 43).

Though McEnery and Hardie also say that web-based concordancers usually do not "extend the range of available analyses" realised in the stand-alone concordancers like AntConc and WordSmith Tools, ICNALE *Online* has three unique features: a frequency graph generation, a user-friendly query panel for keyword analysis, and a multimodal data search.

First, the frequency graph enables users to grasp the change in the usage of a word or a phrase in an intuitive way. Figures 2.4 to 2.5 show the results of the inter-regional and domestic comparison of the frequencies of "think" in learner essays.

Figure 2.4 represents how the frequency of "think" varies across learners from different regions. The system automatically adjusts the raw frequency per million words, and it also limits the learner proficiency levels to B1 Upper and B2+ to enhance the validity of comparison. The graph illustrates that learners in Japan tend to use "think" much more often than ENS and other learners.

Figure 2.5 represents how the frequency of "think" changes across Japanese learners at different L2 proficiency levels. The graph demonstrates that the overuse trend gradually decreases as proficiency levels go up, though even learners at B2+ level still use "think" considerably more than ENS.

Second, ICNALE *Online* adopts a newly designed query panel for keyword analysis (Figure 2.6). Keyword analysis as a CL technique is not novel at all, but what to set as a target and what to set as a reference is often confusing, especially for those who are not familiar with CL.

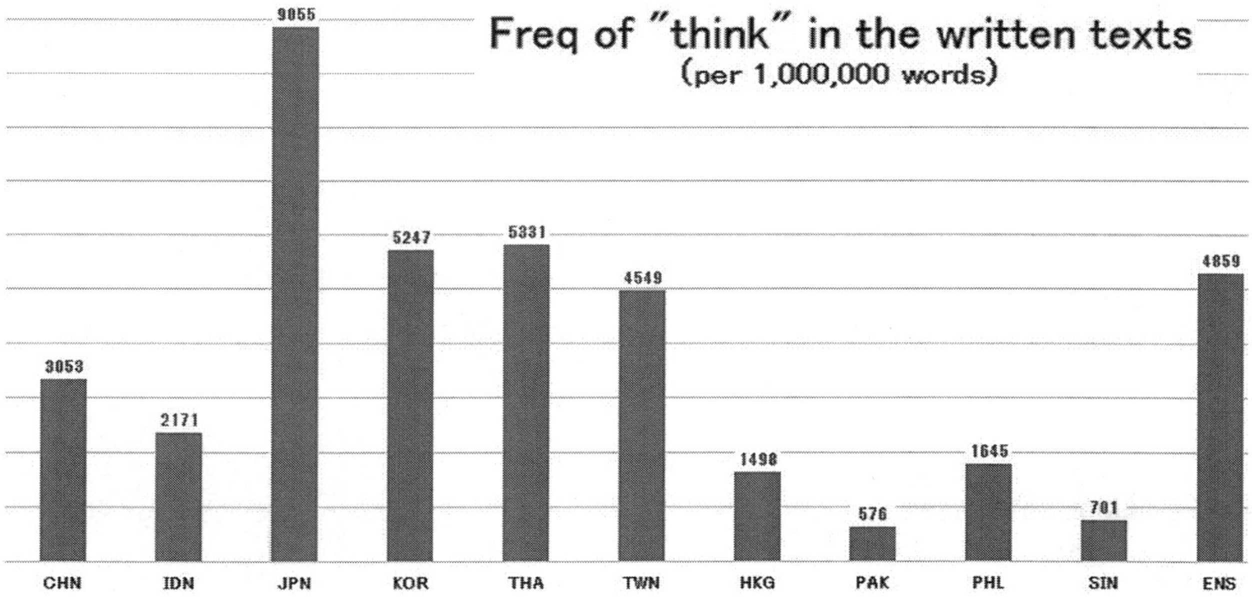

FIGURE 2.4 Frequency graph from the inter-regional comparison

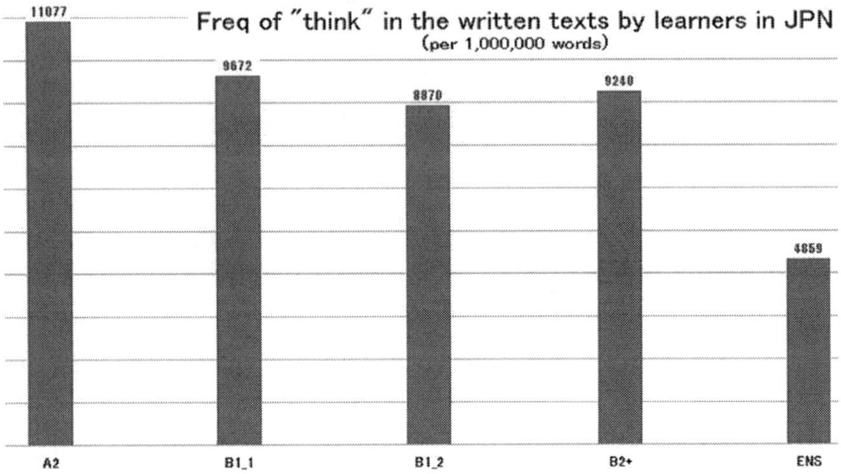

FIGURE 2.5 Frequency graph from the domestic comparison

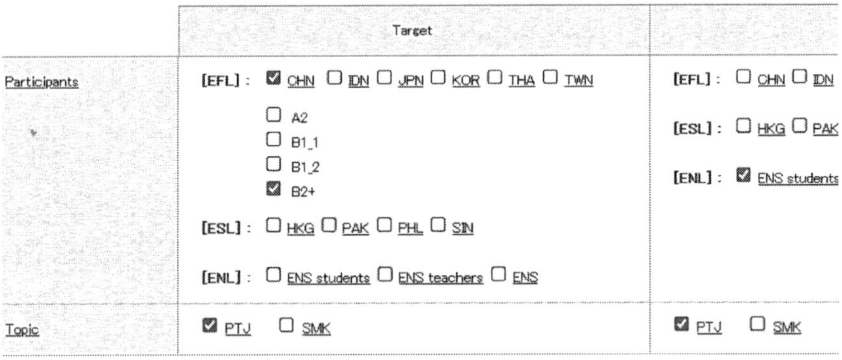

FIGURE 2.6 Query setting panel for the keyword analysis

The query panel presents the complex structure of the included data in an easy-to-understand manner, which enables users to appropriately choose a target group, a reference group, and the type of essays to be compared. The setting above, for example, identifies the words overused and underused by Chinese learners at B2+ level when compared to the ENS student-writers in part-time job (PTJ) essays. Users can attempt various types of data comparisons, which leads to a deeper understanding of the aspects of L2 use of a target learner group.

Finally, ICNALE *Online* gives users easy access to the audio and video data, which is linked to text data (Figure 2.7).

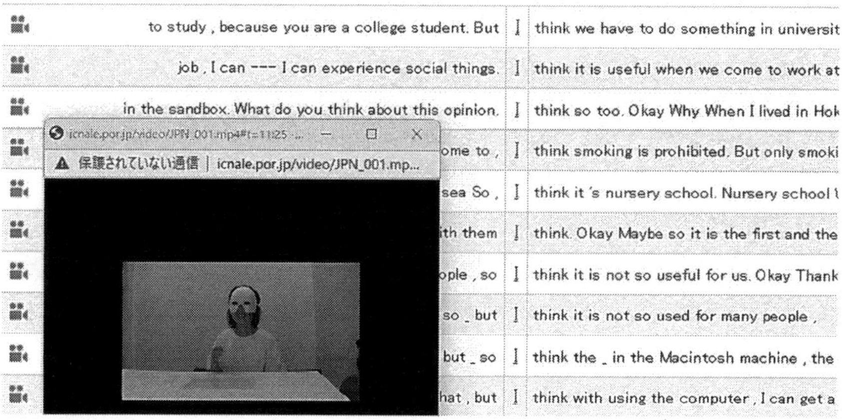

FIGURE 2.7 Text/video link in the query result

Users will find an audio or video link button at the left of the concordance lines. By clicking it, they can listen to the audio file or watch a video clip with checking the transcript, which significantly enhances the efficiency of the analysis.

3

ICNALE

Modules

3.1 Introduction

As discussed in Section 2.1, the International Corpus Network of Asian Learners of English (ICNALE) currently comprises three core modules: Written Essays (WE), Spoken Monologues (SM), and Spoken Dialogues (SD); and two additional modules: Edited Essays (EE) and Global Rating Archives (GRA). The outline of each module is shown in Table 3.1.

In all, 3,955 learners and 370 L1 English native speakers (ENS) participated in the data collection for the three core modules, and 14,250 output samples were collected.

3.2 ICNALE Written Essays

3.2.1 Background

The ICNALE project dates back to 2007, when the author began to collect essays from Japanese college students. Then, he collected additional data from a small number of ENS and Chinese college students. All the essays were written about two common topics. The essays collected at this early stage were released as the Corpus of English Essays Written by Asian University Students (CEEAUS) in 2008. It included 770 essays written by Japanese learners, 146 essays by ENS, and 92 essays by Chinese learners. Although the CEEAUS gained some attention from local scholars, it was too small to discuss the general tendency seen in Asian learners of English.

Therefore, in 2010, the author began a new project to collect comparable essay data from learners in ten countries and regions in Asia. He formed an international network of collaborating researchers, each of whom was in charge of collecting

DOI: 10.4324/9781003252528-4

TABLE 3.1 Outline of the five ICNALE modules

Type	*Release**	*Included data*	*Data size*
Core modules			
WE	2012	200–300-word topic-based essays (two topics)	2,800 participants 5,600 samples 1,300,000 words
SM	2015	60-second topic-based monologue speeches (two topics and two trials)	1,100 participants 4,400 samples 500,000 words
SD	2019	Dialogue speeches collected in approx. 40-minute interviews, which include 10 kinds of tasks	425 participants 4,250 samples 1,600,000 words (Learner utterances: 770,000 words)
Additional modules			
EE	2017	Fully edited versions of 656 topic-based essays sampled from WE	328 participants 656 samples 150,000 words
GRA	2023 (planned)	Ratings of the 140 topic-based essays and 140 roleplay speeches sampled from WE and SD	100+ raters 10,000+ ratings

Note: The year of release is based on the year when version 1.0 was officially released.

the data from local students. The staple aim of this project was to develop a new international learner corpus (LC) that enables a "sophisticated" contrastive interlanguage analysis (CIA) for Asian L2 English learners (Ishikawa, 2013). When deciding the details of the data collection scheme, the author learned a great deal from the International Corpus of Learner English (ICLE), whose first and second editions were released in 2002 and 2009.

The collected essays were released in 2012 under the name of the ICNLAE Written (Ishikawa, 2013), which was renamed the ICNALE Written Essays in 2017.

3.2.2 Participants

In ICLE, the number of essays in a single national subcorpus varies between 243 (Turkish) and 982 (Chinese) (Granger et al., 2020, p. 33). With this in mind, the ICNALE team aimed to collect at least 200 essays in one region. As each participant writes two essays in the ICNALE essay collection scheme, this means the team needed to recruit at least 100 learners in one region. Finally, the team were able to collect 200–800 essays from 100–400 learners in one region. The total number of participants is 2,800, and that of the collected essays is 5,600 (Table 3.2).

When recruiting the participants, the team did not strictly adjust the ratio of each of the four proficiency levels. However, the proportion of the B2+

TABLE 3.2 Number of participants in the ICNALE Written Essays

Regions	*A2*	*B1_1*	*B1_2*	*B2+*	*Sum*
CHN	50	232	105	13	400
HKG	1	30	52	17	100
IDN	32	82	83	3	200
JPN	154	179	49	18	400
KOR	75	61	88	76	300
PAK	18	91	88	3	200
PHL	2	11	176	11	200
SIN			134	66	200
THA	119	179	100	2	400
TWN	29	87	61	23	200
ENS					200
Total	480	952	936	232	2,800

Note: Regarding the region codes, see the List of the Abbreviations.

upper-intermediate and advanced learners is naturally larger in the regions of English as a second language (ESL), while that of the A2 novice learners is larger in regions of English as a foreign language (EFL).

3.2.3 Task Design

As discussed in Section 2.2.3, ICNALE aims to collect homogenous and comparable data. The team, therefore, limited the number of the topics to two: "It is important for college students to have a part-time job" (a part-time job) and "Smoking should be completely banned at all the restaurants in the country" (non-smoking). The participants were requested to show whether they agreed or disagreed with each of the statements and why they thought so.

When given a topic that is abstract and conceptually challenging, some of the learners may not be able to write well, not because their L2 writing proficiency is low but simply because they do not know or understand the topic sufficiently. To avoid this, the team chose the above topics, which are easy to understand and familiar to the college students as target learners of ICNALE. In addition, these topics allow the participants a certain range of freedom in the content of the essays.

When collecting the data, international collaborators presented the common instruction shown in Figure 3.1 to the participants. Some of the participants wrote the essays in classes, while others wrote them at home.

As seen above, not only the topic but also various writing-related variables such as time, length, and use of reference tools were controlled, which also guarantees the comparability of the collected data.

What should be noted here is that the team made all the participants use a word processor when writing, which has at least three benefits. First, it naturally urges learners to write longer. Pennington (2003) suggests that the "student writer

Topics

Do you agree or disagree with the following statements? Use reasons and specific details to support your opinion.

(Topic A) It is important for college students to have a part-time job.

(Topic B) Smoking should be completely banned at all the restaurants in the country.

Instructions

1. Clarify your opinions and show the reasons and some examples.
2. You can use 20–40 minutes for each essay. This means that you have 40–80 minutes to complete two essays. Do not finish too early or spend too much time.
3. You must use MS Word or a similar word processor.
4. Do not use dictionaries or other reference tools.
5. Do not plagiarise anyone else's essay.
6. The length of your single essay should be from 200 to 300 words (not letters). Essays that are too short or too long cannot be accepted. You can check the length of your essay using the word count function of MS Word.
7. You must run a spell checker before completing your writing.
8. Finally, copy your essays to the ICNALE Survey file in MS Excel.

FIGURE 3.1 Instruction for participants in the ICNALE Written Essays

working in a computer medium is led to write in a less self-conscious way and with greater engagement, thus writing with a freer mind and less 'rewriting anxiety.'" This undoubtedly leads the participants to produce longer texts. Second, it allows participants to check the number of words before submitting their essays. Third, it saves corpus developers a great deal of time to manually enter handwritten texts.

The team had prepared an Excel file for data collection, which included the sheets for confirmation of research participation, a learner background survey questionnaire, a common vocabulary size test, and two essays. The participants copied and pasted their essays written in Word into this Excel file and submitted it to a local coordinator.

3.2.4 Data Processing

The team checked all the essays collected by international collaborators. The essays that contain the same or quite similar content with the work of someone else, the essays whose lengths do not fall between 200 and 300 words (more precisely, between 180 and 330 words, as the team allowed ±10% of the discrepancy at maximum), and the essays that do not seem to be about the given topics, were all rejected. If one of the two essays written by a student did not meet the requirement, both were excluded. Thus, approximately 15% of the collected samples were rejected.

Finally, the team saved individual essays as the UTF8 text file. Collected essays were distributed in two ways. Registered users can download all the essays and learner metadata, which they can analyse with various analytical software (see Section 2.2.7). They can also access the essay data through ICNALE *Online* (see Section 2.2.7).

3.2.5 Data Samples

Quotes below are the beginning parts of the part-time job essays written by a Chinese learner at B2+ level (CHN_172) and an ENS student (ENS_005).

(1) Today an increasing number of college students take part-time jobs. Have you ever taken a part-time job? There are many advantages for us to take part-time jobs. Firstly, part-time jobs help us keep up with the outside world. They can gain working experience and become more independent. Besides, it's a good chance for us to put what we have learned at college into practice … (CHN_172)

(2) I agree because I am studying at college full-time and also working two part-time jobs which have been a real boon for me. I think that even though it has been a bit of a squeeze to fit everything in a lot of the time, I have learned a lot of tips and tricks to get the most out of my time, cut down the learning curve and for the first time in a long time, I haven't been throwing my money away as much as I used to … (ENS_005)

Just looking at the beginning parts, corpus users soon find out many gaps between a learner and an ENS in terms of vocabulary choice, sentence complexity, and tense control, for instance. Also, these two samples exemplify the merit of topic control in a contrastive study. As the topic is rigidly controlled, the difference in the language of the two writers appears all the more clearly.

3.3 ICNALE Spoken Monologues

3.3.1 Background

Since its release in 2012, ICNALE Written Essays has come to be used by a variety of researchers, teachers, and graduate students in Asia and around the world, but it was clear that speech data was needed for discussion of the whole of Asian learners' L2 English use.

Speeches are subdivided into monologues and dialogues (Crystal, 1995), which are different not only in terms of the number of participants but also in terms of communicative function (see Section 2.2.2). As collecting both monologues and dialogues at the same time seemed difficult, the author decided to begin by collecting monologue speeches. The project was commenced in 2012 (Ishikawa, 2014).

First, the author thought of asking international collaborators to record their students' monologue speeches with IC recorders but soon realised that it may not guarantee the comparability of the collected data. To collect the data for contrastive studies, one needs to control the content of instructions, the timings to give them, and the duration of speeches, all in a rigid way. In particular, time control is an essential factor because one of the aims of this project was to develop a dataset to discuss the difference in oral fluency between ENS and learners and then between learners with different backgrounds.

Thus, prior to the data collection, the author developed an automatic monologue speech collection system installed on a server, which was connected to the international telephone network. As the system gives the same instructions in the same order and with the same timings to all the participants, and it automatically stops recording after the pre-set time, it enabled the collection of highly homogeneous, that is, comparable monologue speeches produced under controlled conditions.

In 2013, after one year of preparation, the author formed a new international network of collaborating researchers and asked them to recruit local participants. Also, the author developed a sound morphing system to protect the privacy of the participating students (see Section 2.2.5). Part of the collected data was released as the ICNALE Spoken Baby in 2014 (Ishikawa, 2014), and the full data was released in 2015 as the ICNALE Spoken, which was renamed the ICNALE Spoken Monologues in 2017.

3.3.2 Participants

Considering the number of samples collected in the ICNALE Written Essays, the ICNALE team aimed to collect at least 200 monologue samples in one region. In the data collection scheme, one participant was required to speak four times (i.e., speaking twice about each of the two topics), meaning that the team needed to recruit at least 50 learners in one region. Finally, the team could collect 200–600 monologues from 50–150 learners in one region. The total number of participants is 1,100, and that of the collected monologue speeches is 4,400 (Table 3.3).

TABLE 3.3 Number of participants in the ICNALE Spoken Monologues

Regions	*A2*	*B1_1*	*B1_2*	*B2+*	*Sum*
CHN	14	48	78	10	150
HKG		1	23	26	50
IDN	26	37	34	3	100
JPN	30	47	43	30	150
KOR	6	15	43	36	100
PAK	5	6	88	1	100
PHL		7	81	12	100
SIN			29	21	50
THA	2	19	25	4	50
TWN	17	41	25	17	100
ENS					150
Total	100	221	469	160	1,100

As in the case of the essay module, the ratios between proficiency levels were not strictly controlled. In ESL regions, the proportion of upper-intermediate and advanced learners is higher, while in EFL regions, the proportion of novice learners is higher. The number of speakers is zero or only a few in some cases, which users need to note.

3.3.3 Task Design

To make a new corpus module fully comparable with the ICNALE Written Essays, the team decided to use the same two topics for monologue speeches: "It is important for college students to have a part-time job" and "Smoking should be completely banned at all the restaurants in the country."

Also, to elicit homogenous and comparable outputs from the international participants, the team fixed the content and the sequence of the instructions as well as the duration of a speech recording, which were all programmed as a scenario in the automatic data collection system stored in the server. Figure 3.2 is a part of the leaflet given to the participants beforehand, which explains how the recording proceeds in detail.

Instruction for the ICNALE Speech Data Collection

Sentences shown in bold are the instructions you will hear on the phone. Topics for your speeches will be presented on the day of the telephone interview.

Welcome to the ICNALE speech data collection system. Now, kindly respond to the following 10 questions.

This recording will last for approximately 10 minutes. If you stop performing the tasks halfway, you will have to do them all over again from the beginning. You are advised to complete all the tasks within a single session.

> Q1: After the beep, please key in your student number provided by your college using the keys on your phone.
> If your student number includes alphabets or symbols, please ignore them and key in just the numbers. (e.g., 123A45XYZ → 12345) Beep → 8 seconds for your key entry
>
> Q2: Please state your family name and first name after the beep. Beep → 5 seconds for your recording (e.g., Shakespeare, William or Obama, Barack)
>
> Q3: Please state the name of your nation or country. Beep → 5 seconds for your recording (e.g., Japan, China, Korea)
>
> Q4: Please state the name of your college or university after the beep. Beep → 5 seconds for your recording (e.g., Kobe University) If this is the first time for your taking this telephone interview, press 0. If not, press 1.
> When you do this task for the first time, press 0 (most of you need to choose 0). Or, if your earlier trial was rejected and you like to retry it, press 1.
>
> Q5: Please record your self-introduction after the beep. You may talk about your hobbies, your academic major, and your dreams; you may choose any topic you like. You have to continue talking for 60 seconds. Beep → 60 seconds for your recording
>
> Q6: You may begin with Speech Task 1. Now, listen to the topic carefully. These days, some people say that XXX (the topic will be given on the day of the telephone interview). Do you

FIGURE 3.2 Instruction for participants in the ICNALE Spoken Monologues

agree or disagree with this statement? Use reasons and specific details to support your claim. You will have 20 seconds to prepare your response. After the beep, start talking immediately and continue for 60 seconds. Do not stop talking before the time is up. Do you like to listen to the topic once more again? If yes, press 1. If no, press 0 and prepare for your speech. Do not mention persons' names in your speech.
♪Chime → 20 seconds for your preparation → Beep → 60 seconds for your recording

Q7: This is your second trial for your speech on XXX. You will have 10 seconds to prepare. You can repeat the same points, but this time, try to speak more. After the beep, start talking immediately.
♪Chime → 10 seconds for your preparation → Beep → 60 seconds for your recording

Q8: You may begin with Speech Task 2. Now, listen to the topic carefully. These days, some people say that YYY (the topic will be given on the day). Do you agree or disagree with this statement? Use reasons and specific details to support your claim. You will have 20 seconds to prepare. After the beep, start talking immediately. Do not stop talking before the time is up. Do you like to listen to the topic once more again? If yes, press 1. If no, press 0 and prepare for your speech.
♪Chime → 20 seconds for your preparation → Beep → 60 seconds for your recording

Q9: This is your second trial for your speech on YYY. You will have 10 seconds to prepare. You can repeat the same points, but this time, try to speak more. After the beep, start talking immediately.
♪Chime → 10 seconds for your preparation → Beep → 60 seconds for your recording
Do not hang up the receiver of your phone till you hear your task completion code

Q10: This is the last question. How was your speech today? Press the number on your phone after the beep. "Very well", press 3. "Well", press 2. "So-so", press 1. "Bad", press 0.
Beep → 5 seconds for your key entry

Now you have completed all the tasks. Your task completion code is X. Don't forget to fill the blank on your Excel sheet with this code. Thank you very much for your cooperation with the ICNALE project.

FIGURE 3.2 (Continued)

So that all the participants could fully understand the instructions, the team took three measures. First, international collaborators gave the leaflet above to all the participants beforehand. Second, they also explained the flow of the recordings to the participants in the students' L1s. Third, all the instructions were recorded in easy-to-understand English as a lingua franca (ELF) pronunciation.

As shown in the leaflet above, this project required the participants to make five 60-second monologue speeches, including a self-introduction speech (Table 3.4).

Prior to the development of a recording scenario, the author conducted several pre-experiments with Japanese learners at varied proficiency levels and found out that even advanced learners often could not continue to speak for more than one minute. Therefore, the duration of a speech was set as 60 seconds. All the participants were asked to continue to speak as much as possible until the time was up.

In the recording, the participants first made a self-introduction speech, which is not included in the corpus. This initial task was given to make the participants feel

TABLE 3.4 Five speeches recorded in the ICNALE Spoken Monologues

Topic	*Tasks*
Self-introduction	Trial (60 second)
Part-time job	Preparation (20 second) + 1st Trial (60 second)
	Preparation (10 second) + 2nd Trial (60 second)
Non-smoking	Preparation (20 second) + 1st Trial (60 second)
	Preparation (10 second) + 2nd Trial (60 second)

relaxed, get accustomed to the speech recording on the phone, and get a feel for the length of 60 seconds.

Then, the participants were given two chances to speak about each topic. This is also based on the results of the pre-experiments above, which showed that even when given enough time for preparation, some felt very nervous and could not begin speaking immediately. Therefore, the team gave all the learners two chances to talk about the same topic. Repeating the same points was not prohibited, but most of the participants used somewhat different lexical items and phrases even when trying to convey a similar idea.

After finishing all the speeches, the participants were asked to self-evaluate their own speeches on a scale of 0 (very poor) to 3 (very good), which is one of the four kinds of assessment data offered in ICNALE (see Section 2.2.4.2).

3.3.4 Data Processing

The participants' speeches were automatically recorded and individually stored as different WAV files on the server. The team accessed all data through the online data management interface shown in Figure 3.3.

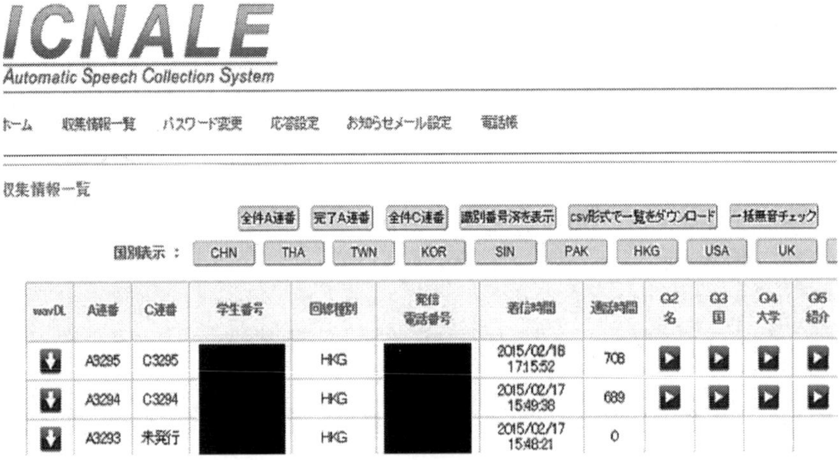

FIGURE 3.3 The ICNALE automatic speech collection system

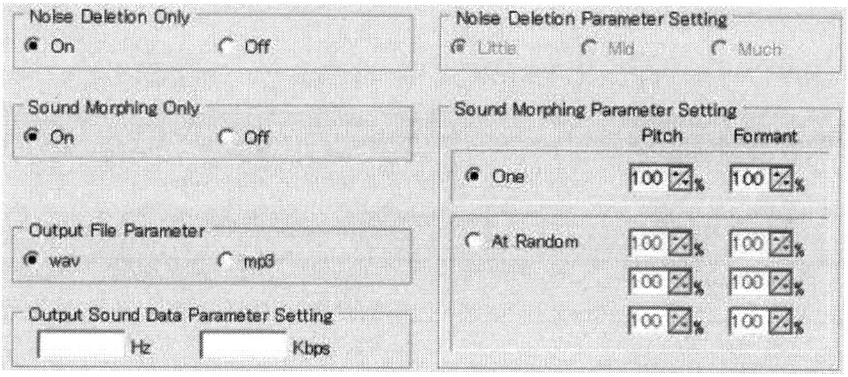

FIGURE 3.4 The ICNALE sound morphing system

This interface enabled the team to easily identify who completed the task and who did not. For example, Speaker A3293 made a phone call but did not leave any messages. Thus, only the speeches of the participants who completed all the tasks were downloaded and manually transcribed by the expert team.

Then, as a preparation for the distribution of the audio data, the team adjusted the pitch and formant of the original WAV file, using a sound morphing system developed for this project (Figure 3.4).

Sound morphing changes the acoustic image of the original speaker's voice to the degree that hearers cannot identify who the speaker is, even if they know the speaker very well. Morphing, however, does not influence the sound wave itself, meaning that corpus users can conduct a fundamental acoustic analysis even with the morphed sound data. In addition, as the same morphing parameter is applied to all the files, the differences across individual speakers and/or across speaker groups are retained.

Registered users can download the whole audio files together with the transcripts and the speaker metadata to analyse them with various analytical software (see Section 2.2.5). They can also access the audio data through ICNALE *Online* (see Section 2.2.7).

3.3.5 Data Samples

Quotes below are the whole of a first-trial speech about the part-time job topic by an Indonesian learner at B1_1 level (IDN_023) and an ENS student (ENS_073).

(3) Okay, I am agree because we have part-time job can help us to get more experience and we can get more pocket money than before. So we have money without asking the parents. And I am disagree if it is school and part-time job, part-time job is on, it will make us more tired than not we just a student and we have time to learn just … (IDN_023)

(4) As a college student, I think it's definitely important to always consider either having a part-time job or securing a part-time job for yourself or full time after graduation, and in that regard I think that you are—you fall into either two categories where in the first category you are—well, in my case I'm studying overseas and for students who travel overseas, either they have some kind of scholarship system which supports them in which case they are financially rather stable. But then, there's also different cases where that financial support falls out and the student has to worry about their income and finances by themselves where they don't have support from parents or from scholarship programs, and in that case I think is almost mandatory ... (ENS_073)

As expected, a learner's speech includes many grammatical errors and deviant word choices. However, what attracts our attention is an essential gap in terms of fluency between a learner and an ENS. The former produces 68 words, while the latter produces 128 words during the same duration. The data collection scheme of the ICNALE Spoken Monologues, which controls the topic, the duration of speaking, and other related variables, enables us to compare various aspects of L2 English speeches of Asian learners on reliable evidence.

3.4 ICNALE Spoken Dialogues

3.4.1 Background

After releasing the ICNALE Spoken Monologues in 2015, the author considered the possibility of collecting learners' dialogue speeches, which seem to reflect learners' L2 communicative skills more directly than their monologues. Therefore, the author started a new project to collect learners' dialogue speeches in 2017.

Dialogue data is usually collected through L2 interviews. By learning from the design of the existing learner interview corpora, such as the NICT-JLE Corpus (Izumi et al., 2003) and the Louvain Interlanguage Database of Spoken English Interlanguage (LINDSEI) (Gilquin et al., 2010), the author developed a protocol for the interviews, which include ten kinds of tasks loosely related to the two common topics of the ICNALE project: a part-time job and non-smoking. The data collection began in Japan. Next, the author again recruited international collaborating researchers, gave them a training session, and asked them to conduct interviews to collect the data from local students in 2018.

The data collected in the early stage of the project was released as the ICNALE Spoken Dialogue Baby in 2018, and the complete data was released in 2019 as the ICNALE Spoken Dialogues (Ishikawa, 2019).

TABLE 3.5 Number of participants in the ICNALE Spoken Dialogues

Regions	*A2*	*B1_1*	*B1_2*	*B2+*	*Sum*
CHN	3	11	17	19	50
HKG		10	9	11	30
IDN	6	6	16	2	30
JPN	31	29	28	12	100
KOR		3	7	10	20
MYS	2	4	14		20
PAK	5	6	13	1	25
PHL	1	1	34	4	40
THA	7	12	19	2	40
TWN	11	7	16	16	50
ENS					20
Total	66	89	172	78	425

Note: As the team could not find a collaborator in Singapore in the dialogue collection, Malaysian learner data were collected instead.

3.4.2 Participants

Each of the national subcorpora of LINDSEI includes the data of 50 learners, and the length of interviews is approximately 14 minutes (Gilquin et al., 2010, pp. 25, 31). As the length of the ICNALE interview is approximately 30–40 minutes, it suggests that the ICNALE team needed to collect at least 25 learners to obtain the roughly same amount of learner outputs. Finally, the team collected the data from 20–100 learners in one region. The total number of participants is 425. As one interview is classified into ten kinds of task speeches, the total number of collected dialogue speech samples is 4,250 (Table 3.5).

Regarding the proficiency levels, the numbers of learners at A2 and B2+ levels were zero or a few in some cases. Users need to be careful when dealing with these small data.

3.4.3 Task Design

What tasks should be included in the interviews depends on the aims of the corpus development. For example, the interviews for LINDSEI include three kinds of tasks: set topic, free discussion, and picture description (see Section 1.2.1). Meanwhile, those for the NICT-JLE Corpus, which collects the data from the Standard Speaking Test (SST) administered by a Japan-based test agency, consist of a sequence of warm-up, picture description, roleplay, storytelling (description of serial pictures), and wind-down; and those for the Trinity Lancaster Corpus (TLC), which collects the data from the Graded Examinations in Spoken English (GESE) administered by Trinity College London, include tasks such as prepared presentation, discussion, and interactive conversation (see Ishikawa, 2019 for a detailed review of the structures of major interview LC).

Analysing the tasks adopted in these interview LC and considering the aim of the ICNALE project, the team made four decisions about the structure of the interviews. First, the interview should include three tasks to elicit different types of learner speeches: free conversations (introductory Q&A about English learning, Q&A about task-related contents, and final reflection), serial-picture descriptions, and roleplays. Second, each of them should be related to the two common topics in ICNALE—a part-time job and non-smoking—which guarantees the compatibility of a dialogue module with the other ICNALE modules. Third, the same tasks should be given to all the participants. This is different from the task design in the existing corpora: the LINDSEI participants could choose a topic from the three options, and the SST interviewers could choose a prompt from several options. The ICNALE interview does not allow a choice by the participants and the interviewers, which enhances the homogeneity of collected data. Fourth, the interview should include a short L1 reflection at its end, where the interviewer and interviewee talk in their L1. This unique additional task is intended to collect baseline data for discussion of the participants' L2 fluency.

Next, the team decided on a task sequence in the following manner, which comprises four modules: Introduction (Icebreaking), Part-time Job Task Set, Non-smoking Task Set, and Reflection (Table 3.6). Each task set includes four subtasks; a serial picture description, a Q&A session about the pictures, a roleplay, and a Q&A session about the content of the roleplay. The mean duration of an interview was approximately 32 minutes, which was followed by approximately 6 minutes of L1 reflection. The total duration was around 40 minutes, which is much longer than the duration of the interviews in the existing dialogue corpora.

The picture prompts and the roleplay prompts (role cards) used in the interviews are shown in Figures 3.5–3.8. The former includes the instruction of "A few weeks ago" on the top, which means that the participants need to begin their speeches with this phrase. This is intended to obtain the data to discuss the accuracy of the participants' tense control. The latter was presented bilingually in English and the participants' L1.

The team also prepared a detailed interview protocol book for the interviewers, which clearly regulates what the interviewers should do and say, though some freedom was given to them only in the roleplay tasks. Figure 3.9 is a part of the protocol book, which shows the instructions regarding the introduction and the part-time job task module.

In the roleplays, the interviewers were told to continue refuting students' claims. This is because one of the purposes of the task was to see how a learner deals with a challenging communicative mission to persuade someone who has a different opinion.

3.4.4 Interviewers

In many of the existing learner interview corpora, ENS teachers have been appointed as interviewers. However, the team asked local non-native college English teachers

TABLE 3.6 The ICNALE interview structure

Task module	*Contents*
Introduction (Icebreaking)	[1] Introductory Q&A: An interviewee answers easy questions about their English learning.
Part-time Job Task Set	[2] Picture Description: The interviewee describes six serial pictures about a boy having a part-time job at a computer shop to earn money to go swimming with his friends.
	[3] Picture-related Q&A: The interviewee answers questions about the contents of the pictures (swimming and computers) and gives an opinion on the college students' use of smartphones.
	[4] Roleplay: The interviewee plays the role of a college student wishing to continue their part-time job. The interviewee is told to persuade their supervisor, who firmly believes that students should not have part-time jobs, to allow him/her to continue working.
	[5] Roleplay-related Q&A: The interviewee answers questions related to the topic of roleplay (part-time jobs) and gives an opinion on the college students' part-time jobs.
Non-smoking Task Set	[6] Picture Description: The interviewee describes six serial pictures about a mother with her son who tells a nearby smoker to stop smoking in the park.
	[7] Picture-related Q&A: The interviewee answers questions about the contents of the pictures (a park and the depicted woman) and gives an opinion about the cleanness of public parks.
	[8] Roleplay: The interviewee plays the role of a customer who had a meal with their friend at a restaurant that allows smoking. The interviewee is told to persuade a restaurant owner to refund their money because their friend could not enjoy the meal due to too much smoking.
	[9] Roleplay-related Q&A: The interviewee answers questions related to the topic of the roleplay (restaurants) and gives an opinion on the ban on smoking at restaurants.
Reflection	[10] L2 Reflection: The interviewee answers questions about the whole interview.
	[11] L1 Reflection: The interviewee answers questions about different tasks in the interview in their L1.

to do the interviews. As a rule, one teacher was in charge of all interviews in one region, but in some cases, the team appointed two or more teachers.

There are many merits in appointing a non-native English teacher as an interviewer. First, it suits the actual status of the English language in the modern world, where English is often used as a means for communication between non-native speakers who have different L1 backgrounds rather than for communicating with ENS. From such an ELF viewpoint, it would be natural for a non-native teacher to serve as an interviewer. Second, a non-native interviewer usually makes the participants—especially those who have had limited opportunities to talk with ENS before—feel less nervous, which is vital in eliciting spontaneous oral outputs from

FIGURE 3.5 Picture prompt based on a part-time job topic

FIGURE 3.6 Picture prompt based on a non-smoking topic

> You are a college student, and you work part-time now. An examiner is your supervisor at your college. Recently the supervisor told you to stop working immediately because your job would negatively influence your study and research. However, you like to continue to work part-time. Please explain why you need to continue it, and try to persuade the supervisor to permit you to continue working.

FIGURE 3.7 Role card based on a part-time job topic

> You recently went to a restaurant with your friend to have a meal. As the restaurant did not prohibit smoking, many people smoked, and your friend said s/he could not endure the smell of cigarettes there. So, you and your friend had to leave the resultant, although you two had not finished meals yet. Now you make a phone call to the restaurant owner. You request the owner to refund (pay back) both of you and your friend.

FIGURE 3.8 Role card based on a non-smoking topic

> ICNALE Spoken Dialogue Learner Interview Scenario
>
> Check the battery of your IC recorder and the video camera. Then, switch on your IC recorder first, then the video camera. You also need to have prepared (a) two picture cards and (b) two role cards to be presented to the interviewees. You should have added L1 translation to the role cards. Do not forget to collect these materials after the interviews. Participants are required to make the content of the interview secret.
>
> **Introduction (3–5 min)**
>
> Thank you for attending this interview. As you know, this is an English interview. So, can I ask you several questions?
>
> (1) First, do you like speaking in English? (Yes) Why do you like it? (No) Why do you not like it?
>
> (2) How often do you speak in English a week? (With whom? In which situation? Topics?)
>
> (3) Do you want more chances to speak in English?
> (Yes) What kinds of topics do you like to talk about in English? (No) Why do you want no more chances to speak in English?
>
> (4) As you know, speaking in English is not easy for many learners. In your case, what do you usually do to improve your English-speaking ability? (Talking to a foreigner, or recording your own speech, for example. If the student says, "I watch English-language movies" or something similar, please ask why it is related to the development of speaking ability rather than listening ability.)
>
> (5) OK. As you know, there are different types of speaking. For example, a one-to-one conversation like this and a group discussion. Which do you like better? Why?
>
> (6) Finally, as you know, there are four basic language skills: Listening, reading, speaking, and writing. In your opinion, which do you think is the most important skill? Please explain why you think so …
>
> Thank you.
>
> **Picture Description 1 (6–8 min)**
>
> OK. Let's move on to our first task, a picture description (you show a card to the interviewee). Now I will give you a picture card. There are six pictures on it, from No. 1 to No. 6. They make one same story. So, please describe those pictures to me. But there is one rule. You have to begin your description with "A few weeks ago …" You understand? Please begin when you are ready.

FIGURE 3.9 Instruction for interviewers in the ICNALE Spoken Dialogues

(If the examinee says "one" or "first," tell them not to count the number. And if the examinee says, "A few weeks ago, I …" stop their speech and tell them to begin with "A few weeks ago, a man …")

Following Q&A

Thank you. Now let me give you several questions.

(1) As you can see, the boy in the picture enjoys swimming. Do you like to swim? (Yes) Why do you like it? (No) Why do you not like it?

(2) Perhaps you have some experience of swimming in the sea. Please introduce your memory [experience] to me.

(3) Also, the boy in the picture is trying to sell a computer to the customers. Do you have a computer? Is it a Windows machine or a Macintosh machine? (Win/Mac …) Why did you choose it? What do you think is the biggest difference between Win and Mac?

(4) Finally, as you know, now many of college students prefer using smartphones. They don't use computers very often, and they cannot use computers very well. So, some business people say that this is a very bad trend. What do you think about this point? (…) Do you have any good ideas to make college students use computers more often?

Thank you.

Roleplay 1 (6–7 min)

OK. Now let's move on to our new task, a roleplay. Here is a roleplay card. (You show a card and then give it to the examinee. The examinee receives the card and reads it silently. You wait for some time.) Did you understand the situation? (Yes …) You are a student, and I am your supervisor. I mean, I am your teacher. You have to persuade me to permit you to continue doing your part-time job. When you are ready, please begin.

Role card for the examiner: *You are a college teacher. An examinee is a college student you are supervising. Recently you have told your student to stop working part-time immediately because you strongly believe that it is bad and it negatively influences the student's study and research. However, your student tries to persuade you to permit them to continue to work part-time. You should behave as a stubborn teacher and continue to reject your student's appeal. Please do not accept the student's claims easily. You are required to continue rejecting what they say.*

Following Q&A

Thank you very much. Good job! Now let me give you several questions.

(1) First, have you ever worked part-time? Do you have some part-time job now? (Yes) Please introduce the job you are doing now. … Maybe there were various jobs available for you. Then why did you choose that particular job? (No) Why didn't you try working part-time?

(2) Maybe, as you know, teaching is one of the popular part-time jobs for college students. There are several types of teaching jobs. For example, a home tutor, you teach at a student's house, and a cram school teacher, you teach at a school. If you teach, which do you like to try? Why?

(3) Finally, some people say that it is important for college students to have a part-time job. Do you agree or disagree? Why do you think so?

Thank you...

FIGURE 3.9 (Continued)

them. Third, it is usually easier for the participants to understand the speech of the non-native interviewers than that of ENS interviewers. Thus, participants can focus on speaking rather than on listening during the interview. Fourth, only a local non-native interviewer can initiate an L1 reflection to be added to the ICNALE interviews. Finally, it is expected to prevent our project from unintentionally contributing to the imposition of ENS centrism on Asian learners and teachers of English (see Section 2.2.6).

As a preparation for the interview, the team sent a set of interview materials to international collaborators: a video camera, an IC recorder, picture prompts, role cards, and a mask for the students to wear. Then, the team required all the interviewer candidates to read the interview protocol (see Section 3.4.3) most carefully, and after that, do a test interview and submit its video to the team. The team scrutinised whether the interview was appropriately conducted and gave them detailed feedback when needed. After this training session, an interviewer was allowed to resume the remaining interviews. These measures ensure greater comparability of collected data.

3.4.5 Data Processing

The interview videos were sent to the team through a cloud-based storage service. The team accessed the data remotely, and a group of experts transcribed it manually. Registered users can download all the video files, the transcripts, and the speaker metadata, and analyse them with various analytical software programs (see Section 2.2.5). They can also access the video data through the ICNALE *Online* (see Section 2.2.7). The multimodality realised in the ICNALE Spoken Dialogues will expand the scope of learner corpus research (LCR).

3.4.6 Data Samples

Quotes below are the output data of a Taiwanese learner at B1_2 level (TWN_34) in an introductory conversation, a picture description, and a roleplay. The two main tasks concern a part-time job topic. In the transcripts, [T] and [S] stand for a teacher (interviewer) and a student (interviewee).

First, in the introductory conversation, the participant answers the questions about his English learning.

(5) [T] … First, do you like speaking in English? / [S] Umm, not really, but I can—I can speak English. So, I think I like it. / [T] Okay. And why do you like it? / [S] Um, I don't know because I can—I started in English since I—in maybe 10 years old. / [T] Mm-hmm. / [S] I don't know, I forgot it. / [T] Uh-huh. / [S] So I—I don't—cannot really say if I really like it or not. / [T] So, it's kind of like your habit/ [S] Maybe …

Then, the participant describes the six pictures of a boy who does a part-time job to earn money to go swimming.

(6) [S] The boy named Peter really wanted to go to beach for swimming or playing other activities, but the problem is—the problem was he did not have that much money for him to go to the beach and then he saw a wanted—job wanted. So, he—he saw the job wanted, so he go—went to apply this job. And since he applied this part-time job, he got the salaries and in this case, he could go—he could go to the beach with his friends and have a good time.

After dealing with the question related to the content of the picture, the participant begins a roleplay and tries to persuade an interviewer, playing a college supervisor, to allow him to continue working.

(7) [S] Um, excuse me, professor. / [T] Yeah. / [S] I really need to get a part-time job. / [T]Um, I—I thought you are having a part-time job. You—you—you do have a part-time job now, right? [S] Yes. / [T] Um, but I—I hope that you can quit your job? / [S] Um, but I really cannot because my family has some financial problems. So, I really need to keep on this part-time job. / [T] Um, well, you know, you are a student and you are supposed to study hard and I found that, uh, recently as I have been seeing you in my class, tired and exhausted and which is not good for your study. [S] Yes. And … / [S] I'm really sorry about that, but if I don't get the part-time, I can—if I can't continue my part-time job, I could be starving. I—I mean because my—you know, my dad's company was bankrupt last month and so our credit line just being lower and lower … [T] I feel so sorry about this really and … / [S] And my mom just need XXX operation next month. If we don't have the money, then we could be starving and cannot just—cannot live. I don't know. [T] Um, you want to try borrowing money from the bank? …

It is clear that different tasks effectively elicited different types of L2 oral outputs from a participant. This kind of data, especially when analysed with the corresponding video, is a good source for analysis of the participant's skills in L2 lexis, grammar, pragmatics, and communication in general.

3.5 ICNALE Edited Essays

3.5.1 Background

One of the limitations of the ICNALE Written Essays is that the included essays are neither error-tagged nor assessed, and therefore, a corpus user cannot directly discuss what type of errors tend to occur in learner essays, how the errors should be corrected, and what degree of linguistic quality the individual essays possess.

One possible solution to this limitation is annotating all the samples with a set of error tags (e.g., Dagneaux et al., 2008). Granger (2003) introduces an error classification framework developed for the FRIDA corpus, which consists of three layers of error annotations: error domain, error category, and word category. Granger emphasises that LC are "especially useful when they are error-tagged, that is, when all errors in the corpus have been annotated with the help of a standardised system of error tags," but as Granger admits, drawing a line between a correct use, a mistake, and an error is highly challenging, and it cannot help being a subjective judgment. A computer-aided error analysis is regarded as one of the staple analytical methods of LCR (Callies, 2015, p. 40), but it does not seem to have spread widely yet due to several practical limitations. First, deciding what is an error and what is not an error is extremely difficult, even if a detailed tagging manual is prepared. Second, error tagging focuses on grammar problems, and it usually does not deal with non-grammatical problems seen in learner essays, though they often account for the non-nativelikeness of learner outputs. Third, error tagging does not explain the overall quality of learner essays.

Considering these points, the author chose another approach and decided to ask professional proofreaders to assess and edit learner essays. This new project began in 2015. Part of the data collected in the early stage was released as the ICNALE Proofread. Then, the whole dataset was released in 2017 as the ICNALE Edited Essays (Ishikawa, 2018a).

3.5.2 Sample Selection

Considering cost and time, the ICNALE team decided to choose ten learners as a sample from each of the four proficiency subgroups in each region. However, the numbers of learners at A2 and B2+ levels were zero or a few in some regions. As each learner wrote two essays, the team assessed and edited 656 essays written by 328 learners in total (Table 3.7).

3.5.3 Assessing and Editing

In this project, the team hired six professional proofreaders (A–F). Each of them was in charge of assessing and editing some of the 656 essays written by 328 learners.

TABLE 3.7 Number of participants in the ICNALE Edited Essays

Regions	*A2*	*B1_1*	*B1_2*	*B2+*	*Sum*
CHN	10	10	10	10	40
HKG		10	10	10	30
IDN	10	10	10	3	33
JPN	10	10	10	10	40
KOR	10	10	10	10	40
PAK		10	10	3	23
PHL		10	10	10	30
SIN			10	10	20
THA	10	10	10	2	34
TWN	10	10	10	10	40
ENS					
Total	60	90	100	78	328

Notes: The total number of learners was 320 for v1.0 and v .2.0. However, the data of B2+ learners from Indonesia, Pakistan, and Thailand were added for v 3.0.

TABLE 3.8 Proofreader backgrounds

Rater	*Age*	*Gender*	*Degree*	*Experience*	*L1*	*Num.*
A (LC)	28	Female	BA	3 years	Canadian	80
B (NH)	32	Female	MS	5 years	Australian	122
C (MH)	27	Female	BS	3 years	American	138
D (JES)	38	Female	BS	10 years	British	220
E (JAC)	31	Female	PhD	2 years	Australian	80
F (Mic)	NA	NA	NA	29 years	NA	16

Notes: LC, NH, MH, etc., are the proofreader identification codes. "Num." in the right column represents the number of essays of which each proofreader was in charge.

TABLE 3.9 Descriptors for the content category in the ESL Composition Profile

Score	*Descriptors*
10–12	EXCELLENT TO VERY GOOD: • knowledgeable • substantive • thorough development of thesis • relevant to assigned topic
7–9	GOOD TO AVERAGE: • some knowledge of the subject • adequate range • limited development of thesis • mostly relevant to topic but lacks detail
4–6	FAIR TO POOR: • limited knowledge of the subject • little substance • inadequate development of topic
1–3	VERY POOR: • does not show knowledge of the subject • non-substantive • not pertinent • OR not enough to evaluate

All the proofreaders have experience in editing academic papers that have appeared in prestigious international journals (Table 3.8).

Essay assessment is usually based on a common rating rubric. The team, therefore, decided to adopt the ESL Composition Profile (Jacobs et al., 1981), one of the most widely used rubrics for an essay assessment. The Profile includes five assessment criteria: content (CON), organisation (ORG), vocabulary (VOC), language use (LNU), and mechanics (MEC). With each of these criteria, proofreaders were required to see the level descriptor, whose sample is shown in Table 3.9, and decide the score.

In the original rubric, different weights were given to different criteria, meaning that different ranges of scores were assigned to them. The team, however, modified

```
Now many parents and teachers disagree that college students should
have their own part-time jobs b~~. B~~ecause they ~~are~~ believe that
students will spend their study~~-~~ time on working. But I do not think
so~~,~~. I think a part-time job is one of the most important things in
college life. It will be the precious experience in your whole life
for several reasons. Firstly~~.~~, a ~~P~~part-time job is a good way to fill
```

FIGURE 3.10 Editing on the essay of CHN_001

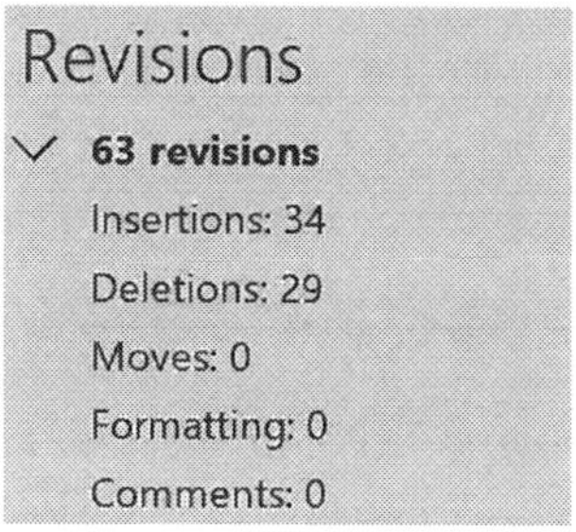

FIGURE 3.11 Number of edits given to the essay of CHN_001

it and asked proofreaders to score all the categories using the same 1–12 point scale, which helped proofreaders assess different aspects of learner essays more efficiently and consistently. Then, the team calculated two kinds of integrative scores: a simple sum of the five categories and an adjusted sum reflecting the weights suggested in the original rubric.

After completing the assessment tasks, proofreaders edited learner essays so that the clarity of the essays was improved and they became fully intelligible. They were required to retain the original texts as much as possible. Making additions, deletions, and alternations in terms of content were prohibited. They did an editing job by using MS Word's track change function, which automatically recorded any change they made.

The quote below (Figure 3.10) is a part of the edited version of the part-time job essay written by a Chinese learner at B1_1 level (CHN_001).

As shown in Figure 3.10, corpus users can easily see which word was inserted and which word was deleted by a proofreader. Also, they see how many revisions were given in total in Word's revision pane (Figure 3.11). The total number of edits, which is sometimes called an edit distance, can be used as an index for the lack of grammatical accuracy in an essay.

3.5.4 Data Processing

Assessment data obtained from six proofreaders were integrated into a single Excel file. Then, edited essays were collected in the form of Word files. They were also saved as UTF8 text files to be analysed with concordancers.

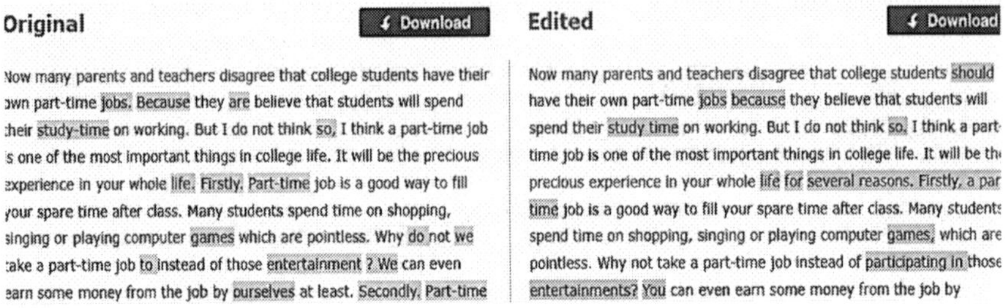

Original Download

Now many parents and teachers disagree that college students have their
own part-time jobs. Because they are believe that students will spend
their study-time on working. But I do not think so, I think a part-time job
is one of the most important things in college life. It will be the precious
experience in your whole life. Firstly, Part-time job is a good way to fill
your spare time after class. Many students spend time on shopping,
singing or playing computer games which are pointless. Why do not we
take a part-time job to instead of those entertainment ? We can even
earn some money from the job by ourselves at least. Secondly, Part-time

Edited Download

Now many parents and teachers disagree that college students should
have their own part-time jobs because they believe that students will
spend their study time on working. But I do not think so. I think a part-
time job is one of the most important things in college life. It will be the
precious experience in your whole life for several reasons. Firstly, a par
time job is a good way to fill your spare time after class. Many students
spend time on shopping, singing or playing computer games, which are
pointless. Why not take a part-time job instead of participating in those
entertainments? You can even earn some money from the job by

FIGURE 3.12 Query results on the ICNALE *Online*

Note: The words added, deleted, and changed by the proofreaders are grey-shaded.

Registered users can download the whole of the original and edited essays and analyse them with various analytical software programs (see Section 2.2.5). Also, they can search for some words or expressions and see how the original version was revised in the edited version on ICNALE *Online*. Figure 3.12 shows the result of the query of a part-time job essay by CHN_001.

In this project, six proofreaders assessed and edited different parts of 656 essays. This means that the difference among the proofreaders may have influenced the assessment scores as well as the number and the content of the edits. Therefore, the team conducted an independent verification study and asked five proofreaders (excluding F) to assess and edit the same additional set of eight essays written by learners with different L1 and proficiency backgrounds. The details of this study are reported in Section 3.6.4.

3.5.5 Data Samples

The quotes below are the beginning parts of the non-smoking essay written by a learner at B1_2 level from Thailand, followed by its edited version.

(8) Today ours human being have more things to addict. Some thing are good and the others are bad. But bad thing must also attractiveness by peer pressure such as alcohols, weeds and cigarettes etc. The easily thing that you can take them in any place and every time that you comfort is cigarette. When you walk on the street you can find the person who was smoking along the ways you would see at least one person. Because there is no smoking prohibited … (THA_004, Original)

(9) Today, human beings have more things to get addicted to. Some things are good and others are bad, but bad things are also attractive by peer pressure, such as alcohol, weed, cigarettes, etc. The easiest thing that you can take any place and any time that comforts you is a cigarette. When you walk on the street, you can find a person who is smoking along the way. You would see at least one person because smoking is not prohibited… (THA_004, Edited)

A comparison of the two versions illustrates how problems seen in the original essay were appropriately identified and corrected by a proofreader. By such a text-based comparison, corpus users can discuss not only the grammar errors but also various types of problematic L2 use by Asian learners.

3.6 ICNALE Global Rating Archives

3.6.1 Background

ICNALE collected learners' output data and their L2 proficiency data estimated from the external test scores (see Section 2.2.4.2), but it did not include output assessment data.

An exception was a small number of essay assessments experimentally collected for the ICNALE Edited Essays. The ICNALE team asked five proofreaders to assess the same set of eight essays based on the five-category rubric. The author analysed collected assessment data and confirmed three facts. First, the essay quality judged by the proofreaders and the writers' proficiency levels estimated from their test scores were not necessarily in accordance, which suggests the importance of collecting more output assessment data. Second, there were several cases where different proofreaders assigned considerably different scores to the same learners' essays, which exemplifies that when collecting assessment data, it would be better for a rater to assess all the samples rather than some of them. Third, there were considerably strong correlations among the five categories in the rubric used for the project, which means that existing rubrics may evaluate only the limited aspects of the learner outputs, and one needs to increase the number of rating categories to appropriately assess the overall quality of learner outputs.

Thus, in 2020 the author began a unique project to collect the output assessment data of Asian learners' speeches and essays from more than 100 raters with varied L1, regional, and occupational backgrounds. Part of the data collected in the early stage was released as the ICNALE Global Rating Archives version 0.1 in 2021 (Ishikawa, 2020b). The full dataset is scheduled to be released by 2023.

3.6.2 Sample Selection

As mentioned above, based on the analysis of essay assessment data experimentally collected, the ICNALE team confirmed that a rater should be responsible for assessing the whole set of target samples (speeches or essays) rather than only a part of them. This means that the team needed to decrease the number of speeches and essays to be assessed in a new project to a reasonable volume. Therefore, the team made four decisions.

First, regarding the topic, the team decided to include only the samples about the part-time job.

Second, regarding the speech type, the team decided to include only the dialogues. Then, from the interview data, the team clipped only the initial 90 seconds

TABLE 3.10 Number of samples assessed in the ICNALE Global Rating Archives

	Speeches					*Essays*				
Regions	*A2*	*B1_1*	*B1_2*	*B2+*	*Sum*	*A2*	*B1_1*	*B1_2*	*B2+*	*Sum*
CHN	2	6	6	6	20	5	5	5	5	20
HKG				4	4				4	4
IDN	6	6	6	2	20	5	6	6	3	20
JPN	5	5	5	5	20	5	5	5	5	20
KOR		3	7	10	20	5	5	5	5	20
PAK			3	1	4			1	3	4
PHL				4	4				4	4
SYN/ MYS			4		4				4	4
THA	6	6	6	2	20	6	6	6	2	20
TWN	5	5	5	5	20	5	5	5	5	20
ENS					4					4
Total	24	31	42	39	140	31	32	33	40	140

of the persuasion roleplays related to the part-time job topic. The team thought that the roleplays reflect a wider range of a learner's speech skills, including fluency, pronunciation, grammar, pragmatics, and willingness to communicate (WTC) (MacIntyre, 1994; MacIntyre et al., 1998).

Third, regarding the target learners, the team decided to focus mainly on Asian learners in EFL regions.

Finally, regarding the number of samples, the team considered a balance between coverage in sampling and practicality in assessment and chose 140 essays and 140 roleplay speeches (Table 3.10). Twenty samples were taken from each of the EFL regions and four from each of the ESL regions, as well as an ENS group. The team regards the assessment data of ESL learners and ENS as a kind of reference to discuss the linguistic quality of the outputs of EFL learners.

The team paid attention to the balance between proficiency levels, but when the number of available samples was limited in the original dataset, the team flexibly adjusted the numbers. All the samples above were anonymised and randomised in order, which enabled raters to assess each of them without any prior knowledge about the background of a speaker/writer.

3.6.3 Rater

At the beginning of the rater selection, there were two things that the team needed to decide: how many numbers and what type of raters should be recruited.

First, the team decided to collect the assessment data from at least 50 raters for each of the essay and speech assessments, meaning recruiting at least 100 raters in total. Considering that the number of raters assessing an L2 learner output is usually one or two even in high-stakes tests, this is an overwhelming number. However, the team thought that the quality of a learner's output should be decided by the collective knowledge of a sufficient number of experts.

Next, regarding the type of raters, the team aimed to recruit raters with varied L1, regional, and occupational backgrounds. In the field of language teaching, many believe that a learner's output can be assessed in a reliable manner only by experienced ENS teachers. Such a belief, which is also seen in the choice of a yardstick for contrastive interlanguage analysis (CIA) (see Section 1.3.2), seems to be bound by two kinds of groundless dogmas: ENS centrism and teacher centrism (see Section 2.2.6). Regarding the so-called native speakerism, Holliday (2006) suggests that English language teaching has been strongly influenced by the belief that "'native-speaker' teachers represent a 'Western culture' from which spring the ideals both of the English language and of English language teaching methodology." However, such deification of ENS teachers would not be appropriate any longer when thinking of the rapid spread of ELF in Asia and the world and the shift from a teacher-centred to a learner-centred approach in modern communicative language teaching (CLT). More and more researchers have joined the trend of the "non-native speaker (NNS) movement," which empowers non-native English teachers in the world (Braine, 2018).

Thus, aiming to expand regional and mother tongue diversity, the team recruited raters not only from the Inner Circle, where English is spoken as a mother tongue, but also from the Outer Circle, where English is used as a second or an official language, and also from the Expanding Circle, where English is learned at schools as a foreign language (see Section 2.2.1). At the time of writing this chapter, rater nationalities cover three countries in the Inner Circle (US, Australia, and Canada), five countries and regions in the Outer Circle (Hong Kong, India, Malaysia, Pakistan, and the Philippines), and ten countries in the Expanding Circle (Cambodia, China, Indonesia, Japan, Jordan, Korea, Laos, Taiwan, Thailand, and Vietnam), whose L1s cover 17 languages (Arabic, Cantonese, Mandarin Chinese, English, Filipino, Hmong, Indonesian, Japanese, Konkani, Korean, Lao, Malay, Punjabi, Thai, Urdu, Uyghur, and Vietnamese).

Also, aiming to expand occupational diversity, the team collected data from business people (media/advertisement, software development, accounting, biomedical engineering, and customer service), graduate students with non-English majors (economics, engineering, and science), college teachers with non-English majors (psychology and history), in addition to English teachers and graduate students with English majors. Inclusion of assessment by business people is especially important because they are key players in global ELF communication. For instance, the Vienna–Oxford International Corpus of English v2.0 (VOICE) (see Section 1.2.4), which is one of the most widely used ELF corpora, collects only 25.5% of the whole data from the "educational" domain and 10.1% from the "professional research and science" domains, while it collects 54.5% from the business domains ("professional business" and "professional organizational") (from "Statistics VOICE 2.0 Online").

Recruitment of raters with varied backgrounds is based on the key philosophy of ICNALE. It has consistently paid careful attention to keeping a reasonable distance from the imposition of a narrow ENS model on corpus users as well as L2 teachers and learners in Asia. Thus, the team collected the output data from varied types of ENS (Written Essays and Spoken Monologues), recorded the oral instructions in ELF (Spoken Monologues), and invited non-native interviews (Spoken Dialogues). Together with these existing modules, the ICNALE Global Rating Archives is expected to neutralise the conventional ENS/teacher centrism inherent in LCR (see Section 2.2.6).

3.6.4 Rating

After deciding how many numbers and what type of raters should be recruited, the team then considered what type of rubric should be adopted and how a rating process should be controlled.

To develop a new rubric for this project, the team first re-examined the results of the verification study conducted in the ICNALE Edited Essays project, in which five proofreaders assessed and edited the same set of eight essays (see Section 3.5.4). When assessing, they used the ESL Composition Profile (Jacobs et al., 1981), which includes five rating criteria: content (CON), organisation (ORG), vocabulary (VOC), language use (LNU), and mechanics (MEC). These criteria seemed to cover a wide range of aspects of essay quality, but the correlation analysis revealed that the correlations between ORG and CON, between VOC and LNU, and between LNU and MEC were all strong (Table 3.11), and the Profile may have assessed only two or three aspects (Ishikawa, 2018b).

Thus, the team decided to double the number of rating categories in the new rubric. Also, the team decided to use the same rubric for both speech assessment and essay assessment, which enables researchers to discuss the quality of Asian learners' spoken and written outputs on the same ground.

A new rubric includes both a holistic rating and an analytical rating. The latter covers three basic aspects that may influence the quality of learners' L2 outputs: language, content, and attitude, each of which is subdivided into two to four categories (Table 3.12).

The ICNALE rubric is unique in that it includes two attitude markers. Willingness to communicate is defined as "a readiness to enter into discourse at a particular time with a specific person or persons, using a L2" (MacIntyre et al.,

TABLE 3.11 Correlations between five criteria in the ESL Composition Profile

	CON	*ORG*	*VOC*	*LNU*	*MEC*
CON	1.00				
ORG	0.93	1.00			
VOC	0.51	0.62	1.00		
LNU	0.32	0.36	0.76	1.00	
MEC	–0.04	0.01	0.09	0.68	1.00

TABLE 3.12 Rubric structure of the ICNALE Global Rating Archives

Language	*Content*	*Attitude*
Intelligibility	Comprehensibility	Willingness to communicate
Complexity	Logicality	Involvement
Accuracy	Sophistication	
Fluency	Purposefulness	

1998), and it is caused by "a combination of communication apprehension and perceived competence which have their roots in introversion and self-esteem" (MacIntyre, 1994). Meanwhile, involvement usually concerns the overt presence of a speaker/writer and a listener/reader in a discourse. As surveyed in Petch-Tyson (1998), involvement level tends to increase in speeches than in essays, in informal discourses than in formal discourses, and in interactive discourses than in monodirectional discourses. In comparison to the language and content categories, these two attitude categories can be more independent of learners' L2 proficiency levels. It is possible that low-proficiency learners produce more willing and engaging utterances. In this sense, the ICNALE rubric enables raters to assess the quality of learner outputs from a more balanced viewpoint.

To make an assessment valid and reliable, the team needed to clearly define each criterion and make all the raters fully understand it. Thus, the team prepared a detailed rater handbook, where each category was explained in the following manner (Figure 3.13).

The rating was conducted in two stages. First, raters were asked to decide on a holistic rating score of 0–100 points. Then, they were asked to give an analytical rating score of 0–10 points for each of the 10 categories. The former should be based on the overall impression of a learner's output, and the latter should be decided by examining each aspect. Also, raters were required to write short comments about the strong and weak points of each output sample (Figure 3.14).

Then, another problem the team needed to think about was how to control the rating process, especially in terms of scoring strictness, a yardstick for scoring, and acquaintance with the rubric.

First, regarding scoring strictness, the verification study mentioned above proved that among only five proofreaders, the rating scores were not necessarily stable. Table 3.13 lists the means of the scores that different raters gave to the same set of eight samples, as well as the total means and standard deviations (SD).

This shows that Rater B tends to assign relatively higher scores, while Rater A tends to assign relatively lower scores, and Rater D tends to give similar scores to different samples. Based on this finding, the team decided to require all the raters who join a new project to ensure that the mean of their rating scores falls within the range of 45–55 for a holistic score (/100) and 4–6 for a category score (/10) to fill the possible gap between a generous grader and a strict grader. Furthermore, controlling a variance in the rating scores, the team required all the raters to confirm

Overall

(0) Holistic: First, read or listen to the entire sample and grasp its overall quality. Here you do not need to analyse it in detail.

Language-related categories

(1) Intelligibility: To what extent can you "decode," that is, verbally understand what is said/written? In speech evaluation, factors such as pronunciation and intonation will influence the degree of intelligibility. In essay evaluation, factors such as spelling and sentence structures may influence it. Please note that "intelligibility," which concerns the understandability of the language, should be distinguished from "comprehensibility," which concerns the understandability of the content. You may sometimes find a speech/essay that is intelligible but not comprehensible, such as a logical but nonsensical statement. Meanwhile, you do not usually find a speech/essay that is comprehensible but unintelligible because if the text cannot be decoded, its content cannot be conveyed.

(2) Complexity: To what extent do you think the speaker/writer uses morphologically and/or semantically complex words, phrases, expressions, constructions, and grammar? Complexity is seen at many levels of language. For example, "I speculate ..." usually sounds more complex than "I think" (vocabulary). "It is speculated that ..." may sound more complex than "I speculate" (voice, construction). "If I were a bird" may sound more complex than "If I am a bird" (subjunctive, grammar).

(3) Accuracy: To what extent do you think the sample is error-free in terms of vocabulary and grammar? In addition, you should examine the elements such as pronunciation and intonation in speech evaluation and the elements such as punctuation in essay evaluation. Please note that you should ignore minor and isolated errors, which may be a mistake rather than an error. And please note that the standard for evaluation should be a proficient non-native ELF speaker, not an English native speaker.

(4) Fluency: To what extent do you think the speaker/writer is fluent in the speeches/essays? Fluency needs to be evaluated in two ways: fluency and disfluency. If someone talks/writes more, the fluency score should increase, while if they use more disfluency markers, the score may decrease. Disfluency markers include fillers (e.g., "uh," "well," "oh," "hmm"), pauses, false starts (e.g., "I thin ... thin ... no, I thought ..."), etc. in speeches; and unnecessary connectors (e.g., "and," "but," "so," "because") and semantically empty phrases ("I think" most typically), etc., in essays. Please note that using these disfluency markers once or twice usually does not cause any problems in communication.

Content-related categories

(5) Comprehensibility: To what extent can you understand the content of the speech/essay? Please note that comprehensibility, which concerns the understandability of the content, should be distinguished from intelligibility, which concerns the understandability of the language. If a speaker/writer presents a logically reasonable idea, the score should increase.

(6) Logicality: To what extent do you think the idea presented in the speech/essay is logical and reasonable? In speech evaluation, you need to examine the reasons presented by the speaker to explain why they need to continue working. In essay evaluation, you need to examine whether the reasons and the conclusions are logically connected.

(7) Sophistication: To what extent do you think the ideas presented in the speech/essay are sophisticated and critically thought out, unique, original, and innovative?

(8) Purposefulness: To what extent do you think the speaker/writer consistently and consciously pays attention to the purpose of the task? In a speech, the participant was asked to persuade a supervisor to allow them to continue working; and in an essay, the participant was asked to share their own opinion about part-time jobs for college students. You must examine whether the participant fully understands the purpose of the task and consistently sticks to it. Purposefulness is closely related to task completion.

FIGURE 3.13 Rating rubric for the ICNALE Global Rating Archives

Attitude-related parameter

(9) Willingness: To what extent do you think the speaker/writer is willing to communicate? A participant with a limited L2 proficiency may show a high level of willingness to communicate (WTC), and a participant with a high L2 proficiency may show a relatively low level of WTC. In a speech, factors such as the quantity of talk, the frequency of turn-taking, change of tones, and the use of body language may reflect the participant's WTC. In an essay, factors such as the quantity of writing, the number of ideas presented, and the use of various amplifiers (e.g., "very," "surely," "definitely," and "I strongly believe") may represent the participant's WTC.

(10) Involvement: To what extent do you think the participant tries to present themselves and involve or engage the hearer/reader in their discourse, rather than speaking/writing one-sidedly? Factors such as the use of the second-person pronouns (e.g., "You know," "as you see," "as you expect") and mentioning the hearer/reader are usually related to the degree of involvement.

FIGURE 3.13 (Continued)

[Strong points] Supports the reason with details. Grammar is well controlled, though awkward word choices from time to time.

[Weak points] The listener must be patient, as the speech is choppy throughout. Perhaps an alternative reason could be provided.

FIGURE 3.14 Rater comment samples

TABLE 3.13 Scores assigned by five proofreaders

Rater	*CON*	*ORG*	*VOC*	*LNU*	*MEC*	*Mean*	*SD*
A	7.88	7.88	7.25	7.25	8.38	7.73	0.93
B	9.88	10.38	8.38	7.63	8.25	8.90	1.40
C	9.13	8.88	8.25	8.00	8.50	8.55	0.86
D	8.38	8.13	7.88	7.25	8.00	7.93	0.67
E	7.50	8.00	8.25	7.75	8.38	7.98	0.71

that the standard deviation (SD) of their rating scores falls within the range of 20–30 for a holistic score (/100) and 2–3 for each category score (/10). As these values are automatically calculated on the Excel-based rating sheet, raters can correct their scores anytime, as needed.

However, even with such a scoring rule, different raters may have different views about the standard in their rating. If some raters regard an eloquent ENS orator as the standard for rating, and others regard a non-native speaker only with a basic survival level of English skills as a standard, their ratings would not be comparable. Therefore, regarding the yardstick, the team decided to regard "a professional and proficient ELF speaker who regularly uses English for their business/research purposes" rather than an ideal ENS as a standard in the rating. As the team expected that some of the raters might not be familiar with the ELF concept, the rating guide explained what it is in detail (Figure 3.15).

What is ELF?

Each sample should be evaluated from the viewpoint of English as a lingua franca (ELF), a type of English used mainly for professional communication between non-native speakers who have different mother tongues (e.g., between L1 Japanese and L1 Thai speakers). According to recent research, more than 75% of English communication in the fields of business and research occurs between non-native speakers. Raters are expected to fully understand the status of English in the current world. Therefore, "Excellent" in the rating scale, for example, should be understood NOT as excellent in comparison to English native speakers but excellent as a professional ELF speaker.

FIGURE 3.15 Definition of ELF in the ICNALE rating guide

Q4: Analytical evaluation should be done ...
- (a) before the overall (holistic) evaluation
- (b) after the overall (holistic) evaluation
- (c) before or after overall (holistic) evaluation

Q5: The middle (average) point should be ...
- (a) 60/100 (or 6/10)
- (b) 50/100 (or 5/10)
- (c) decided by each rater

Q6: Closeness to English native speakers ...
- (a) is the most important in rating
- (b) is not necessarily the most important in rating
- (c) should be appropriately considered in rating

FIGURE 3.16 Check test for raters (Questions 4–6)

Notes: The answers to Q4–6 are (b)

As shown above, the team prepared a detailed rater guidebook that explains the project aim, the outline of the rubric, detailed specifications of each rating category, the ELF concept as a key philosophy, and the details of a rating process. However, some raters may begin the rating without fully understanding the content of the guide, which would subsequently undermine the reliability of the collected assessment data. Therefore, the team asked all the raters to take an online test. The test includes ten questions about the content of the guidebook (Figure 3.16).

If the score was below 9, a rater was asked to take a retest. When a rater finished the test successfully, a confirmation code was issued, which a rater needed to enter on the rating sheet. This test system guarantees that all raters understood the project aim and the rating scheme appropriately.

3.6.5 Data Processing

Assessment data obtained from raters were integrated into a single Excel file. Registered users can download and analyse it for their research aims. They can easily calculate the means of the scores given to a particular sample or a set of samples. Thus, it is possible to compare the overall qualities of the outputs by different regional groups (e.g., Thai learners vs. Japanese learners), by different proficiency groups (e.g., A2 learners vs. B2+ learners), and in different production modes (i.e., speeches vs. essays), for example. Also, users can compare different rater groups (e.g., ENS raters vs. non-ENS raters or teacher-raters vs. non-teacher-raters). Such comparisons can be conducted not only for the rating scores but also for the rater comments.

In addition to the assessment data, the ICNALE Global Rating Archives includes the edit data of learner essays, which makes it possible for users to analyse the relationship between the overall quality of an output sample and the number of edits given to it.

3.6.6 Data Samples

Tables 3.14 and 3.15 show four raters' (001, 004, 005, and 012) ratings and comments on a part-time job essay written by a Taiwanese learner at B1_2 level (TWN_005).

The sample rating data above show that the gap in scores given by different raters may be much more significant than usually expected. The discrepancy between

TABLE 3.14 Ratings on a sample essay (TWN_005)

Rater profile	*R_001*	*R_004*	*R_005*	*R_012*
Job	Business	TESOL	Testing	Grad
Age	30s	20s	30s	30s
Gender	Male	Male	Female	Female
L1	Japanese	English	Filipino	Lao
Degree	BA	BA	BA	MA
CEFR (Self-reported)	C1	ENS	C1	B2
Holistic Score	85	60	75	69
Analytical Score Sum	88	49	70	69
Intelligibility	9	4	7	6
Complexity	9	6	8	6
Accuracy	9	3	6	7
Fluency	9	6	7	5
Comprehensibility	9	6	7	6
Logicalness	9	6	7	7
Sophistication	9	5	7	6
Purposefulness	9	3	8	9
Willingness	8	2	6	8
Involvement	8	8	7	9

Note: "Grad" represents a graduate student.

TABLE 3.15 Rater comments on a sample essay (TWN_005)

	Strong points	*Weak points*
R_001	Clear and coherent context along with good examples to justify the argument.	A couple of minor grammar mistakes and inaccurate use of words.
R_004	Decent logical flow and good attempts at advanced language	Many points of inaccuracy. Should elaborate more
R_005	Complexity shown. Instead of saying "important" → "necessary." Minor grammatical errors shown.	Difficulty in explaining that the writer wants to work after military responsibility
R_012	There is one clear, well- focused topic. Main ideas are clear and are well supported by detailed and accurate information.	Most sentences are well constructed, but have a similar structure. Makes several errors in grammar, and spelling that interfere with understanding.

the maximum and the minimum values reaches 25 points in a holistic score and 39 points in an analytical score sum. It seems that R_004 (teacher) is a relatively stricter rater, while R_001 (business person) is a lenient rater. Such a dataset would offer a new angle to discuss the quality of Asian learners' L2 speeches and essays.

PART II

Aspects of Asian Learners' L2 English Use

4
VOCABULARY

4.1 Introduction

4.1.1 Vocabulary in LCR

4.1.1.1 Background

Vocabulary is a core of learners' L2 linguistic knowledge. In second language acquisition (SLA), it has been known that people with more extensive vocabulary tend to have a higher L2 proficiency (Meara, 1992). However, the relationship between vocabulary knowledge, L2 proficiency, and actual L2 performance is not very clear. Thus, "understanding how it [vocabulary] is learned and used by individual speakers and writers is of paramount importance to the field of applied linguistics as a whole" (Szudarski, 2018, p. 35).

It is expected that learners use a smaller number, a narrower range, and a lower difficulty level of words than L1 English native speakers (ENS), and they often use some sets of words in a deviant manner. To investigate these aspects, learner corpus (LC) researchers examine lexical fluency, lexical diversity, and lexical sophistication in learner texts, and they scrutinise how various sets of words are used by learners.

Lexical fluency is measured by the total number of running words in a text. Lexical diversity, which represents the proportion of unique words in a text, is measured by the type/token ratio (TTR) or its modified indices such as Corrected TTR (Carroll, 1967), *R* (Guiraud, 1960), *C* (Herdan, 1960), *D* (Malvern & Richards, 2002), and mean segmental TTR (Johnson, 1939). Some researchers also discuss lexical density as its variant, which represents the proportion of lexical or content words in a text. Then, lexical sophistication, which represents the proportion of the

DOI: 10.4324/9781003252528-6

advanced vocabulary in a text, is measured by the ratio of the difficult words that are not included in basic word lists or, more simply, by the mean word length (i.e., the mean number of letters in a word). It is also called lexical difficulty.

The target of these vocabulary studies is not limited to single words. It also includes word sequences, which are called multi-word units (MWU), lexical bundles, clusters, *n*-grams, and phraseology in learner corpus research (LCR). Firth (1957) says, "You shall know a word by the company it keeps" (p. 17). These word sequences are regarded as one of the markers distinguishing ENS and learners (Granger & Bestgen, 2014).

4.1.1.2 Spoken Vocabulary Use

LC-based vocabulary studies have discussed aspects of L2 learners' vocabulary use in speeches and essays. Here we will survey some of the recent studies discussing how learners use L2 vocabulary in their speeches. What should be noted here is that the boundary between vocabulary studies and grammar studies is often fuzzy in LCR. Some of the vocabulary-related studies are also reviewed in Section 5.1.

There are many studies discussing the general patterns seen in learners' oral vocabulary use. First, regarding the vocabulary level and its distribution, Jones et al. (2018) analyse an interview test corpus and find out that approximately 97% of the words used by learners belong to the top 2,000-word level and little difference exists across learners at B1, B2, and C2 levels, though the cumulative ratios of the top 20 words decrease by five points in per cent (pp. 40–41, 45), and learners particularly overuse the words such as "we," "er(m)," "think," and "can" (pp. 47–64). Crossley et al. (2014) analyse one-year longitudinal conversations between ENS and L2 learners studying at a US university and report that the ENS vocabulary shows a normal Zipfian distribution (i.e., the frequency of a word steadily decreases as its frequency rank goes down), which, however, is not seen in learners' vocabulary use because they often use high/low-frequency words in a unique way. Thus, the authors conclude that the quantity of L2 input may not lead to a change in learners' speech vocabulary. Second, as regards lexical innovations, Brunner et al. (2016) report that in English as a lingua franca (ELF) Skype conversations, European college students adopt a variety of innovative forms in order to accommodate themselves to the interaction. Finally, as regards the range of speech vocabulary, Smith et al. (2020) analyse the contents of the TOEFL speaking tasks and report that existing academic vocabulary lists may not wholly cover the range of the needed vocabulary.

Several studies pay attention to multi-word sequences in learner speeches. Pęzik (2015) applies a new distributional technique to *n*-gram extraction and succeeds in extracting discourse functional *n*-grams (including unigrams) semi-automatically from a conversation corpus. Wang (2017) reports the frequency, form, and function of four-word lexical bundles used in academic ELF speeches vary across speech types (lectures and seminars) as well as disciplinary genres (medicine, social sciences, and natural sciences). Cervantes and Gablasova (2018) analyse speeches of a variety of learners and reveal that the frequency of phrasal verbs (e.g., "turn off") steadily increase from B1/2 to C1/2 levels, and L1 Chinese learners particularly overuse them.

Learners' vocabulary use in speeches is closely related to their oral fluency. Brand and Götz (2011) compare L1 German learners' temporal fluency, which was estimated from the numbers of unfilled pauses, and the number of errors and reveal that fluency and accuracy are not significantly correlated. However, fluency measurement may be a problematic process. Götz (2019) reports that the number of filled pauses is influenced not only by learners' proficiency levels but also by the place of their origin, the age of their L2 acquisition, and even the experiences of an interviewer.

4.1.1.3 Written Vocabulary Use

Next, our attention is paid to learners' written vocabulary use. Earlier studies based on the analysis of the International Corpus of Learner English (ICLE) show that European learners tend to overuse or underuse specific types of words. For example, Ringbom (1998) shows many European learners commonly overuse core nouns (e.g., "people" and "things"), core verbs (e.g., "think" and "get"), modals (e.g., "be" and "can"), vague quantifiers (e.g., "all" and "very"), and conjunctions (e.g., "but" and "or"). Lorenz (1998) reports that L1 German learners overuse particular adjectives (e.g., "important" and "good") and a variety of scalar intensifiers, especially amplifiers in the phrases of intensifying adverbs + adjectives. Altenberg and Tapper (1998) suggest that L1 Swedish learners overuse several connectors (e.g., "for instance" and "of course") but underuse the others (e.g., "therefore," "though," and "yet"). Petch-Tyson (1998) reports that many European learners commonly overuse the first/second-person pronouns, hedges (e.g., "kind of" and "sort of"), and the words referring to the situation of writing and reading (e.g., "here" and "now"), which the author attributes to a higher level of writer-reader visibility seen in learner essays. Granger and Rayson (1998) show that L1 French learners overuse the words like "as," "a," "is/are," "it," "they," and "have," while they underuse the words like "the," "and," "that," "for," and "he/his." Then, Hasselgren (1994) reports that advanced Norwegian learners often depend too much on "lexical teddy bears," that is, a limited set of easy words that are similar to their L1 words and learned at an earlier stage. By using them, learners maintain a certain level of fluency without making serious errors.

Recent studies have come to discuss learners' written vocabulary from more diversified viewpoints. Many of them focus on the general patterns seen in it. First, as regards lexical overuse/underuse, Callies (2013) observes that learners overuse first-person pronouns and subject placeholders ("it" and "there"), while they underuse inanimate noun subjects and use limited types of reporting verbs. Leedham (2015) reports that L1 Chinese students studying at UK colleges use longer words but produce shorter sentences than ENS, and they tend to overuse connectors (e.g., "besides," "in other words," "meanwhile"), informal words (e.g., "besides," "what's more," "lots"), first-person pronouns of "we," and reference-related vocabularies (e.g., "according to," "as below," "figure," "table") (pp. 41–58). Chitez (2014) shows that L1 Romanian learners overuse verbs, prepositions, and adverbs, and underuse nouns and determiners by more than three points in per cent in comparison to ENS, and they tend to make errors most often with prepositions, then with determiners and verbs (pp. 66–71, 73). Next, as regards lexical errors, Huiping and Yongbing (2014) report that L1 Chinese students often make errors in the usage of high-frequency verbs, many of which they suggest can be explained from the viewpoint of conceptual transfers. Also, regarding lexical innovations, which are said to characterise the status of English as a second language (ESL), Callies (2016) reveals that L2-based innovations in derivational morphology are seen in the writings of learners both in ESL regions and English as a foreign language (EFL) regions. The author insists that ESL/EFL speakers may share a common cognitive mechanism to enhance morphological transparency and explicitness of form-meaning connections in L2. Then, when discussing the quality of learners' vocabulary use from a macro viewpoint, researchers often examine lexical diversity, which is usually calculated from the numbers of tokens and types. Jarvis and Hashimoto (2021) reconsider the methods to quantify lexical diversity in L1 and L2 texts by comparing five kinds of word type definitions (forms, lemmas, POS-based lemmas, POS-based lemmas with manual correction, and word families including all the derivative forms) and three kinds of measures (a measure of textual lexical diversity [MTLD], moving average MTLD with wrap-around measurement, and moving average TTR). A statistical comparison with the human-rated scores proves that there are no significant differences between different measures.

Next, some studies discuss multi-word sequences in learner essays. First, regarding the method to identify them, O'Donnell et al. (2013) compare the set of multi-word formulas extracted from four kinds of criteria: *n*-gram frequency, *n*-gram association, semi-productive phrase-frames (e.g., "it is * to"), and native norms (i.e., items included in the ENS' academic formula list) and suggest that the choice of a criterion may influence the relationship between writers' backgrounds and their formula use. Second, as regards the relationship between collocation frequency in corpora and collocation knowledge of learners, Durrant (2014) conducts a meta-analysis of the related studies and reveals that they are moderately correlated. Third, regarding the effect of learners' L1, Paquot (2013) shows that lexical bundles adopted by French learners are partly influenced by their L1, which the author calls priming transfer. Edwards and Lange (2016) report that in terms of the usage of three-word clusters, no clear difference is observed between ESL and EFL speakers, though the gaps between ENS and learners and those between learners from different regions are suggested. Chen (2013) notes that the frequency of phrasal verbs greatly varies, even between British and American students. Finally, as regards the development in learners' multi-word sequence use, Garner (2016) analyses a quasi-longitudinal dataset (see Section 1.2.4) and reports that L1 German learners' use of phraseology (phrase-frames) in essays becomes more varied and complex according to the increase in proficiency, while Chen (2018) analyses a longitudinal essay corpus and reports that the number and the variety of phrasal verbs used by L1 Chinese learners may not increase so steadily.

In addition to these, there are many studies focusing on the usage of particular groups of words. First, regarding nouns, Flowerdew (2010) reveals that learners use shell nouns (aka signalling nouns), which are a kind of container nouns whose meanings depend on the context (attitude, consequence, difficulty), less than ENS, while they use a particular type of shell nouns with cataphoric functions across clauses relatively more often. Schanding and Pae (2018) report that shell nouns are used in different lexicogrammatical patterns by ENS and learners. Next, as regards adverbs, Pérez-Paredes and Sánchez-Tornel (2014) report that young learners begin to use adverbs sufficiently after grade 10. Schweinberger (2020) reports that learners use "very" as an adjective modifier in a different manner from ENS, which the author suggests is due to the gap in the collocations of particular types of adjectives. Finally, regarding reference and aboutness markers, Rankin and Schiftner (2011) report that L1 German learners overuse those markers, especially "concerning," without noticing the semantic difference between reference and aboutness.

4.1.2 ICNALE Case Studies

In Section 4.2, we will first discuss the overall quantitative aspects of Asian ESL and EFL learners' vocabulary use in speeches and essays. The data are taken from the ICNALE Spoken Monologues and the ICNALE Written Essays. Our analytical attention is paid to three kinds of quantitative indices: lexical fluency, lexical diversity, and lexical sophistication.

Next, in Section 4.3, we will focus on the keywords characterising Asian EFL learners' speeches and essays taken from the corpus modules mentioned above. We will compare the learner outputs and ENS outputs to identify what vocabulary is overused or underused by learner groups at different proficiency levels or from different regions. Our focus is put mainly on the keywords common to most of the learner groups.

Finally, in Section 4.4, we aim to reconsider the features of Asian ESL and EFL learners' written vocabularies from another angle by comparing the learners' essays and their fully edited versions. The data is taken from the ICNALE Edited Essays. Identifying the keywords and keyphrases (trigrams) characterising each of the original and edited versions would help us deepen our understanding of the communicative problems in learner essays. Here we attempt to expand the conventional keyword analysis as a powerful technique of contrastive interlanguage analysis (CIA) in two ways by applying it not only to individual words but also to multi-word sequences and by comparing learners' outputs with the edited versions rather than the ENS' outputs.

4.2 Quantitative Aspects of Learner Vocabulary

4.2.1 Aim and RQs

As mentioned in Section 4.1, we usually assume that learners use a smaller number, a narrower range, and a lower difficulty level of words than ENS. However, whether it applies to both speeches and essays of Asian learners and how learner-related variables such as regions of origin and L2 proficiency levels as well as task-related variables such as topics and speech trial numbers influence it is not necessarily clear. Thus, this study examines the following research questions:

RQ1 To what extent do learner/task-related variables influence lexical fluency in learners' speeches and essays?
RQ2 To what extent do learner/task-related variables influence lexical diversity in learners' speeches and essays?
RQ3 To what extent do learner/task-related variables influence lexical sophistication in learners' speeches and essays?

4.2.2 Data and Method

In this study, we analyse the output data of ESL and EFL learners taken from the ICNALE Spoken Monologues and the ICNALE Written Essays. For RQ1 (fluency), we examine the total number of words in speeches and essays. Then, for RQ2, we examine the mean segmental TTR (STTR) values, which are adjusted by 10 words for speeches and by 50 words for essays. Finally, for RQ3, we examine the mean word length (MWL), that is, the mean number of letters in single words. Though word length does not directly reflect its difficulty, it is usually supposed that the longer a word is, the more complex and difficult it can be.

When discussing the effect of proficiency, we analyse all the learner data included in the corpus, while when discussing the other effects, we use the data of learners only at B1 level (B1_1 and B1_2) to control the possible proficiency effect. We conduct a between-subjects ANOVA when examining the effects of learner-related parameters, and a within-subjects ANOVA when examining the effects of task-related parameters.

4.2.3 Results and Discussion

4.2.3.1 RQ1 Lexical Fluency

Lexical fluency in the outputs by different participant groups, which we define as the mean numbers of words in a single speech or essay, is shown in Figures 4.1, 4.2.

Comparing speeches and essays, we realise that the gaps between groups are much more prominent in speeches than in essays, which can be explained by several

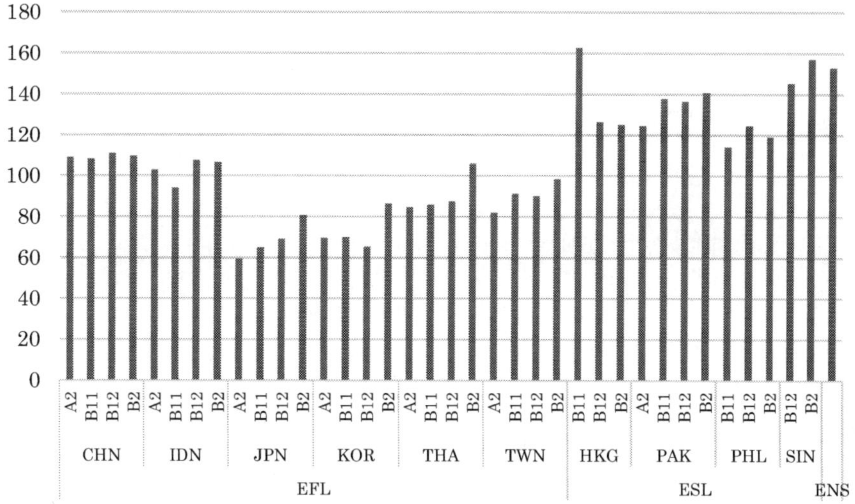

FIGURE 4.1 Mean numbers of words in speeches

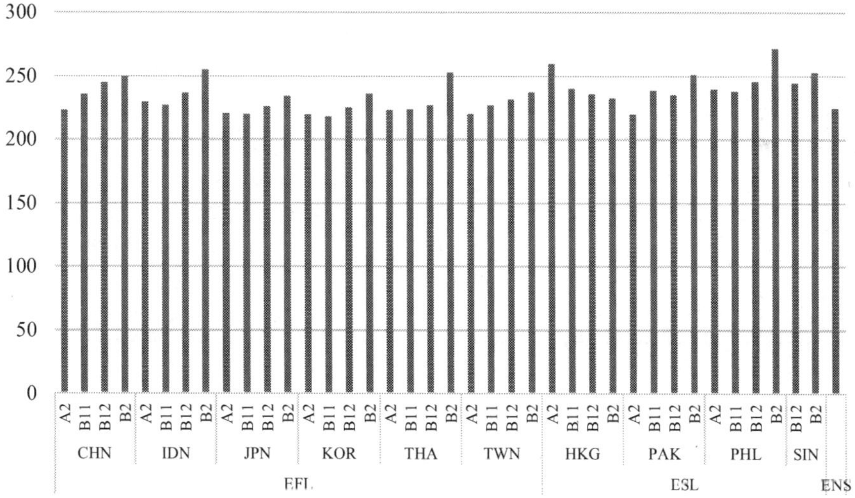

FIGURE 4.2 Mean numbers of words in essays

factors. First, there was a difference in data collection methods. When collecting monologue speeches, we required the participants to speak as much as possible in 60 seconds, but how much they actually spoke during the time depended on individuals. Meanwhile, when collecting essays, we required the participants to write 200–300 words and accepted only the samples meeting the requirements. Second, there may exist a gap in difficulty between the two tasks. Speaking can be a cognitively more challenging task—speakers need to control many elements such as pronunciation, stress, rhythm, and intonation in a limited time span—and it is usually marginalised in traditional "comprehension-based" language teaching (Lazaraton, 2001, p. 103). Contrary, when writing, people can spend time as long as they like, and as writing "enjoys special status" in the communicative framework of language teaching (Olshtain, 2001, p. 201), many learners have experience writing essays in classes.

Then, how do learner-related and task-related variables influence the number of words? Regarding speeches, the main effects of proficiency levels (F (4, 4395) = 387.114, $p < .001$, η_p^2=.261), regions (F (10, 3349) = 444.916, $p < .001$, η_p^2 =.571), topics (F (1, 1679) = 146.27, $p < .001$, η_p^2 =.080), and trial numbers (F (1, 1679) = 210.775, $p < .001$, η_p^2 =.112) were all significant. Also, regarding essays, the main effects of proficiency levels (F (4, 5595) = 69.931, $p < .001$, η_p^2 =.048), regions (F (10, 4165) = 31.425, $p < .001$, η_p^2 =.070), and topics (F (1, 2087) = 168.690, $p < .001$, η_p^2 =.075) were all significant.

Post-hoc tests (Holms) revealed the orders between different participant groups or between different task variables, as shown in Table 4.1.

In terms of proficiency, participants' speeches are classified into three groups: ENS, B1_2/B2+, and B1_1/A2, and their essays are classified into four groups: B2+, B1_2, ENS/B1_1, and A2. The difference between learners and ENS is clear in speeches but not so in essays, which is because the essay length is controlled, as mentioned above. We might say that learners come to speak and write more as their overall proficiency levels go up. According to the data, the number of words produced by learners at A2 level is 44% smaller in speeches but only a few per cent smaller in essays when compared to ENS. Then, the value for learners at B2+ level is 30% smaller in speeches, and they write 8% longer than ENS.

Second, regarding regions, participants' speeches are classified into eight groups: ENS, SIN, PAK, HKG/PHL, CHN, IDN, TWN/THA, and JPN/KOR, while

TABLE 4.1 Effects of four variables on lexical fluency

Variables	*Speech*	*Essay*
Proficiency	ENS (153.073) > B1_2 (110.347) ≈ B2+ (107.289) > B1_1 (90.193) ≈ A2 (85.867)	B2+ (243.522) > B1_2 (237.052) > ENS (224.705) ≈ B1_1 (228.028) > A2 (221.886)
Region	ENS (153.073) > SIN (145.414) > PAK (136.553) > HKG (127.875) ≈ PHL (123.582) > CHN (109.927) > IDN (100.454) > TWN (90.780) ≈ THA (86.795) > JPN (66.994) ≈ KOR (66.642)	PHL (244.816) ≈ SIN (244.552) ≈ CHN (238.255) ≈ HKG (237.177) ≈ PAK (236.796) ≈ IDN (231.715) ≈ TWN (228.676) ≈ THA (224.735) ≈ ENS (224.705) ≈ KOR (222.168) ≈ JPN (221.072)
Topic	PTJ (115.391) > SMK (109.958)	PTJ (236.069) > SMK (227.441)
Trial Number	2nd (115.621) > 1st (109.727)	

Notes: Regarding the region codes, see the List of the Abbreviations. The symbol ">" represents that the difference between adjacent pairs is significant, while "≈" represents that the difference is not significant at α= .05.

TABLE 4.2 Sample monologue speeches (CHN_006 and ENS_025)

Speaker	*Speech (All)*
CHN_006 1st Trial (89 words)	These days some people say that it's important for college student to have a part-time, part-time job. First, from the material point of view, at this year, the Ministry of Education has made further adjustment of college tuition. Part-time jobs will undoubtedly ease economic burden for those not so rich families. Secondly is the shortcomings of China's exam-oriented education, most of the students cannot communicate with others or confront difficulties alone in the society. Part-time jobs can make them adjusted to the society gradually.
ENS_025 1st Trial (153 words)	Ah, my answer is dependent on a particular individual's previous experiences. Ah, I think if kids have had a part-time job experience in high school, uh, then they don't necessarily need to have part-time jobs in college. However, for students who haven't, I think it's an important part of, ah, learning. It's an important life skill to develop. Um, part time jobs come with different responsibilities and obligations and tasks and skills and things like that than purely academic study does and there isn't really an opportunity afforded to college students in a classroom or in a lecture to learn those particular skills. Uh, like I said on the other hand though, if a student has already had experience with that, ah, there's really no need for them to develop the skills as they probably already have them and part-time work can interfere with the student's ability to learn academically.

clear grouping was not seen in essays. The difference in speech fluency is seen not only between learners and ENS but also between ESL and EFL learners. In the outer circle, Singaporean learners speak more, and Philippine learners speak less, while in the expanding circle, Chinese learners speak more, and Japanese and Korean learners speak less. Here we like to have a look at the speeches of a Chinese learner at B1_2 level (CHN_006) and an ENS teacher-participant (ENS_025) (Table 4.2).

The learner, who tries to present a well-thought idea, seems to think and speak at the same time. This leads them to speak considerably less than ENS.

Finally, regarding topics and trial numbers, it was suggested that the part-time job topic elicits significantly more outputs than the non-smoking topic. This is presumably because a part-time job is a familiar topic for participants, many of whom have experienced working part-time before. Then, the data showed that the participants spoke significantly more in the second trial than in the first trial. When talking about the same topic again, they get accustomed to the task and feel more relaxed, which seems to lead to greater fluency.

4.2.3.2 RQ2 Lexical Diversity

Lexical diversity of the outputs by different groups, which we define as the STTR, is shown in Figures 4.3 and 4.4.

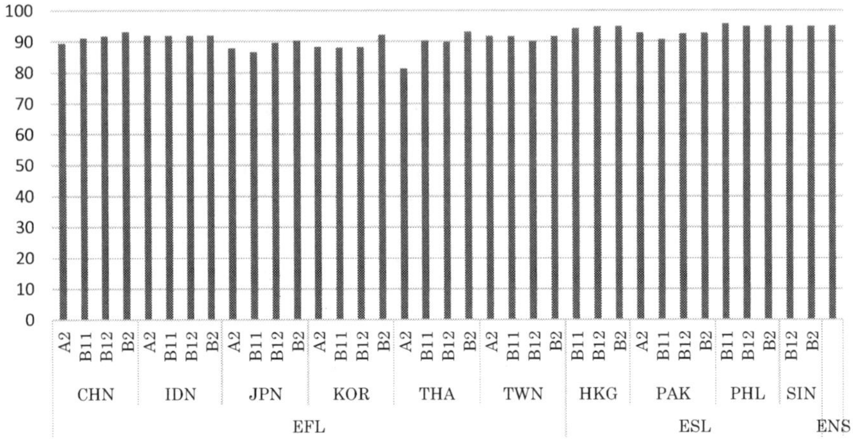

FIGURE 4.3 Mean STTR values in speeches

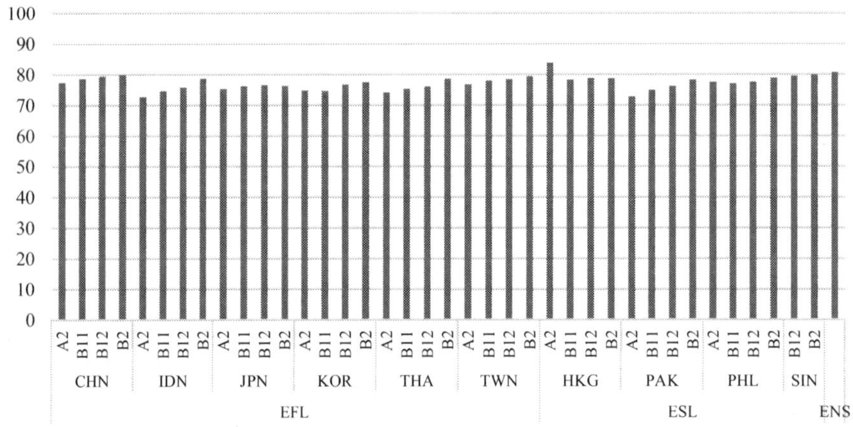

FIGURE 4.4 Mean STTR values in essays

Regarding speeches, the main effects of proficiency levels (F (4, 4395) = 116.651, p < .001, η_p^2 =.096), regions (F (10, 3349) = 106.182, p < .001, η_p^2 =.241), and topics (F (1, 1679) = 69.268, p < .001, η_p^2 =.04) were significant, but the main effect of trial numbers (F (1, 1679) = 0.109, p = .742, η_p^2 =.000) was not significant. Then, regarding essays, the main effects of proficiency levels (F (4, 5595) = 149.631, p< .001, η_p^2=.097), regions (F (10, 4165) = 80.834, p < .001, η_p^2=.163), and topics (F (1, 2087) = 77.168, p < .001, η_p^2=.036) were all significant.

Then, post-hoc tests (Holms) proved the orders between groups and between variables, as summarised in Table 4.3.

Comparing speeches and essays, we see that the STTR values seem to be considerably lower in the latter. This is because the essays, all of which fall within 200–300 words, are much longer than monologue speeches, which are approximately 80–160 words long.

TABLE 4.3 Effects of three variables on lexical diversity

Variables	*Speech*	*Essay*
Proficiency	ENS (95.082) > B2+ (92.846) > B1_2 (92.083) > B1_1 (90.253) ≈ A2 (89.959)	ENS (80.552) > B2+ (78.567) > B1_2 (77.579) > B1_1 (76.516) > A2 (74.977)
Region	ENS (95.082) ≈ SIN (94.972) ≈ PHL (94.917) ≈ HKG (94.756) > PAK (92.424) ≈ IDN (91.859) ≈ CHN (91.566) ≈ TWN (91.121) ≈ THA (90.003) > KOR (88.168) ≈ JPN (87.965)	ENS (80.552) > SIN (79.501) ≈ CHN (78.864) > HKG (78.538) ≈ TWN (78.185) > PHL (77.530) > JPN (76.317) ≈ KOR (75.909) ≈ THA (75.540) ≈ PAK (75.480) ≈ IDN (75.276)
Topic	PTJ (92.644) > SMK (91.630)	SMK (77.806) > PTJ (76.952)

In terms of lexical diversity, participants' speeches are classified into four groups: ENS, B2+, B1_2, and B1_1 and A2; and their essays are classified into five groups: ENS, B2+, B1_2, B1_1, and A2. This suggests that learners speak and write with a narrower vocabulary than ENS, though advanced learners use a relatively more expansive range of vocabulary than novice learners. The difference between learners and ENS and between learners at different proficiency levels can be observed more clearly in lexical diversity than in the total number of words. According to the data, the range of the vocabulary of learners at A2 level is approximately 5% narrower in speeches and 7% narrower in essays when compared to that of ENS vocabulary. Then, the value for learners at B2+ level is only 2–3% narrower in speeches and essays.

Second, regarding regions, participants' speeches are classified into three groups: ENS/SIN/PHL/HKG, PAK/IDN/CHN/TWN/THA, and KOR/JPN, while their essays are classified into five groups: ENS, SIN/CHN, HKG/TWN, PHL, and JPN/KOR/THA/PAK/IDN. The STTR values are higher for ESL learners than for EFL learners, though we see several exceptions. Also, the values are relatively higher for Singaporean learners and lower for Pakistani learners among ESL participants, while they are relatively higher for Chinese learners and lower for Japanese and Korean learners (in speeches) and Indonesian learners (in essays). Here we have a look at the essay samples of an Indonesian learner at A2 level and an ENS student (Table 4.4).

The Indonesian learner repeats and reuses not only the words but also the phrases (e.g., "many people say …") and the structures (e.g., "because in X, S+V"). By such repetitions, the student may try to compensate for their lack of vocabulary knowledge and complete writing. Meanwhile, the ENS writer hardly repeats the words. In the ENS essay, therefore, the discourse is going forward without going back and forth. Lexical diversity highlights the gap between two texts.

Finally, regarding topics, different results are shown between speeches, where the part-time job topic elicits more varied vocabulary, and essays, where the non-smoking topic does so. Generally speaking, a social topic is more complex, and it is likely

TABLE 4.4 Sample essays with a high/low STTR value (IDN_063 and ENS_100)

Writer	*Essay (initial part)*
IDN_063 STTR=53.5	*We know that time is very interesting for us. And many people say* "Time Is *Money.*" Many people say time is money, *because in everyday* many people *work to find* money. To find *job* is very *difficult,* because in *the world, all of human life from* job. Everyday, *every* time in *our* life is *use* to work to find the money …
ENS_100 STTR=88.4	*Advising college students to sacrifice what little available time they possess away from their studies in the pursuit of Mammon's glittering bounty is both wrong-headed and short-sighted. Anyone who has ever known a university or college student appreciates* the *focus* and *dedication* they *bring* to the *acquisition* of a *diploma* …

Notes: The italicised words occur the first time in the text.

to elicit a greater variety of vocabulary than a personal topic. In speeches, however, participants often do not have enough time to consider what to say and therefore try to depend on a familiar vocabulary to avoid making pauses, which may explain why the participants use a narrower range of words when discussing non-smoking in speeches. What should be noted here is that lexical diversity seems to be influenced by both the task difficulty and the topic difficulty.

4.2.3.3 RQ3 Lexical Sophistication

Lexical sophistication of the outputs by different groups, which we operationalise as the mean word length (MWL), is shown in Figures 4.5 and 4.6.

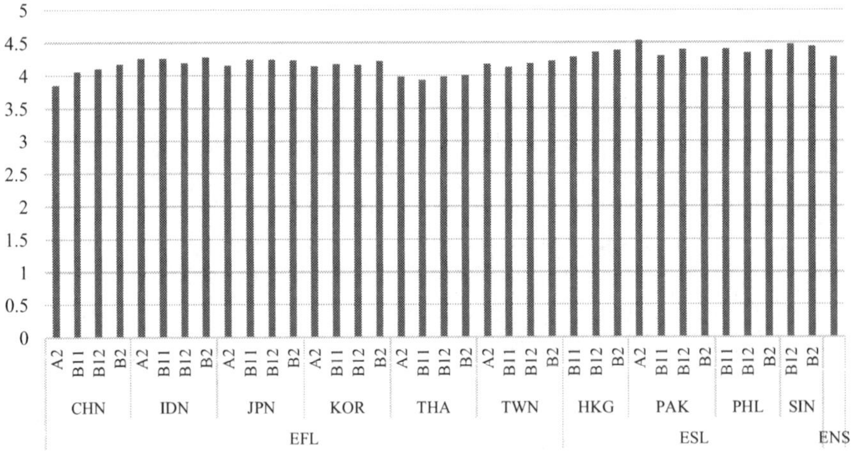

FIGURE 4.5 Mean numbers of letters per word in speeches

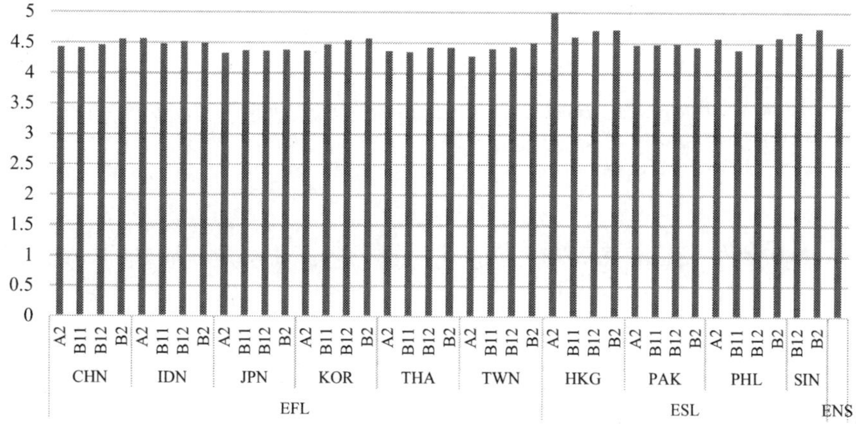

FIGURE 4.6 Mean numbers of letters per word in essays

TABLE 4.5 Effects of four variables on lexical sophistication

Variables	*Speech*	*Essay*
Proficiency	ENS (4.278) ≈ B2+ (4.278) ≈ B1_2 (4.266) > B1_1 (4.159) ≈ A2 (4.157)	B2+ (4.602) > B1_2 (4.518) > ENS (4.435) ≈ B1_1 (4.413) > A2 (4.373)
Region	SIN (4.469) ≈ PHL (4.400) ≈ PAK (4.388) ≈ HKG (4.347) ≈ ENS (4.278) ≈ JPN (4.242) ≈ IDN (4.228) ≈ KOR (4.165) ≈ TWN (4.149) ≈ CHN (4.085) > THA (3.959)	SIN (4.683) ≈ HKG (4.675) > KOR (4.509) ≈ IDN (4.496) ≈ PHL (4.494) ≈ PAK (4.489) ≈ ENS (4.435) ≈ CHN (4.429) ≈ TWN (4.418) ≈ THA (4.373) ≈ JPN (4.366)
Topic	SMK (4.333) > PTJ (4.147)	SMK (4.572) > PTJ (4.352)
Trial number	2nd (4.247) > 1st (4.233)	

Regarding speeches, the main effects of proficiency levels (F (4, 4395) = 26.157, p < .001, η_p^2=.023), regions (F (10, 3349) = 55.036, p < .001, η_p^2=.141), topics (F (1, 1679) = 475.369., p < .001, η_p^2=.221), and trial numbers (F (1, 1679) = 3.971, p = .046, η_p^2=.002) were all significant. Likewise, regarding essays, the main effects of proficiency levels (F (4,5595) = 85.049, p < .001, η_p^2 =.057), regions (F (10, 4165) = 43.398, p < .001, η_p^2 =.094), and topics (F (1, 2087) = 1311.19, p < .001, η_p^2 =.386) were all significant.

Then, post-hoc tests (Holms) proved the orders between groups and between variables, as summarised in Table 4.5.

Comparing speeches and essays, the MWL values tend to be lower in the former. When speaking, participants seem to use shorter and easy-to-recollect words to keep their speeches going smoothly.

TABLE 4.6 Sample speeches with a high/low value in word length (THA_016 and SIN_028)

Speaker	*Speech (initial part)*
THA_016 MWL=3.340	*It*—smoking *is the bad*—*the bad way to*—*to* [***] *my*—other people when *I see the man* smoking, *I* think *it*—*it's not* polite. *It can die to him. I*—*I* don't [***] *it and I* [***] more people allow [***] because smoke *is bad*....
SIN_028 MWL=5.067	*I* agree that smoking should *be* banned *in* restaurants across *the* country. Firstly, this *is for* hygiene reasons. *If* consumers *in* restaurants *are* allowed *to* smoke while they consume their food, *the ash* from their cigarettes....

Notes: [***] represents the word(s) that the transcriber could not understand.

First, in terms of lexical sophistication, participants' speeches are classified into two groups: ENS/B2+/B1_2 and B1_1/A2; and their essays are classified into four groups: B2+, B1_2, ENS/B1_1, and A2. This suggests that ENS do not necessarily use longer words than learners, but advanced learners tend to use somewhat longer words than novice learners. The differences between proficiency groups are more salient in essays, where participants have enough time to sophisticate the vocabulary, and they can try using longer words when needed than in speeches. According to the data, the length of the words used by learners at A2 level is approximately 3% shorter in speeches and 5% shorter in essays when compared to that by ENS. Then, the value for learners at B2+ level is almost the same as that for ENS in speeches, and they use 3–4% longer words than ENS in essays.

Second, regarding regions, participants' speeches are classified only into two groups: THA and the others; and their essays are classified into SIN/HKG and others. Here we have a look at the non-smoking speeches in the first trials of a Thai learner at B1_1 level (THA_016) and a Singaporean learner at B1_2 level (SIN_028). In the quotes in Table 4.6, which show the initial parts of two learner speeches, shorter words consisting of one to three letters are shown in italics, and longer words consisting of seven or more letters are shown with underlines.

The Thai learner repeatedly uses shorter words such as "I," "it," and "to," while longer words rarely occur except for *ing*-forms ("smoking") and basic words ("because"). Meanwhile, the Singaporean learner seldom adopts shorter words except for a set of function words and instead uses longer words such as "firstly," "hygiene," and "consumers."

Finally, regarding topics and trial numbers, it was revealed that the non-smoking topic encourages the participants to use longer words than the part-time job topic. Also, as naturally expected, participants were proven to use somewhat longer words in the second trial, where they could develop their original claims by adopting more sophisticated vocabulary.

TABLE 4.7 Summary of the findings: effects of learner/task-related variables on three kinds of lexical aspects

	Fluency	*Diversity*	*Sophistication*
Speeches			
P	ENS > [B1_2/B2+] > [B1_1/A2]	ENS > B2+ > B1_2 > [B1_1/A2]	[ENS/B2+/B1_2] > [B1_1/A2]
R	SIN > PAK > [HKG/PHL] > CHN>IDN > [TWN/THA] > [JPN/KOR]	[SIN/PHL/HKG] > [PAK/IDN/CHN/TWN/THA]>[KOR/JPN]	[Others] > THA
T	PTJ > SMK	PTJ > SMK	SMK > PTJ
TT	$2^{nd} > 1^{st}$	(*ns*)	$2^{nd}>1^{st}$
Essays			
P	B2+ > B1_2 > [ENS/B1_1] > A2	ENS > B2+ > B1_2 > B1_1 > A2	B2+ > B1_2 > [ENS/B1_1] > A2
R	(*no clear grouping*)	[SIN/CHN] > [HKG/TWN] > PHL > [JPN/KOR/THA/PAK/IDN]	[SIN/HKG]>[Others]
T	PTJ > SMK	SMK > PTJ	SMK > PTJ

Note: P, R, T, and TT represent Proficiency, Region, Topic, and Trial Times, respectively.

4.2.4 Summary

In this section, we analysed the data from the ICNALE Spoken Monologues and the ICNALE Written Essays to examine the quantitative aspects of learners' L2 vocabulary use. Major findings are summarised in Table 4.7. Regarding regions, ENS groups are excluded.

The gap between A2 and B2+ levels and that between two topics were confirmed in all three indices in both speeches and essays. In addition, the gap between ESL and EFL regions was suggested in fluency and diversity in speeches, and partly in sophistication in essays.

These findings, which suggest a relatively large effect of learner/task-related variables on learners' vocabulary use, seem to be in accordance with what has been reported in the recent LCR. For example, Gablasova et al. (2017) analyse learners' use of epistemic forms such as "maybe," "kind of," and "actually" in four kinds of speech tasks adopted in the Trinity Lancaster Corpus (TLC) (see Section 1.2.2), and they reveal that learners' stance-taking style drastically changes across task types (especially between monologic and dialogic tasks) and even across individual speakers. Also, as mentioned in Section 4.2.1, Pérez-Paredes and Díez-Bedmar (2019) analyse the same corpus and report that the usage of certainty adverbs changes across learners' L2 proficiency levels and also across task types. These results strongly suggest that we need to consider varied learner/task-related parameters when discussing learners' L2 vocabulary use. In this sense, easy generalisation of the findings should be carefully avoided.

4.3 Keywords in Speeches and Essays

4.3.1 Aim and RQS

SLA researchers once tended to pay attention solely to learners' errors. However, keyword analysis or frequency-based identification of the lexical items significantly overused or underused by a target group (see Sections 1.3.1 and 1.3.2) enables us to discuss misuse (errors), overuse, and underuse in combination.

Previous keyword studies in LCR, many of which are based on ICLE, have revealed noteworthy facts about over/underuse in essays by advanced learners in Europe, but whether they also apply to the speeches and essays of Asian EFL learners and what words characterise Asian EFL learners in general rather than a part of them has remained largely unclear.

Therefore, we conduct two kinds of keyword analyses here based on the comparisons between learners and ENS and between learners with different proficiency and regional backgrounds, which follows the standard analytical procedures in CIA. Thus, this study examines the following research questions:

RQ1 What are the spoken keywords for Asian EFL learners at different proficiency levels and from different regions?
RQ2 What are the written keywords for Asian EFL learners at different proficiency levels and from different regions?

4.3.2 Data and Method

In this study, we analyse the output data of EFL learners taken from the ICNALE Spoken Monologues and the ICNALE Written Essays. For both RQs, we identify the keywords based on the log-likelihood ratios (LLR). LLR is a slightly modified version of a chi-squared value (χ^2), and it shows to what extent an observed value deviates from the value expected when the difference in frequency between the two texts is not significant. Like χ^2, when LLR is higher than 3.84, 6.63, 10.83, and 15.13, the difference is said to be significant at α = .05, .01, .001, and .0001. However, as frequency comparisons are repeated countless times with all the words appearing in the target and/or reference texts, it would be safer for us to apply a stricter threshold to control the Type 1 error. Thus, we discuss only the top 20 overused or underused keywords whose LLRs are 30 or higher.

When discussing the overall trend in the vocabulary use of Asian EFL learners, it is crucial for us to distinguish the keywords common to most of them from the keywords characterising only one or a few particular subgroups. Therefore, we first subdivide the target learners into four proficiency-based groups (A2, B1_1, B1_2, and B2+) and the learners at B1 level (B1_1 and B1_2) into six region-based groups (CHN, IDN, JPN, KOR, THA, TWN), and then compare their outputs with ENS outputs. Analysing the learners only at B1 level when comparing the regions is because learners' proficiency levels are not controlled between different region modules. Next, we extract the 20 keywords from each of the groups and regard the keywords common to more than three proficiency-based groups as the keywords characterising Asian EFL learners in general and the keywords common to more than four region-based subgroups as the keywords characterising Asian EFL learners at the intermediate level.

4.3.3 Results and Discussions

4.3.3.1 RQ1 Speech Keywords

First, the top 20 keywords identified by the comparisons between learner speeches and ENS speeches are shown in Table 4.8, where the words appear in the decreasing order of the LLR.

TABLE 4.8 Keywords overused or underused in learner speeches

	Overuse	*Underuse*
Proficiency		
A2	we, our, agree, can, bad, smoking, is, will, harm, make, so, uh, because, money, many, my, student, smoker, he, opinion	that, 's, believe, would, um, where, able, be, hand, restaurants, a, it, 're, going, are, studies, them, into, been, while
B1_1	we, our, can, agree, is, job, smoking, because, part, many, make, I, money, us, will, bad, so, harm, statement, opinion	that, would, believe, be, able, while, um, where, a, it, going, 're, you, hand, are, 's, into, of, to, whether
B1_2	we, our, uh, can, agree, is, will, smoking, opinion, part, the, money, my, many, make, job, harm, I, must, uhh	that, would, able, be, believe, uhm, going, it, where, while, are, a, hand, 's, restaurants, being, you, having, 're, to
B2+	we, can, our, is, agree, so, many, uhh, statement, part, harm, smoking, opinion, job, student, because, earn, money, bad, first	um, that, would, a, believe, able, 're, be, going, 's, while, into, hand, where, an, being, work, go, you, then
Common, (3+/4)	[4/4] agree, can, harm, is, many, money, opinion, our, smoking, we [3/4] bad, because, job, make, part, so, will	[4/4] a, able, be, believe, going, hand, 're, 's, that, where, while, would [3/4] are, into, it, um, you
Regions (B1 level only)		
CHN	uh, we, our, can, some, us, will, society, opinion, harm, the, harmful, part, make, more, many, first, is, smoking, may	that, would, be, able, they, believe, you, work, while, going, where, being, go, working, 're, or, it, area, having, are
IDN	we, can, our, because, the, make, agree, passive, smoker, money, English, active, will, parents, cigarette, dangerous, buy, student, must, get	uh, um, restaurants, would, you, believe, to, able, should, hand, going, into, 't, where, while, that, might, think, go, are

(*Continued*)

TABLE 4.8 (Continued)

	Overuse	*Underuse*
JPN	we, is, agree, so, statement, this, I, smoking, with, many, money, opinion, our, disagree, study, bad, because, can, part, my	a, that, you, be, it, 's, would, really, just, believe, 're, hand, as, are, able, to, into, them, then, while
KOR	uhh, I, is, we, so, smoking, agree, money, part, bad, job, student, because, my, very, many, opinion, smoker, our, umm	that, it, a, you, be, restaurants, 're, would, able, 's, as, where, in, to, uhm, of, around, are, hand, while
THA	agree, the, make, we, I, you, student, can, will, bad, because, part, time, uhh, restaurant, many, job, our, money, destroy	restaurants, be, would, students, are, believe, hand, where, of, going, 's, those, while, could, to, banned, as, all, it, own
TWN	I, we, think, our, will, agree, completely, job, can, because, my, smell, restaurant, learn, smoking, part, important, harm, hate, Taiwan	um, that, 're, as, able, of, would, them, believe, going, smokers, where, which, while, on, non, even, being, around, out
Common (4+/6)	[6/6] our, we [5/6] agree, because, can, part [4/6] I, many, money, smoking, will	[6/6] while, would [5/6] able, are, believe, that, where [4/6] as, be, going, hand, it, 're, to, you

Common overused and underused keywords, identified by two kinds of analyses based on learners' proficiency levels and their regions, clearly illustrate the gaps between the speeches of Asian EFL learners and ENS. Here we focus on the six points.

First, Asian learners refer too much to themselves ("I," "we," "our") in speeches, while ENS also refer to hearers ("you"). This may explain why learner speeches sound subjective and sometimes even one-sided, while ENS speeches sound more involved and interactive. As mentioned above, Petch-Tyson (1998) revealed that European learner essays are characterised by a higher degree of "writer visibility" and "reader visibility." Our analysis, however, showed that Asian EFL learner speeches are characterised by a higher degree of "speaker visibility" and a lower level of "listener visibility." Two quotes below exemplify these points (italics mine).

(1a) *I*'m the one who have a part-time job … after *I* finished class …, *I* have a part-time job at department store. *I* work about … *I* got a big experience after *I* work …. *We* have to open *our* mind … (THA_019_B1_2_PTJ2)

(1b) … and, *you* know, we can't really control people in their action because if *you* ban smoking, even then people can still go and smoke. (ENS_149, SMK1)

Second, Asian learners tend to emphasise the relationships between causes and results ("because," "so"), which may reflect that their discourses may not be sufficiently logical in themselves, while ENS prefer presenting two views in contrast ("while," "[on the other] hand") to discuss the matter from a more balanced view.

(2a) I agree with this opinion *because* as we all know smoking is harmful for people's body, *so* if somebody is smoking … *So* I think the restaurants should ban … (CHN_030_B1_2_SMK1)

(2b) … it [a part-time job]'s a good thing for some students. Uh, but *on the other hand*, um, not all students should have a part-time job … (ENS_134_PTJ1)

Third, learners tend to express modality with simple non-epistemic modals ("can," "will"), while ENS use semi-modals ("be able to," "be going to") and control a speaker's stance flexibly with epistemic modals ("would") and emphatic verbs ("[I] believe that"). Ringbom (1998) mentioned that European learners overuse modals in their essays, but our analyses showed that there exists a gap in terms of the types of modals adopted in speeches between Asian learners and ENS.

(3a) Firstly, it [i.e., a part-time job] *can* strengthen their skills … in the society, it *will* teach them a lot of more things … and they *will* learn how to, for example, communicate with others … (CHN_081_B1_2_PTJ1)

(3b) Now, I always *believe* that it *would* help people, uh, reduce smoking in public restaurants if the government *would* assist in passing a—a law or where—where it [i.e., smoking], uh, *would* be banned. (ENS_011_SMK2)

Fourth, learners tend to overuse vague quantifiers ("many"), which agrees with the findings in Ringbom (1998). A similar trend was not seen in the speeches of ENS.

(4) We know that—uh—smoke contains *many*—uh—the harmful—harmful things…I think, so *many* people—I know *many* of my friends … (CHN_072_B1_2_SMK1)

Fifth, learners hardly use contractions, while ENS repeatedly use the contraction forms ("'s," "'re"). This may be caused by the difference in terms of pronunciation and intonation, which we can easily confirm in the sound data offered in the corpus. Learners often pronounce each word separately and put a relatively long pause between adjacent words, while ENS pronounce several words together as chunks, where *be* verbs (and sometimes the negation "not") are shortened.

Then, finally, learners often reuse the words presented in the prompt sentences ("agree," "opinion") or those directly related to two kinds of topics ("part," "job," "money," "smoking," "bad," "harm"), presumably to compensate for their lack of vocabulary knowledge, while ENS use a greater range of words and try to modify them in various ways (NP + "that"/ "where" …).

(5a) I *agree* with the *opinion* that we, college students, should try some *part*—uh—some *part*-time jobs in our free time .... (CHN_090_B1_2_PTJ2)

(5b) ... it [i.e., a part-time job] also taught me about managing about my own money *that* I make ... some students do not know how to do these kinds of things because they come from a family *where* all of that was done for them ... (ENS_036_PTJ2)

In addition to these common overuses and underuses, we also identified several tendencies applicable only to particular Asian learner groups. For example, among four proficiency-based groups, "first" is overused only by learners at B2+ level, who often list the contents in sequence and mention each of them with the discourse markers such as "first" and "second." Meanwhile, "been" is underused only by learners at A2 level, who may not be able to use the perfect tense appropriately yet. Werner et al. (2021) suggest that the choice between simple past and present perfect by ENS is determined by persistence (structural priming/repetition), semantics, time adverbials, and mode, and they also reveal that persistence is the most important factor explaining the gap between learners and ENS.

Then, among six region-based groups, words such as "first," "may," and "some" are overused by Chinese learners, and "very" is overused by Korean learners alone. Interestingly, with some words, different learner groups showed different patterns: "think" is overused by Taiwanese learners but underused by Indonesian learners, and "you" is underused by many of the EFL learners but rather overused by Thai learners.

4.3.3.2 RQ2 Essay Keywords

The top 20 keywords identified by the comparisons between the essays of learners and ENS are shown in Table 4.9, where the words appear in the decreasing order of the LLR value.

TABLE 4.9 Keywords overused or underused in learner essays

	Overuse	*Underuse*
Proficiency		
A2	we, money, people, you, smoke, smoking, can, part, job, restaurant, must, but, bad, completely, time, because, our, smoker, person, society	would, that, Japan, their, as, believe, simply, any, been, just, bans, Japanese, on, governments, and, ban, upon, this, being, an
B1_1	we, can, people, job, our, you, smoking, part, money, smoke, restaurant, time, smoker, country, must, bad, but, completely, society, place	would, Japan, that, and, Japanese, simply, been, I, any, bans, studies, to, believe, upon, this, bit, was, as, well, already

(*Continued*)

TABLE 4.9 (Continued)

	Overuse	*Underuse*
B1_2	can, we, job, part, people, money, you, smoking, our, time, smoker, smoke, country, completely, must, the, society, but, earn, nowadays	Japan, would, that, I, Japanese, and, been, this, any, simply, were, was, to, enough, bans, believe, able, governments, my, states
B2+	money, can, people, part, job, smoking, smoke, earn, country, we, experiences, students, second, society, completely, time, smoker, smokers, restaurant, moreover	that, Japan, I, and, would, Japanese, bans, any, just, simply, was, my, been, well, this, were, government, governments, work, business
Common, (3+/4)	[4/4] can, completely, job, money, part, people, smoke, smoker, smoking, society, time, we [3/4] but, country, must, our, restaurant, you	[4/4] and, any, bans, been, Japan, Japanese, simply, that, this, would [3/4] believe, governments, I, was
Regions (B1 level only)		
CHN	we, our, can, us, society, part, public, people, more, time, job, smoking, harm, jobs, you, nowadays, others, completely, knowledge, the	I, Japan, would, that, and, Japanese, work, was, they, or, this, any, able, their, me, simply, were, allow, bans, enough
IDN	can, smoker, we, job, our, restaurant, because, must, active, passive, disturb, cigarette, people, Indonesia, part, country, money, smoke, make, time	I, would, to, my, me, and, that, restaurants, been, on, up, these, simply, this, believe, any, think, was, governments, were
JPN	we, money, people, smoking, smoke, completely, seats, so, think, but, smoker, job, society, 't, seat, example, earn, bad, part, can	would, just, as, that, and, well, studies, been, any, believe, financial, their, while, an, government, simply, issue, on, was, to
KOR	job, part, money, smoking, people, cigarette, you, smoker, smoke, time, tuition, Korea, damage, but, can, university, we, lots, area, is	Japan, that, would, Japanese, and, believe, ban, any, as, their, them, been, or, enough, to, governments, same, just, way, allow
THA	you, money, job, your, people, can, good, bad, make, because, time, must, will, smoke, restaurant, part, smoker, smoking, stop, person	Japan, would, I, that, been, on, of, this, able, to, just, was, believe, a, as, bans, studies, ban, were, upon
TWN	people, we, you, can, job, the, country, learn, completely, smoke, second, smell, our, part, smoking, earn, Taiwan, experiences, your, besides	Japan, that, and, Japanese, would, as, this, of, able, bans, been, simply, were, enough, any, while, bit, already, was, degree
Common (4+/6)	[6/6] can, job, part, people [5/6] smoke, smoking, we [4/6] money, smoker, time, you	[6/6] that, would [5/6] and, any, been, was [4/6] as, believe, Japan, simply, this, to, were

One thing that should be noted here is that words such as "Japan" and "Japanese" are included in the underused keywords of several learner groups. This derives from the fact that some of the ENS writers, who were informed that this project began in Japan, tried to mention Japan in their essays. As it is quite natural that non-Japanese learners did not do so, this should be excluded from the discussion.

Then, based on the common keywords obtained from two kinds of essay analyses, we discuss four gaps observed between Asian learners and ENS. Some of them are similar to the gaps seen in learner speeches already discussed, but others seem to be rather specific to essays.

First, learners overuse first-person plural and second-person pronouns ("we," "our," "you") as well as nouns referring to a vague group of people ("people," "society"), while ENS often adopt first-person singular pronouns ("I"). Unlike speeches, the essay data analysis showed that a higher level of "writer–reader visibility" seen in European learner essays (Petch-Tyson, 1998) is also appliable to Asian learner essays. Another finding that should be added is that Asian learners prefer making a claim from the viewpoint of collective identity such as "we," "people," and the "society," rather than that of "I" as a marker of personal identity. Asian learners may consciously or unconsciously try to avoid taking responsibility for their own claims by hiding themselves in an anonymous group of people.

(6a) ... job is the way *we* can realize *our* dream and can fulfill *our* needed as *people*... (IDN_045_A2_0_PJJ)

(6b) ... for these reasons *I* do not agree with a blanket ban on smoking in restaurants. (ENS_109_SMK)

Second, learners overuse contrastive conjunctions ("but"), while ENS use additional and causal conjunctions ("and," "as"). Considering that learners also overuse "because" and "so" in speeches, they may have a common tendency to explicitly show how each content should be logically connected, which is presumably because the logic flow in learner essays is often complicated and difficult to follow. Meanwhile, in the essays of ENS, discourses seem to develop more naturally and smoothly, and we can easily follow the flow of logic even without so many explicit logical signposts.

(7a) I know it may be difficult for people to stop smoking in the restaurants *but* this policy is necessary... (CHN_144_B1_1_SMK)

(7b) Getting high grades is of paramount importance to my future, *as* I wish to become a doctor... (ENS_114_PTJ)

Third, learners often use non-epistemic modals ("can," "must"), while ENS adopt epistemic modals ("would") and various emphasisers ("any," "simply," "believe") to control the writer's position more effectively. This tendency was also seen in speeches.

(8a) In order to be independent, we *must* be financial independent first. And using the money made by ourselves *can* make us feel very good. (CHN_123_B1_1_PTJ)

(8b) As an accountant, I *believe* that this [i.e., having a part-time job] is important and *would* go a long way towards improving student's financial education … (ENS_150_PTJ)

Finally, as we saw in speeches, learners tend to reuse the words included in the topic sentences or related directly to the topics ("part," "time," "job," "money," "smoke," "smoker," "smoking," "completely," "restaurant," "country"). In addition, they also depend almost solely on the present tense. Meanwhile, ENS use various paraphrases, as seen in the use of the noun form "ban" instead of "banned" included in the topic sentence. They also use not only the present tense but the past tense ("was," "were") and the perfect tense ("been"). By adopting a narrower range of vocabulary and simpler tense structure, learners seem to try to avoid making errors.

In addition, we also found tendencies specific only to particular Asian learner groups. Among proficiency groups, the conjunction "because," which marks the relationship between causes and results, is overused only by learners at A2 level, and the adverb "moreover," marking the addition of information, is overused only by learners at B2+ level. We could see that learners come to pay more attention to the parallel listing of the information as their proficiency levels rise. Then, among regional groups, the conjunction "so" and expressions of "(I) think" and "(for) example" are overused only by Japanese learners, while "besides," another information addition marker, is overused only by Taiwanese learners, and "will" is overused only by Thai learners. Meanwhile, indefinite articles ("a," "an") are often dropped in essays by Thai and Japanese learners, and third-person plural pronouns ("they," "their," "them") do not appear much in essays by Chinese and Korean learners.

4.3.4 Summary

By conducting statistical keyword analyses, we identified the words overused or underused by Asian EFL learners in speeches and essays. Major findings are summarised in Table 4.10.

Summarising these findings, we could conclude that the oral and written productions of Asian EFL learners are often characterised by *I*-centred subjective claims, vague and ambiguous discussions about a larger theme, weaker control of a stance in claims, limited attention to the relationship between a speaker/writer and a hearer/reader, dependence on the limited range of vocabulary and tense, and excessive emphasis on the logical connections of the presented elements. Learner speeches and essays include features of both casual and formal discourses, which leads them to sound less elaborated and consistent, especially in comparison to ENS speeches and essays.

TABLE 4.10 Summary of the findings: keywords for speeches and essays

Overuse	*Underuse*
Speeches	
[Personal pronoun] First-person	[Personal pronoun] Second-person
[Conjunction] Cause and effect	[Conjunction] Contrast
[Modal] Non-epistemic	[Modal] Epistemic; Semi-modals
[Emphasis] N/A	[Emphasis] Emphatic verbs
[Quantifier] Vague quantifiers	[Quantifier] N/A
[Contraction] N/A	[Contraction] Contraction markers
[Item reuse] Repetition	[Item reuse] N/A
[Modification] N/A	[Modification] NP modification
Essays	
[Personal pronoun] First-/Second-person	[Personal pronoun] First-person singular
[Noun] Vague nouns	[Noun] N/A
[Conjunction] Contrast	[Conjunction] Addition, cause
[Modal] Non-epistemic	[Modal] Epistemic
[Emphasis] N/A	[Emphasis] Emphasisers
[Item reuse] Repetition	[Item reuse] N/A
[Tense] Present	[Tense] Past, perfect

It is, of course, true that L2 learners do not always need to follow the way ENS speak and write, but informing the learners of these gaps could be pedagogically beneficial, as it naturally leads them to reflect on their own L2 productions. The findings from the keyword analysis help learners to be more "conscious" speakers/writers.

4.4 Vocabularies in the Original and Edited Essays

4.4.1 Aim and RQs

Keyword analysis, which we conducted in Section 4.3, can be extended both in terms of the target lexical unit and the comparison type. In this study, we apply the method of keyword analysis not only to individual words but to the trigrams, that is, any type of word string consisting of three words. Phraseology-based data analysis will enable us to discuss learners' L2 vocabulary use from a new angle. Also, we attempt a comparison between learners' essays and their edited versions, which leads to the identification of the problems that may exist in learner essays. Thus, this study examines the following research questions:

RQ1 What are the keywords characterising learners' original essays and their edited versions?

RQ2 What are the keyphrases characterising learners' original essays and their edited versions?

4.4.2 Data and Method

In this study, we analyse the essays of ESL and EFL learners at B1 level (B1_1 and B1_2) and their edited versions taken from the ICNALE Edited Essays.

For both RQs, we identify the keywords and keyphrases (key trigrams) based on the log-likelihood ratios (LLR) as in the previous section. We discuss the top 20 items overused in the original versions and those overused in the edited versions. The former, which are the items deleted by the proofreaders, reflect the problems existing in learner essays, while the latter, which are the items added by them, suggest how they should be corrected.

4.4.3 Results and Discussions

4.4.3.1 RQ1 Keywords in the Original and Edited Essays

Table 4.11 shows the list of words characterising each of the original (Or) and edited (Ed) essays. All words are listed in the descending order of LLR.

First, learners tend to overuse non-hyphenated open compound words ("part time," "non smoker," "[second] hand"), inappropriate word forms ("specially,"

TABLE 4.11 Keywords for the original and edited essays

Keywords for original essays				*Keywords for edited essays*			
Words	*Or*	*Ed*	*LLR*	*Words*	*Or*	*Ed*	*LLR*
part	503	98	291.05	part-time	631	1054	115.44
time	899	489	115.35	a	1984	2320	32.96
smoker	209	91	45.50	jobs	248	384	32.11
manner	24	0	32.82	cigarettes	91	181	32.07
the	3686	3156	31.73	smokers	314	431	20.72
non	28	1	31.00	manners	4	28	20.70
parent	22	0	30.09	restaurants	502	635	18.20
restaurant	341	210	29.03	non-smokers	54	101	15.38
student	213	122	23.35	areas	34	70	13.41
place	156	82	22.02	cannot	62	106	12.50
fee	16	0	21.88	relationships	3	18	12.17
self	14	0	19.15	secondhand	13	36	11.67
hand	73	29	18.80	their	778	902	11.64
specially	10	0	13.68	places	97	147	11.28
study	176	117	10.88	students	774	887	9.97
cigarette	155	101	10.48	fires	0	7	9.84
relationship	19	4	10.35	lives	21	45	9.39
skill	23	6	10.32	studying	52	86	9.12
costumers*	7	0	9.57	are	774	881	9.08
sometime	7	0	9.57	causes	41	71	8.71

"*costumers," "sometime"), and sometimes contractions. All of them are replaced by hyphenated or solid compounds ("part-time," "non-smokers," "secondhand"), correct forms ("especially," "customers," "sometimes"), and non-contraction forms ("cannot"). These edits suggest that many learners, even if they are already at the intermediate level, do not wholly understand the mechanics of the target language, such as spelling, punctuation, and hyphenation. In the quotes below, the italics are mine.

(9a) I think I *can't* answer you directly. Because I'm the one who never have the part-time job. (THA_030_B1_1)
(9b) I will think that I *cannot* answer you directly because I'm someone who never had a part-time job. (Edited)

Second, learners have a clear tendency to use nouns as singular forms ("restaurant," "student," "place," "manner," "cigarette," "relationship," "smoker," "non-smoker," "study," "skill"). The use of a singular-form noun in a general claim may sometimes sound inappropriate. Thus, editors delete them and add many plural forms ("restaurants," "students," "places," "manners," "cigarettes," "relationships," "smokers," "non-smokers," "areas," "fires," "lives," "causes"). As a result of this, *be*-verbs responding to the plural nouns ("are") and pronouns for plural nouns ("their") are also added by proofreaders. Then, some of the singular nouns ("study") are changed into gerunds ("studying").

(10a) They might even choose to sit in an area sectioned off for *smoker* or *non-smoker* ... (IDN_004_B1_1)
(10b) They might even choose to sit in an area sectioned off for *smokers* and *non-smokers* ... (Edited)
(11a) As to *study*, what is known to all is that appropriate practice contributes to *study* by combining the theory to practice. (CHN_013_B1_2)
(11b) As for *studying*, what is known to all is that appropriate practice contributes to *studying* by combining theory and practice. (Edited)

Third, when using nouns, learners often drop needed articles as we saw in (10a), or add definite articles ("the") even when the nouns are not contextually specified. Many of them are replaced with indefinite articles ("a").

(12a) They do *job* or also give *proper time* to their studies. (PAK_025_B1_2)
(12b) They can do *a job* and assign *a proper amount of time* to their studies. (Edited)
(13a) And, instead of collecting money, experience is more wonderful present we got from doing *the* part time job. (IDN_009_B1_2)
(13b) And, instead of collecting money, we can get wonderful experiences from doing *a* part-time job. (Edited)

Chuang and Nesi (2006), who analysed the essays of L1 Chinese learners, also note that errors in the article system are the most problematic for learners. The same problem is observed in our data.

Summarising these, we could conclude that understanding the language mechanics (spelling, punctuation, and notation), controlling the number of nouns, and choosing the appropriate articles are the major problems seen in the essays of Asian ESL and EFL learners at an intermediate level.

4.4.3.2 RQ2 Keyphrases in the Original and Edited Essays

Table 4.12 shows the list of trigrams characterising each of the original (Or) and edited (Ed) essays. All the trigrams are listed in the descending order of LLR.

Keyphrase analysis underpinned the patterns observed in the keyword analysis. Learners tend to use open compounds ("part time job," "take part time [job]," "second hand smoke"), many of which are changed into hyphenated compounds ("a part-time job," "part-time jobs are," "part-time jobs for," "from a part-time [job]"). Next, learners often use definite articles even when the items referred to are not contextually specified ("the part time," "smoking in the," "the college students," "the

TABLE 4.12 Keyphrases for the original and edited essays

Keyphrases for original essays				*Keyphrases for edited essays*			
Trigrams	*Or*	*Ed*	*LLR*	*Trigrams*	*Or*	*Ed*	*LLR*
part time job	364	56	246.59	a part-time job	317	650	123.46
part time jobs	61	8	45.15	part-time jobs are	8	37	20.82
time job is	71	13	42.97	do part-time jobs	3	23	17.83
the part time	31	0	42.39	have a part-time	127	197	16.60
a part time	134	50	38.23	smoking in restaurants	28	64	15.16
doing part time	25	0	34.19	at a part-time	1	15	14.97
do part time	21	0	28.72	how hard it	0	8	11.24
have a part	54	12	28.12	as college students	0	8	11.24
time job in	13	0	17.78	of a part-time	0	8	11.24
time job can	23	3	17.07	work at a	0	8	11.24
smoking in the	38	10	16.89	hard it is	0	8	11.24
the college students	12	0	16.41	part-time job is	76	121	11.24
second hand smoke	16	1	15.68	having a part-time	69	112	11.15
smoking in restaurant	16	1	15.68	for several reasons	1	11	9.94
in the public	20	3	13.75	students do part-time	0	7	9.84
for college student	10	0	13.67	part-time jobs for	2	13	9.22
time jobs are	10	0	13.67	in restaurants because	2	13	9.22
second hand smoking	10	0	13.67	all of the	3	15	8.96
the restaurant in	9	0	12.31	it is to	4	17	8.91
take part time	9	0	12.31	from a part-time	1	10	8.72

restaurant in"). In some cases, these are appropriately deleted ("as college students," "smoking in restaurants," "in restaurants because"). It should be noted that learners' wrong article choices may also be related to the lack of knowledge about the number of nouns because the use of bare nouns is usually permitted only when they are plural.

In addition, a survey of the trigrams characterising the edited texts suggests some more problems seen in learners' original texts. First, some learners may not be able to use "all" as an intensifier in an appropriate way, which explains why the expression of "all of the" occurs more often in edited texts.

(14a) In *every funds* that they will get it helps a lot to build a foundation for the street children in order to have the proper education. (PHL_113_B1_1_SMK)
(14b) *All of the funds* that they will get can be used to help build a foundation for street children so they can have a proper education. (Edited)

Second, not a few learners tend to use "because of" with indefinite reasons, which usually collocates with concrete and specific reasons. Thus, the expression "because of some [several] reasons" that learners often use is replaced by "for several reasons."

(15a) And I don't think it is important for students to have a part time job *because of several reasons*. (HKG_025_B1_1)
(15b) However, I don't think it is important for students to have a part-time job *for several reasons*. (Edited)

Third, some learners seem not to fully understand the construction of "it is X to do," and they often drop "it." Thus, the expressions such as "how hard is …" are corrected by proofreaders.

(16a) And also, they will know *how hard is to make and collect* money by take part time job. (IDN_035_B1_2)
(16b) Also, they will find out *how hard it is to make and collect* money by working at a part-time job. (Edited)

It might attract our attention that learners prefer using the constructions with subject extraposition, which seem syntactically more complex and difficult. Larsson and Kaatari (2019) compare leaner essays with ENS students' essays as well as expert writing and report that learners, who are generally said to prefer informal writing style, often resort to such complex constructions. Castello (2015) analyses longitudinal data and reports that L1 Italian learners come to use a greater number of *it*-extraposition constructions.

Summarising these findings, we confirmed that Asian ESL and EFL learners have problems in understanding the language mechanics (especially the appropriate use of hyphens), choosing the articles (indefinite, definite, and no articles), and using basic words, phrases, and constructions correctly (especially, "all," "because of," and "it is… to do"). These suggest that even intermediate learners are not free from language problems.

TABLE 4.13 Summary of the findings: common problems in learner essays

Type	*Common problems (corrections)*
Mechanics	(1) misspelt words
	(2) open compound forms (➔ hyphenated compounds)
	(3) contraction forms (➔ spelt out)
Noun forms/Articles	(4) inappropriate singular noun forms (➔ plural forms)
	(5) nouns with no articles or unnecessary definite articles
Usage	(6) inappropriate word usages ("every," "because of," "[it] is to do")

4.4.4 Summary

By applying statistical keyword analysis and keyphrase analysis to learners' original essays and their edited versions, we could identify some of the problems widely seen in the essays of Asian ESL and EFL learners at an intermediate level. Major findings are summarised in Table 4.13.

As we demonstrated in this section, a combination of keyword analysis and keyphrase analysis seems to be an effective analytical method in LCR. When the same results are obtained from the two analyses, we can rely more on the validity of the findings. Also, keyphrase analysis often helps us realise the differences that could not be identified in the keyword analysis alone. Our analyses have exemplified the fact that even the intermediate learners, who are usually expected to complete mastery of the basics of the target language, still have problems in terms of mechanics, article choice, and usage of basic words and expressions, which would need to be appropriately considered in English language teaching.

In this section, we attempted to apply the keyword and keyphrase analysis as a central analytical technique of CIA to the comparison of learner texts and edited texts rather than to the conventional comparison of learner texts and ENS texts. Though we used the edit data obtained from ENS proofreaders in this analysis, we can also ask local non-native English teachers to edit learner outputs. By doing so, we could explore the possibilities of CIA more freely without the risk of imposing the ENS model on learners and teachers. Keyword and keyphrase analysis based on the comparison of learner outputs and their edited versions by non-native proofreaders seems to be a promising approach to the new type of CIA.

5

GRAMMAR

5.1 Introduction

5.1.1 Grammar in LCR

5.1.1.1 Background

Like the vocabulary that we discussed in Chapter 4, grammar is also a core of learners' L2 linguistic knowledge. Learner corpus (LC)-based grammar studies are often closely related to the analytical approaches of modern linguistics, such as cognitive linguistics, construction grammar, and lexicogrammar.

Cognitive linguistics, according to McEnery and Hardie (2012), is a functional approach to language, and it aims "to explain language in terms of what is known about how the mind works (cognition)," especially conceptualisation or "how people construct abstract concepts and schemata to think about the world." Construction grammar, which is a major theory within cognitive linguistics, sees any type of syntactic and idiomatic structure as a construction. Constructions, which usually consist of concrete words and abstract slots, are thought to be stored in people's mental lexicon. It assumes that we produce language by filling the slots in the constructions with words (pp. 169, 240, 241, 246). By examining the corpus frequency, we can guess what constructions are stored in learners' L2 mental lexicon. Then, lexicogrammar (aka lexical grammar), according to Paquot et al. (2020), refers to an analytical approach focusing on "a level of linguistic structure where lexis and grammar are not seen as independent, but rather as mutually dependent." Corpus data has exemplified that many words have particular patterns in "lexicogrammatical coselection." For example, a set of verbs such as "arrest," "elect," "name," and "estimate" are known to occur twice as frequently in the passive forms as in the active forms. Lexicogrammar has developed together with construction grammar, both of which are usage-based approaches.

DOI: 10.4324/9781003252528-7

Regarding the affinity between LC-based grammar studies and cognitive/constructionist approaches, Rankin (2015) suggests that both avoid depending on a particular linguistic theory, reject the dichotomy between competence (language ability) and performance (linguistic outputs), which is proposed by Noam Chomsky, focus on the patterns and syntactic regularities emerging from data, regard syntax and lexis as an inseparable set, and put a particular emphasis on the frequency, which is regarded as a marker of entrenchment, conventionalisation, and typicality (p. 234).

Like the LC-based vocabulary studies, LC-based grammar studies also adopt the analytical framework of contrastive interlanguage analysis (CIA). Thus, they often discuss the differences seen between learners and L1 English native speakers (ENS); learners of English as a second language (ESL) and English as a foreign language (EFL); learners with different L1 backgrounds; and learners at different L2 proficiency levels. Among these, proficiency-based CIA leads to the analysis of the development of learners' grammatical skills.

5.1.1.2 Aspects of Learner Grammar

LC-based grammar studies have examined various aspects of learners' L2 grammar use. As mentioned before, they tend to discuss lexis and grammar in combination.

Among a variety of grammatical features, verb usages have been discussed widely. First, regarding *to*-infinitive constructions, Gries and Wulff (2009) investigate whether gerund and infinitival complement patterns (e.g., "try doing" vs. "try to do") are stored as constructions in the interlanguage of L1 German learners through the experiments of sentence completion as well as sentence acceptability rating. Larsson and Kaatari (2019) pay attention to the construction of *to*-infinitive clauses with adjectives and subject-extraposition (e.g., "it is important to remember. ..."). They show that the frequency of the construction is higher in ENS' academic proses and learner essays, while it is lower in ENS' conversations, fiction, and news. It also shows that learners overuse the word pairs of "important to note" and "interesting to see." Then, regarding the subject-verb order, Meriläinen (2021) reports that inappropriate embedded inversions (e.g., "*I don't know what *are you* asking me") often occur in the speeches of L1 Finnish learners, which is because Finnish "differs from English in that it has a similar word order in direct and indirect questions and no subordinating conjunction in Yes/No-questions."

Second, as regards learners' choice of verb tenses, Deshors (2018) analyses L1 French speakers' use of the present perfect and past tenses in L2 English as well as their use of the passé composé, which largely overlaps with those two tenses, in L1 French. The analysis shows that the influence of passé composé is weak, and advanced French learners use the two tenses largely in an ENS-like manner. Meriläinen (2018) reports that the frequency of progressive forms that learners adopt in speeches is influenced by the degree of L2 exposure in their home countries, though not necessarily by their experiences of staying in English-speaking countries. Rautionaho and Deshors (2018) analyse the choice between progressive and non-progressive forms in the multi-genre essays by ESL and EFL writers as well as ENS and show that the difference between different English varieties is not necessarily clear. Fuchs and Werner (2018) report that learners hardly use stative progressives, though previous studies have suggested that learners, including advanced learners, generally tend to extend the progressive to stative verbs. Whether their L1s have a progressive does not directly influence their use of stative progressive. Werner et al. (2021) pay attention to the learners' choice between simple past and present perfect tenses, and the gap between ENS and learners can be explained from the viewpoints of persistence or structural priming. O'Donnell (2015) analyses the essays of L1 Spanish learners at different proficiency levels and reports that the frequency of simple present and present-progressive tenses decreases, while that of simple past, present perfect, and simple modal tenses increases as their proficiency levels increase from A2 to C2 levels. Gerckens and Gans (2015) analyse L1 German learner essays written at three points during the nine-month instructions and report that the tense/aspect error rates rather increase from 4.2% to 6.1%. Then, Van Rooy and Kruger (2016) analyse the innovative progressive aspect seen in Black South African English and report that most of the innovations decrease due to the influence of normative correction and increased proficiency. They also add that these data-based analyses of the linguistic features should be expanded to the use of English as a lingua franca (ELF).

Finally, regarding various types of verb combinations, Lin and Lin (2019) analyse the data from ICNALE and report that Asian EFL learners overuse "make," but they underuse its delexical or light-verb usage (e.g., "make a decision"). Gilquin (2019) analyses the effect of L1 types and task types on the use of light verb constructions (e.g., "take a walk") in learner speeches. The author reports that advanced learners and ESL learners use more light verb constructions in a more complex manner than less advanced learners and EFL learners. Deshors (2016) analyses the usage of phrasal verbs in learner essays. By examining the degrees of mutual attraction between verbs and particles as well as between phrasal verbs and their semantic functions, the author suggests that learners are not necessarily confident in the aspectual use (e.g., completive, inceptive, and continuative) of phrasal verbs and in the verb + object + particle constructions. Meriläinen (2021) reports that inappropriate preposition omission in verb phrases (e.g., "*She went town") often occur in the speeches of L1 Finnish learners as well as in the essays of L1 Japanese and Chinese learners, which is explained by the fact that all of Finnish, Japanese, and Chinese do not have English-like prepositions. Also, Gries and Deshors (2005) analyse the usage of lexical verbs in the dative alternation (e.g., "give him a pen" and "give a pen to him") in ESL and EFL. They conclude that the two English varieties could be regarded as discrete types of varieties rather than different elements of a single continuum or an intermingled whole. Tizón-Couto (2014) pays attention to a complementiser, which is optional in English (e.g., "I think [that] S+V"), partially compulsory in Germany, and fully compulsory in Spanish. The analysis of speech corpora shows that the ratios of using "think" and "say" without complementisers are much lower for Spanish learners than for German learners as well as ENS (p. 211). Schneider and Gilquin (2016) report that both ESL and EFL speakers overuse particular types of verb phrases (e.g., "discuss about"), which they suggest should be considered as innovation rather than an error.

As regards the usage of adverbs, which usually modify verbs, Osborne (2008) reports that learners do not fully understand the appropriate position of adverbs in the construction and therefore tend to choose the ungrammatical order of verb + adverb + object (VAO). This pattern is often seen in the essays of learners with L1s allowing VAO order, but it is also adopted by the other learners. Rankin (2010) notes that L1 German learners tend to choose the VAO pattern when a verb appears in the infinitive, which the author explains may be the result of learners' efforts to avoid the split infinitive. Larsson, Callies, et al. (2020a) report that the adverb position can be influenced by learners' L1 backgrounds in speeches, though an L1 transfer is rather limited in writing. Van Vuuren and Laskin (2017) analyse the usage of pre-subject adverbials and report that L1 Dutch learners overuse circumstance adverbials, linking adverbials, and antecedent-linking adverbials, while they underuse stance adverbials. They also mention that the learners use adverbials in a more ENS-like manner in untimed essays than in timed essays. Schweinberger (2020) reports that learners' usage of "very" as an adjective modifier is considerably different from ENS' usage, which the author suggests is due to the gap in the collocation patterns of particular types of adjectives.

LC-based grammar studies also discuss usages of functional words as well as particular types of constructions (e.g., existential-*there* and *if*-conditionals) in learner outputs. Crosthwaite (2016) uses the data from ICNALE to discuss the accuracy of article use in the essays by three learner groups having article-less L1s (Chinese, Korean, and Thai) at four proficiency levels. The analysis suggests that indefinite and definite articles are generally overused, the accuracy is influenced by learners' L1s and the task types, and L1 Chinese learners are relatively better at the choice of articles. Leńko-Szymańska (2012) analyses the essays by L1 Polish learners at different levels and reports that the frequencies of indefinite and definite articles both increase as their proficiency levels go up, but even the advanced learners underuse definite articles in comparison to ENS. Rankin (2017) analyses reflexive intensifiers (e.g., "The president *herself* answered the phone") in the essays of L1 German learners, who are found to overuse reflexive intensifiers in general, especially inclusive adverbial intensifiers. Lester (2019) analyses learners' use of the optional relativisers (e.g., "the hot tea (that) S + V") in speeches of L1 Spanish and German learners, whose L1s have obligatory relativisers. The statistical analysis shows that, opposite to the case of ENS, learners tend to drop the relativisers in complex and disfluent speeches. Koch et al. (2016) analyse the intrusive "as" constructions (e.g., "this hair-style called as duck tail"), which is said to be a feature of Indian English, and report that it is widely seen in South Asian English varieties, and the difference in ESL and EFL is considerably clear. Gries and Wulff (2013) discuss what variables influence genitive alternation (e.g., "the squirrel's nest" vs. "the nest of the squirrel") in learner English. The statistical analyses show that learners rely on processing-related factors, and their genitive choice patterns vary across their L1s. Then, as regards constructions, Palacios-Martínez and Martínez-Insua (2006) report that an essential gap is seen in the frequency, syntactic complexity, and pragmatics of the existential "there" between L1 Spanish learners and ENS. Winter and Le Foll (2022) analyse the occurrences of *if*-conditionals in EFL textbooks, learner writing, and authentic English use outside the classroom. The analysis shows that textbook typology covers less than 50% of *if*-conditionals appearing in the reference corpora, and it also suggests that learner English seems to be between textbook English and referential English.

As exemplified in some of the studies introduced above, the pattern in learners' L2 grammar use may change qualitatively and quantitatively between speeches and essays. If this is the case, we may need to regard spoken interlanguage grammar as an independent system. Mukherjee (2009) overviews the aspects of lexicogrammatical features seen in the speeches of L1 German learners, which include the patterns in verb-noun collocations, the usage of "you know" as a discourse marker, and performance features such as repetitions and contractions.

When analysing learners' grammar usage or its accuracy, we usually use manually error-tagged data, but its reliability is not necessarily guaranteed. Larsson, Paquot, et al. (2020) mention that very little of the literature in learner corpus research (LCR) reports inter-rater reliability coefficients in grammar feature tagging and add that reliability in coding is a prerequisite for the validity, interpretability, and generalisability of the studies. Another approach we can take is to use automatically tagged data. Automatic annotation of part-of-speech (POS) and/or a variety of lexical and syntactic features help us identify the occurrences of the target items. In comparison to manual coding, it is highly consistent but not always correct. Its reliability is influenced by what type of text to process. Picoral et al. (2021) process academic essays written by ENS and learners with three kinds of taggers (Biber Tagger, Malt Parser, and Stanford Dependency Parser) and report that the rates of precision and recall greatly vary according to the writers' L1 backgrounds. Regarding the assessment of accuracy in learner outputs, Polio and Yoon (2021) report that the corpus-based or usage-based semi-automatic approach (examining the ratio of atypical multiword units seen only in learner outputs and the mean mutual-information scores of all the multiword units) explains 47.6% of the variance of the traditional manual error counts and 28.0% of the variance of the human holistic assessment of accuracy.

5.1.1.3 Development of Learner Grammar

In addition to the studies exploring the aspects of learners' L2 grammar use, many LC researchers have discussed the development of learners' L2 grammatical skills.

As mentioned in Section 1.1, researchers in the field of second language acquisition (SLA) began using learner data in the 1970s to discuss how learners acquire L2 grammar knowledge. For instance, Dulay and Burt (1973) and Krashen et al. (1978) collected learners' speeches and writings to examine whether they acquired grammatical morphemes such as *-ing* (progressive), *s* (plural/third-person/possessive), and articles in a common natural order. If a similar order is observed both for L1 children and L2 learners with different backgrounds, it could powerfully support the hypothesis proposed by Noam Chomsky that language acquisition is controlled by a universal grammar as an innate system. Some of the earlier studies suggested the existence of such a universal acquisition order. Krashen (1977) proposed a four-stage acquisition model of grammatical morphemes: [*-ing*, plural-*s*, copular *be*] → [auxiliary *be*, articles] → [irregular past tense] → [regular past tense, third-person *s*, possessive *'s*]. However, recent studies are revealing that the acquisition order may not be necessarily universal. Analysing the error rate of each morpheme seen in LC data, Murakami and Alexopoulou (2015) show that the order can be influenced by learners' L1 backgrounds.

LC data that can be used for analyses of the development of learners' grammatical skills was scarce in the past, but several longitudinal LC, in addition to large-scale cross-sectional LC that collect data from learners at different L2 proficiency levels, have been compiled (see Section 1.2.2). This has made it possible for us to discuss how learners acquire an L2 grammar system from more diversified viewpoints.

First, regarding overall grammatical complexity, Osborne (2011) reports that fluent speakers come to convey information more efficiently, but their speeches do not necessarily become more syntactically complex. Biber et al. (2020) analyse college students' essays and report that phrasal complexity increases, while dependent clause complexity does not.

Second, as regards basic notation or mechanics, Shatz (2019) reports that capitalisation errors, most of which are classified as under-capitalisation, are seen commonly in the essays of learners with varied L1 backgrounds. The study also suggests that learners with English-like L1s tend to produce more errors, which the author explains is the result of a negative interference, and that the gap between different L1 groups narrows according to the increase in their L2 proficiency.

Third, as regards verb constructions, Römer and Garner (2019) discuss the development of verb-argument constructions in learner speeches. The results show that advanced learners come to use a greater number of target constructions in a more ENS-like style. Zhao and Shirai (2018) report that L1 Arabic learners' acquisition of the past tense markers is influenced by the lexical semantics (i.e., verb types) as well as the phonological saliency, which they conclude supports the aspect hypothesis in SLA. Then, Paquot et al. (2021) analyse the verb + direct object collocations occurring in the longitudinal LC and report that learners' development in phraseological complexity can be explained not by time but by proficiency.

Fourth, regarding noun constructions, Ionin and Díez-Bedmar (2021) analyse the essays written by L1 Spanish and Russian learners and report that the number of correct uses of definite, indefinite, and zero articles increases from B1 to B2 levels for both learners, though the number of incorrect uses of definite and zero articles also increases for Russian learners. Díez-Bedmar and Pérez-Paredes (2020) analyse the syntactic complexity of noun phrases (NP) in the essays of young L1 Spanish students in grades 7, 8, 11, and 12, and reveal that the complexity of premodification gradually increases. Kreyer and Schaub (2018) also analyse the complexity of

NP, which they operationalise as the phrase length and the number of modifiers, in the essays of L1 German learners and conclude that global complexity does not develop between grades 10 and 12, though an individual variation is observed in terms of the frequency of NP modifiers. Alexopoulou et al. (2005) report that learners' usage of relative clauses gradually develops, but it can be influenced by varied parameters such as task effects, formulaic language effects, and L1 effects.

Fifth, regarding multi-word sequences, Leńko-Szymańska (2014) analyses the use of formulaic expressions by students in grades 6, 9, and 12 from six EFL regions and reports that phraseological skills develop according to the increase in proficiency, though they are not directly influenced by learners' age and L1 backgrounds. Xia et al. (2022) analyse the usage of four-word lexical bundles (e.g., "as can be seen") appearing in emails of business English learners at two proficiency levels as well as professionals and report that intermediate learners adopt written-like lexical bundles connoting formality and politeness less often than the others.

Finally, some of the recent studies discuss how to define learners' grammatical proficiency levels on the basis of LC findings. O'Keeffe and Mark (2017) introduce their English Grammar Profile (EGP) project, which aims to modify a reference level descriptor included in the Common European Framework of Reference for Languages (CEFR) and create a new set of grammar competence descriptors. The project team has already made more than 1,200 descriptors.

5.1.1.4 Tagging for Grammar Studies

Annotating LC with a tagging software program makes it possible for us to quickly identify the occurrence of the target grammatical items in learner outputs, and therefore it can be an indispensable step for LC-based grammar studies. Among a variety of tagging software programs, Biber Tagger (Biber, 1988), which was developed by Douglas Biber for his multidimensional analysis (MDA), has been widely used in corpus linguistics (CL).

Biber Tagger automatically processes a bunch of texts and gives 67 kinds of lexicogrammatical tags to each of them. The tagset covers a wide range of linguistic features, including A: tense/aspect (#1–3), B: place/time adverbials (#4–5), C: pronouns/pro-verbs (#6–12), D: questions (#13), E: nominal forms (#14–16), F: passives (#17–18), G: stative forms (#19–20), H: subordination (#21–38), I: prepositional phrases/adjectives and adverbs (#39–42), J: lexical specificity (#43–44), K: lexical classes (#45–51), L: modals (#52–54), M: specialised verb classes (#55–58), N: reduced forms and dispreferred structures (#59–63), O: coordination (#64–65), and P: negation (#66–67).

Biber (1988) examined the frequency of each of the 67 tags appearing in 23 kinds of spoken and written text samples. Then, he conducted a factor analysis, which is a multivariate statistical method to group "the variables that are distributed in similar ways" as a small number of factors (Biber et al., 1998, p. 278). Thus, he identified six factors, which were interpreted as six kinds of text-type dimensions: D1 (involved or informational), D2 (narrative or non-narrative), D3 (explicit or situation-dependent), D4 (overt expression of persuasion), D5 (abstract or non-abstract), and D6 (online informational elaboration) (Biber, 1988, p. 122).

On the basis of these dimension scores, 23 kinds of spoken and written texts were finally classified into eight types: (i) intimate interpersonal interaction, (ii) informational interaction, (iii) scientific exposition, (iv) learned exposition, (v) imaginative narrative, (vi) general narrative exposition, (vii) situated reportage, and (viii) involved persuasion.

In 2013, *Corpora*, one of the CL journals, edited a special issue commemorating the 25th anniversary of the publication of Biber (1988). Since then, many studies in CL have adopted the framework of MDA, though some have doubted the subjectivity in feature selection and dimension interpretation as well as the limited replicability of its findings (McEnery & Hardie, 2012, p. 112). Responding to these criticisms, Biber himself says that a series of criticisms is the "issues that should be addressed in all corpus-based research," and they are never the issues specific to the MDA (Friginal, 2013).

The tagger that Biber used for his MDA was not publicly available, but it has been recently replicated and publicly distributed by Andrea Nini, who combined Stanford POS Tagger and an additional system to conduct MDA. The Multidimensional Analysis Tagger v.1.3 (MAT) (Nini, 2019) is now beginning to be used in CL and also in LCR.

5.1.2 ICNALE Case Studies

As summarised in Section 5.1.1, many of the previous LC-based grammar studies have discussed learners' use of particular types of grammatical features. However, it is also of importance for us to investigate the quality of their overall L2 grammar use.

In Section 5.2, we will first examine how Asian EFL learners' grammar control in essays develops according to the increase in their overall L2 proficiency. The data is taken from the ICNALE Edited Essays. Our analytical focus is put on the number of edits, which roughly represents the quantity of grammatical problems, and the grammar-related rating scores.

Next, in Section 5.3, we pay attention to the speeches of Chinese learners as a representative sample of a variety of L2 English learners in Asia and examine their lexicogrammatical features. The data is taken from the ICNALE Spoken Monologues. After tagging it, we investigate the frequency of each of the 67 kinds of lexicogrammatical features as well as the dimension scores and text types.

5.2 Development of Grammatical Accuracy in Essays

5.2.1 Aim and RQs

It is usually expected that grammar accuracy increases as learners' proficiency levels go up, but whether such a pattern is commonly observed with Asian EFL learners from different regions has not been necessarily clear. Therefore, we analyse the data from the ICNALE Edited Essays and discuss the change in grammatical accuracy. Thus, this study examines the following research question:

RQ Does grammatical accuracy increase according to the increase in learners' overall proficiency levels?

5.2.2 Data and Method

In this study, we analyse the data of the edit and rating that proofreaders gave to the essays of Asian EFL learners at four proficiency levels (A2, B1_1, B1_2, and B2+) and from four different regions (China, Japan, Korea, and Taiwan). All the data is taken from the ICNALE Edited Essays. The data of the participants from Indonesia and Thailand are excluded from the analysis because the numbers of advanced learners are limited in these two groups.

In the essays with higher grammatical accuracy, the number of edits, which include both insertions and deletions, decreases, while the rating score increases. Therefore, we pay attention to the inverse number of edits (INE) as well as the grammar-related rating scores (GRS) as two kinds of indices of grammatical accuracy. To obtain the INE, we first adjust the total number of edits per ten words and then change it into the inverse value. In the case of the part-time job essay by CHN_001, for example, the number of tokens is 275, and the numbers of insertions and deletions are 34 and 29, respectively. As the total number of edits is 63 (34 + 29) and its adjusted value is 2.29 (63/275*10), the inverse number is calculated as 0.437 (1/2.29).

Then, regarding the GRS, we analyse the scores in the category of language use (1–3: "Very poor," 4–6: "Poor to fair," 7–9: "Average to good," and 10–12: "Very good to excellent") that proofreaders determined on the basis of the rubric. They concern the complexity in constructions and the overall language quality in terms of agreements, tenses, numbers, word orders/functions, articles, pronouns, prepositions, and negations. When the language problems cause obscurity in meaning, the point becomes lower than 6.

It should be noted here that both the INE and GRS primarily concern grammatical accuracy, but they may also reflect lexical quality to some extent. As suggested in the concept of lexicogrammar, grammar and lexis are expected to be inseparably correlated.

5.2.3 Results and Discussions

The results of the analysis of INE and GRS are shown in Figures 5.1 and 5.2.

When comparing A2 and B2+ learners, significant increases are suggested in the INE values: 44.6% increase for Chinese learners, 64.6% increase for Japanese learners, 165.9% increase for Korean learners, and 85.4% increase for Taiwanese learners, and similar increases are also suggested in the GRS values: 29.8% increase for Chinese learners, 18.1% increase for Japanese learners, 12.9% increase for Korean learners, and 48.1% increase for Taiwanese learners.

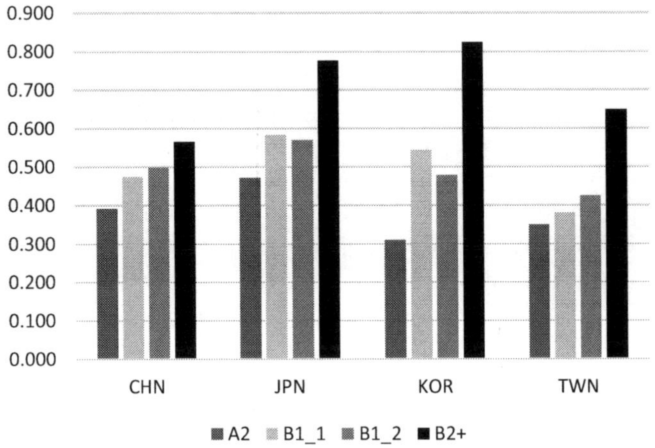

FIGURE 5.1 INE values for learners at different proficiency levels

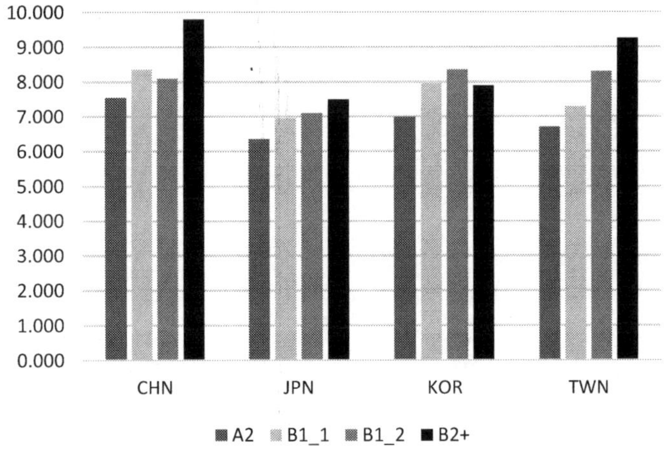

FIGURE 5.2 GRS values for learners at different proficiency levels

Then, two-way ANOVA tests were performed to analyse the effects of proficiency and region on the INE/GRS values. First, regarding the INE, the test revealed that there is not a statistically significant interaction between the effects of proficiency and region (F (9, 304) = 0.752, p = .661, η_p^2 = .022). Then, main effects analyses showed that the effects of region (F (3, 304) = 2.986, p = .031, η_p^2 = .029) and proficiency (F (3, 304) = 12.627, p < .001, η_p^2 = .111) are both statistically significant. Also, post-hoc tests (Holm) proved the order of B2+ (0.704) > B1_1 (0.495) ≈ B1_2 (0.493) ≈ A2 (0.381). The differences between adjacent pairs of JPN (0.600), KOR (0.539), CHN (0.483), and TWN (0.451) are not significant. Thus, we can conclude that the INE values increase between A2/B1 and B2+ for all of the four EFL learner groups. B2+ learners write essays including fewer language problems in comparison to novice and intermediate learners.

Next, regarding the GRS, the test revealed that there is a statistically significant interaction between the effects of proficiency and region (F (9, 304) =2.130, p = .027, η_p^2 = .059). Simple main effects analyses showed that the effects of region (F (3, 304) = 13.368, p < .001, η_p^2 = .117) and proficiency (F (3, 304) = 18.337, p < .001, η_p^2 = .153) are both statistically significant. Also, post-hoc tests (Holm) proved the orders of B2+ (8.613) > B1_2 (7.963) ≈ B1_1 (7.638) > A2 (6.900) in terms of the proficiency levels, and CHN (8.450) > TWN (7.888) ≈ KOR (7.800) > JPN (6.975) in terms of the regions. When seeing each of the four regional groups independently, the difference between different proficiency levels is not significant only for Japanese learners (F (3, 304) =2.057, p = .106, η_p^2 = .075), which is presumably because the degree of increase is rather limited for them.

The results obtained from the two analyses exemplify that learners' grammatical skills generally develop according to the increase in their overall proficiency levels, and this trend is commonly observed with most Asian EFL learners.

The quotes below (Figures 5.3 and 5.4) are the beginning part of the edited versions of the essays written by CHN_228 (B2+, INE: 1.05, GRS: 11) and CHN_045 (A2, INE: 0.303, GRS: 7).

The proofreader's edits on the CHN_228 essay are all about minor lexis-level problems. The writer fails in the control of the number of the nouns ("countries" → "country") and the choice of an appropriate verb phrase ("carry" → "carry out"), verb form ("resulted" → "result"), and verb type ("taking a cigarette" → "having a cigarette"), but these hardly influence the intelligibility of the text.

Smoking has been a serious problem for too long a period. In the whole country~~ies~~, measures have been carried out to prohibit smoking in many public places, such as restaurants. As far as I'm concerned, I'm definitely in favor of this rule. What has been taken into consideration in this rule is first and foremost the health of people. Smoking has been criticized for decades. As is so often pointed out, smoking for a long time is likely to result~~ed~~ in lung cancer. However, there are certain quantities of people who just cannot give up the "terrific" feeling of ~~taking~~ having a cigarette, even though they are clearly aware that they are risking their health. It's not other

FIGURE 5.3 A part of the edited essays (CHN_228)

~~Absolutely~~ I absolutely agree with the point that smoking should be banned at all the restaurants in the country. A ~~R~~restaurant is a place for people to have a nice dinner with their family. Smoking~~es~~ will destroy the warm atmosphere~~. A~~ and ~~this~~ also do harm to people's health. Someone may say that ~~whether~~ smoking~~e~~ depends on personal preferences, but it~~this~~ is a selfish behavior. It will make other people ~~be~~ unhealthy. The important thing is that smoking can shorten one's life. It's very terrible. Personally, I do not like the~~ese~~ people who smoke in public places. As is known to all, smoking just ~~make people~~ increases the risk of cancer in people. ~~And~~

FIGURE 5.4 A part of the edited essay (CHN_045)

TABLE 5.1 Summary of the findings: changes in grammatical accuracy

	INE	*GRS*
Change between A2 and B2+	CHN 44.6%+ JPN 64.6%+ KOR 165.9%+ TWN 85.4%+	CHN 29.8%+ JPN 18.1%+ KOR 12.9%+ TWN 48.1%+
Difference between levels	A2 ≈ B1_2 ≈ B1_1 < B2+	A2 < B1_1 ≈ B1_2 < B2+

Meanwhile, we see pretty many corrections in the CHN_045 essay. The errors can be classified into five major types: (i) confusion in the number of nouns ("restaurant" → "a restaurant," "selfish behavior" → "a selfish behavior," "these" → "this," "place" → "places"), (ii) inappropriate adverb placement ("Absolutely I..." → "I absolutely..."), (iii) problems related to "that" as a complementiser ("the point" → "the point that SV," "that whether SV" → "that SV," "the thing is SV" → "the thing is that SV"), (iv) inappropriate use of causative verbs ("make other people be healthy" → "make other people healthy," "smoking make(s) people increase" → "smoking increases"), and (v) the drop of needed conjunction ("..., this is" → "..., but it is"). These errors considerably deteriorate the readability of the essay.

5.2.4 Summary

In this section, using the data from the ICNALE Edited Essays, we analysed the inverse number of edits (INE) and the grammar-related rating score (GRS) given to Asian EFL learner essays in order to investigate whether we can see a steady increase in terms of the grammatical accuracy. Major findings are summarised in Table 5.1.

The data analyses suggested that both the INE and GRS values significantly increased from A2/B1 level to B2+ level. Though some regional difference was observed with the latter, we could conclude that Asian EFL learners' grammar skills largely develop according to the increase in their proficiency levels. Also, by examining the samples of the edited essays, we confirmed that not only the quantity but also the contents of the edits drastically changed between the essays of novice and advanced learners.

5.3 Lexicogrammatical Features in Speeches

5.3.1 Aim and RQs

Douglas Biber's multidimensional analysis (MDA) (see Section 5.1.1.4) has been widely practised in CL, but the possibilities of MDA-based LCR have not been fully explored. Therefore, we apply MDA to monologue speeches of Chinese learners as well as ENS to discuss how each uses 67 kinds of lexicogrammatical features. Thus, this study examines the following research questions:

RQ1 What difference is seen between Chinese learners and ENS in terms of the frequency of lexicogrammatical features?
RQ2 What difference is seen between Chinese learners and ENS in terms of the dimension scores and the estimated text types?

5.3.2 Data and Method

In this study, we analyse the speech data of Chinese learners at all four proficiency levels, who are regarded as a representative sample of a variety of learners in Asia, as well as ENS. These data are taken from the ICNALE Spoken Monologues.

First, we process all the speech texts with MAT v.1.3 (Nini, 2019). Like the original version of Biber Tagger (Biber, 1988), it identifies 67 kinds of lexicogrammatical features, computes the values of six kinds of factors/dimensions based on the feature-tag frequencies, and chooses the text type closest to the target text (see Section 5.1.1.4). The results obtained from MAT are reported to be almost identical to those from the original tagger (Nini, 2019).

Regarding RQ1, we examine the frequencies of 67 feature tags and adjust them per 100 words. The number of tokens is not adjusted. Then, we calculate the C/E, or Chinese/ENS ratios (%), by dividing the adjusted frequencies in Chinese learner speeches with those in ENS speeches. Tags with 130% or higher C/E ratios are regarded as characterising learners, while tags with 70% or lower ratios are regarded as characterising ENS. All tags whose adjusted frequencies do not reach 0.1 are excluded from the analysis.

Next, regarding RQ2, we compare the six kinds of factor/dimension scores, which are automatically calculated from the tag frequencies, and identify the closest text types for the speeches of Chinese learners and ENS.

5.3.3 Results and Discussion

5.3.3.1 RQ1 Lexicogrammatical Features

Table 5.2 shows the list of lexicogrammatical tags that occur more often in either of the speeches of Chinese learners and ENS. Our analyses reveal that 10 tags characterise Chinese learner speeches, while 14 tags characterise ENS speeches. MAT occasionally gives plural tags to a single word, which are shown in the square brackets in Table 5.2.

Here we introduce some of the words and phrases related to each lexicogrammatical tag. Chinese learners tend to overuse POMD (possibility modals: "can('t)," "could," "may," "might"), FPP1 (first-person pronouns: "I," "we"), DPAR (discourse particles: "well," "now"), PROD (pro-verb *Do*: "do a part-time job," "do harms," "do no good"), AMP (amplifiers: "very," "absolutely," "completely," "greatly," "strongly," "totally"), CONC (concessive adverbial subordinators: "although," "though"), PUBV (public verbs: "agree(d)," "say/said," "add(ed)," "report(ed)"), ANDC (independent clause coordination: "..., and S+V"), DWNT (downtoners:

TABLE 5.2 Overused/underused lexicogrammatical features

Key tags for Chinese learners				*Key tags for ENS*			
Tags	*CHN*	*ENS*	*C/E*	*Tags*	*CHN*	*ENS*	*C/E*
POMD	2.08	1.09	190.8	OSUB	0.11	0.35	31.4
FPP1	6.15	3.28	187.5	EX	0.13	0.33	39.4
DPAR	0.13	0.07	185.7	THVC	0.35	0.73	47.9
[PROD]	0.44	0.25	176.0	PLACE	0.25	0.52	48.1
AMP	0.92	0.53	173.6	[PASS]	0.43	0.87	49.4
CONC	0.10	0.06	166.7	Tokens	8276	15567	53.2
[PUBV]	0.61	0.42	145.2	[PEAS]	0.12	0.2	60.0
ANDC	0.94	0.65	144.6	[WHSUB]	0.21	0.35	60.0
DWNT	0.24	0.17	141.2	[SPAU]	0.25	0.41	61.0
GER	1.64	1.22	134.4	DEMP	0.55	0.86	64.0
				[CONT]	1.56	2.36	66.1
				PHC	0.3	0.44	68.2
				VBD	0.46	0.67	68.7
				SPP2	1.38	1.98	69.7

"[not] only [A but also B]," "almost," "partly," "partially") and GER (gerunds: "smoking," "working").

The quote below is a non-smoking speech of a Chinese learner at B1_2 level. This includes most of the tags characterising Chinese learners, which are shown in bold.

(1) ***I*_FPP1** am_VPRT "_" uh_UH "_" not_XX0 ***totally*_AMP** ***agree*_**VPRT [SUAV] **[PUBV]** with_PIN the_DT statement_NOMZ ._. ***Although*_CONC** ***smoking*_GER** will_PRMD "_" um_NN "_" harm_NN people_NN 's_POS health_NN and_CC "_" uh_UH "_" uh_UH "_" cause_NN "_" uh_UH "_" lung_NN cancer_NN "_" um_NN "_" ***smoking*_GER** also_RB "_" um_NN "_" makes_VPRT some_QUAN people_NN to_TO relax_VB ,_, to_TO relieve_VB pain_NN ._. ***And*_ANDC** "_" uh_UH "_" as_IN "_" uh_UH "_" restaurants_NN is_VPRT [BEMA] a_DT public_JJ place_NN ,_, they_TPP3 should_NEMD be_VB "_" uh_UH "_" satisfy_VB all_QUAN kinds_NN of_PIN people_NN 's_POS need_NN ,_, not_XX0 ***only*_DWNT** the_DT nonsmokers_NN but_CC also_RB the_DT smokers_NN ._. ***And*_ANDC** they_TPP3 "_" uh_UH "_" also_RB the_DT restaurants_NN ***could*_POMD** set_VB a_DT certain_JJ "_" a_DT particular_JJ place_NN for_PIN the_DT smokers_NN they_TPP3 ***can*_POMD** "_" they_TPP3 ***only*_DWNT** ***can*_POMD** smoke_VB there_RB and_CC the_DT nonsmokers_NN in_PIN another_DT place_NN ,_, so_IN they_TPP3 will_PRMD not_XX0 be_VB [BYPA] affected_VBN by_PIN the_DT ***smoking*_GER** ._. ***And*_ANDC** this_DEMP "_" uh_UH "_" in_PIN this_DEMO way_NN ,_,

*we*_**FPP1** *can*_**POMD** respect_VB the_DT rights_NN of_PIN all_QUAN peoples_NN "_" um_NN "_" ***and*_ANDC** they_TPP3 in_PIN the_DT …_: Um_NN._. (CHN_094_B1_2_SMK1)

As suggested in the fact that most of these tags are at the lexis level, Chinese learner speeches are structured less tightly in terms of grammar and constructions. Chinese learners repeatedly mention themselves ("I am …"), their own act of utterance ("I + agree …"), and what people can and cannot do ("restaurants could set …"). Their speeches include many filler-like particles and conjunctions ("And … And …") as well as a strange mix of amplifiers ("totally") and downtoners ("only"). A sense of semantic inconsistency and dissonance observed in their speeches may also be strengthened by the overuse of subordinators serving as heads of concessive clauses ("Although smoking will harm …"), which causes their speeches to sound less smooth and controlled.

Meanwhile, ENS often use OSUB (other adverbial subordinators: "while," "as long as," "since," "so that," "whereas"), EX (existential *there*: "there are people/restaurants," "there should/would be"), THVC (*That* verb complements: "believe/think/feel/find/guess/know + that"), PLACE (place adverbials: "across," "around," "outside," "away from," "as far as," "inside," "near"), PASS (agentless passives: "be + banned/given/involved/worried/exposed/forced/proven/required/supposed"), PEAS (perfect aspect: "have/has + banned/been/chosen/had/noticed/seen/worked"), WHSUB (*WH* [wh-words such as what, who, which] relative clauses on subject position: "people/person/students/customers + who"), SPAU (split auxiliaries: "can/should + actually/also/definitely/easily/just/only + V," "have + already + pp"), DEMP (demonstrative pronouns: "this is because/why…," "this would V," "than/like/with/about/of + this/that"), CONT (contractions: "I'd," "I'm," "you're," "it's," "don't," "I've"), PHC (phrasal coordination: "smoking and nonsmoking," "smokers and nonsmokers," "restaurants and bars/cafes," "college and university," "pros and cons," "quick and efficient," "good and bad," "go and do"), VBD (verb, past tense: "was," "were," "did," "got," "had," "learned," "said," "made," "paid," "smoked," "stated"), and SPP2 (second person pronouns: "you," "your", "yourself"). Also, the difference between Chinese learners and ENS is observed in terms of the number of tokens. Chinese learners speak much less than ENS even in the same topic and time-controlled monologue tasks.

The quote below is a non-smoking speech of an ENS. This includes many of the tags characterising ENS. Except for erroneously tagged cases, these are shown in bold.

(2) It_PIT *'s*_VPRT [**CONT**] [BEMA] a_DT tough_JJ question_NOMZ ._. Personally_RB ,_, I_FPP1 think_VPRT [PRIV] ***that*_THVC** it_PIT does_VPRT ***n't***_XX0 [**CONT**] have_VB to_TO ***be***_VB [**PASS**] ***banned***_VBN completely_AMP in_PIN restaurants_NN ._. I_FPP1 do_VPRT **n't**_XX0 [**CONT**] smoke_VB ._. I_FPP1 do_VPRT ***n't***_XX0 [**CONT**] like_VB smoking_GER ,_, but_CC ***as*_ OSUB** ***long***_NULL ***as***_NULL ***there*_EX**

are_VPRT sections_NOMZ and_CC they_TPP3 ***are***_VPRT [**SPAU**] [**PASS**] ***well***_RB ***ventilated***_VBN ,_, I_FPP1 do_VPRT ***n't***_XX0 [**CONT**] mind_VB it_PIT ._. If_COND it_PIT ***'s***_VPRT [**CONT**] [BEMA] the_DT entire_JJ restaurant_NN smoking_GER ,_, I_FPP1 do_EMPH mind_VB it_PIT and_CC ***that*_DEMP *'s***_VPRT [**CONT**] where_RB I_FPP1 would_PRMD like_VB to_TO see_VB [PRIV] a_DT ban_NN ._. But_CC if_COND they_TPP3 can_POMD divide_VB it_PIT and_CC ***you*_SPP2** actually_RB have_VPRT separate_JJ room_NN with_PIN proper_JJ ventilation_NOMZ ,_, I_FPP1 would_PRMD ***n't***_XX0 [**CONT**] mind_VB ._. I_FPP1 can_POMD see_VB [PRIV] why_RB [WHCL] people_NN would_PRMD mind_VB and_CC ***that*_DEMP *'s***_VPRT [**CONT**] basically_RB because_CAUS of_PIN health_NN reasons_NN ._. I_FPP1 should_NEMD n't_XX0 [**CONT**] ***be***_VB [**PASS**] ***thrown***_VBN into_PIN an_DT environment_NOMZ ,_, especially_RB in_PIN public_JJ restaurant_NN where_RB I_FPP1 come_VPRT to_TO ***eat***_VB ***and*_PHC *have***_VB to_TO breathe_VB in_PIN "_" breathe_VB in_PIN second-hand_JJ smoke_NN ._. it_PIT ***'s***_VPRT [**CONT**] [BEMA] terrible_PRED for_PIN ***you*_SPP2** as_IN second-hand_JJ smoke_NN ***there*_EX *'s***_VPRT [**CONT**] [PASS] been_VBN multiple_PRED "_" more_EMPH than_PIN numerous_JJ scientific_JJ studies_NN of_PIN health_NN related_VBN …_: (ENS_074_XX3_SMK1)

Many of the tags that characterise ENS speeches concern syntax rather than individual words and lexis. This leads ENS speeches to sound more complex and sophisticated in constructions and grammar. Even in speeches, ENS adopt a variety of complex structures, including (i) concessive clauses ("as long as S+V"), (ii) *there*-constructions ("there are …"), (iii) passive voices ("be ventilated," "be thrown"), where adverbs are occasionally inserted ("they are well ventilated"), and (iv) *that* as a complementiser ("think that S+V"). The degree of coherence and consistency is generally higher in ENS speeches, which is underpinned by frequent use of pronouns referring to the preceding contexts ("that's basically because …," "that's where S+V"). ENS also tend to refer to hearers ("you") and present plural lexical items as a set ("eat and have"), which contributes to a higher degree of interaction and structuredness in their speeches.

5.3.3.2 RQ2 Dimension Scores and Text Types

Six kinds of dimension scores (D1: involved or informational, D2: narrative or non-narrative, D3: explicit or situation-dependent, D4: overt expression of persuasion, D5: abstract or non-abstract, D6: online informational elaboration) and the estimated closest text types for the speeches of Chinese learners and ENS are shown in Figure 5.5 and Table 5.3.

Biber (1988) introduces the mean dimension scores for major text types (pp. 122–125). The scores for face-to-face conversations (F-F Conv), telephone

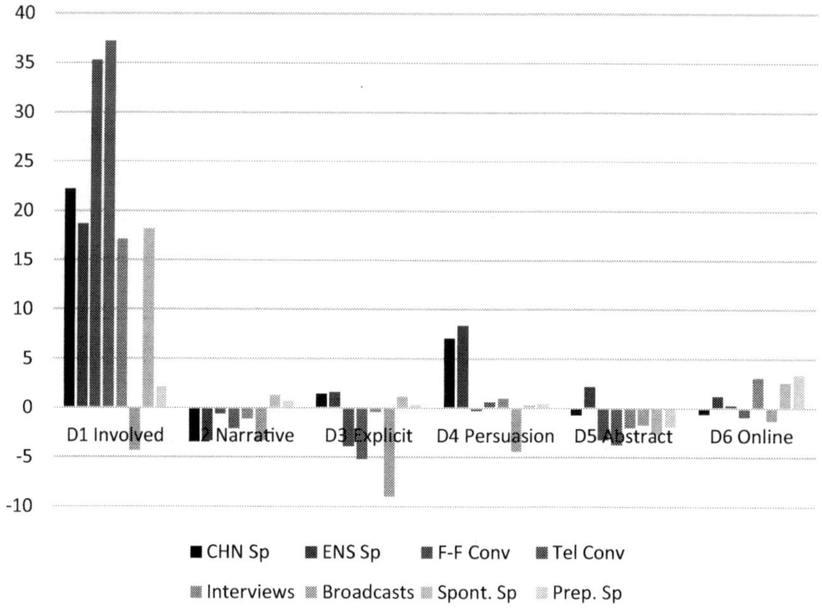

FIGURE 5.5 Dimension scores in the speeches of Chinese learners and ENS

TABLE 5.3 Closest text-types

	Chinese learner speeches	*ENS speeches*
Text-type	Informational interaction	Involved persuasion

conversations (Tel Conv), interviews, broadcasts, spontaneous speeches (Spont. Sp.), and prepared speeches (Prep. Sp.) are shown as references in Figure 5.5.

When compared to other text genres, the monologue speeches of Chinese learners and ENS present relatively similar patterns. For example, both of them show positive values in D3 (explicit or situational), whereas most of the other genres show negative values. They also show relatively higher positive values in D4 (persuasion), whereas the values of the other genres are near zero.

Meanwhile, we observe the difference between Chinese learners and ENS not only in the estimated text types but also in the dimension values. The value for Chinese learners is higher in D1 (involved or informational, CHN: 22.22, ENS: 18.68), and it is almost the same in D2 (narrative or non-narrative, −3.44, −3.32) and D3 (1.46, 1.60). Meanwhile, it is rather lower in D4 (7.07, 8.39), D5 (abstract or non-abstract, −0.73, 2.23), and D6 (online elaboration, −0.62, 1.23). Integrating these findings, we could conclude that when compared to ENS speeches, Chinese learner speeches tend to be somewhat more involved and concrete, but as they are essentially *I*-centred, they cannot be overtly persuasive, and their discourses, which include many fillers and dissonant combinations of lexical items, do not seem to develop naturally and smoothly. Many of these gaps could be attributed to Chinese learners' choice of plain grammar and simpler syntactic constructions, relatively looser control of coherence and consistency, and less attention to the hearers.

5.3.4 Summary

In this section, using the technique of Biber's MDA, which examines the frequencies of 67 kinds of lexicogrammatical features, calculates six kinds of factor/dimension scores, and estimates the type of the target text, we compared the monologue speeches of Chinese learners as a representative sample of Asian learners and ENS. Major findings are summarised in Table 5.4.

Considering that grammar and lexis are often overlapping, Biber's MDA seems quite an attractive approach to exploring various linguistic features of L2 learner outputs. Despite its potential possibilities, Biber's analytical approach has not been widely adopted by LC researchers, which is mainly due to the complex design and the limited accessibility of Biber's original tagger. Kilgarriff (1995) once noted that the MDA "has only been used by Biber and a small group of collaborators" mainly because "the methodology is technically difficult and time-consuming to implement" (p. 613). McEnery and Hardie (2012) also noted that "there is no easy-to-use integrated package publicly available that will perform a full MD analysis from beginning to end in a sufficiently user-friendly way to make it accessible to the majority of linguists" (p. 41).

The release of MAT may change such a situation surrounding LC-based grammar studies. However, we need to remember that even the best tagger can never reach 100% accuracy in complex lexicogrammatical tagging. In MDA, plural tags

TABLE 5.4 Summary of the findings: key lexicogrammatical features

Chinese learner speeches	*ENS speeches*
Key lexicogrammatical features	
[Pronoun] First-person pronouns [Verb] Pro-verbs, public verbs, gerunds [Structure] Independent clause coordination, Concessive adverbial subordinators [Stance] Possibility modals, amplifiers, downtoners [Discourse] Discourse particles	[Pronoun] Second person pronouns, demonstrative pronouns [Tense and aspect] Past tense, perfect aspect, agentless passives [Structure] Adverbial subordinators, existential *there*, *that* verb complements [Discourse] Contractions [Modification] WH relative clauses on subject position, phrasal coordination [Adverbial] Split auxiliaries, place adverbials
Key dimensions and close text-types	
[Dimension] D1 (involved) [Text type] Informational interaction	[Dimension] D4 (persuasion), D5 (abstract), D6 (online elaboration) [Text type] Involved persuasion

may be given to a single lexical or grammatical item. Therefore, one small tagging error may lead to a bigger problem. Regarding a methodological issue existing in a discussion of learners' development in L2 grammar, Durrant et al. (2021) mention, "although many syntactic features are *objective* in that they can be identified through various formal markers, actual stretches of writing are often ambiguous between two or more categorizations." For example, the word "writing" can be interpreted both as a noun and a verb (gerund). This small ambiguity may yield "cascade effects" for other features because syntactic phenomena are essentially interdependent (pp. 108–109).

6 PRAGMATICS

6.1 Introduction

6.1.1 Pragmatics in LCR

6.1.1.1 Background

In the previous chapters, we discussed vocabulary and grammar as two core components of learners' L2 skills. In Chapter 6, we pay attention to pragmatics, which concerns "meaning in relation to a speech situation," that is, "how language is used in communication" (Leech, 1983).

According to Bachman (1990), language competence is divided into organisational competence and pragmatic competence (p. 87). The former includes elements such as vocabulary, syntax, phonology, cohesion, and rhetorical organisation, while the latter covers various illocutionary functions—conventional forces and effects accompanying the utterances—as well as sociolinguistic sensitivity to dialects, registers, and cultures.

Studies in pragmatics have traditionally examined a single text or a few texts mainly from a qualitative viewpoint, but corpus-based pragmatics expands its analytical scope. Rühlemann (2019) notes:

> Corpus pragmatics makes use of the best of two worlds: the vertical-reading methodology of CL [i.e., corpus linguistics] (instructing computer software to plough through myriads of text samples in search of occurrences of a target item) integrated into the horizontal-reading methodology of pragmatics (weighing and interpreting individual occurrences within their contextual environments). The two complementary methodologies can be integrated in two complementary approaches to data analysis: form-to-function and function-to-form.
>
> *(pp. 7–8)*

DOI: 10.4324/9781003252528-8

One of the striking features of pragmatics is diversity in the topics it deals with. It covers speech acts (the effects caused by utterances), politeness (respecting the collocutor's self-esteem and freedom to act), deixis (context-based references), evaluation (positive or negative connotations), pragmatic/discourse markers (expressions to organise a discourse), conversation constituents (turn-opener, turn-taking, overlap, backchannels), and multimodality (body language and acoustic features), for instance.

6.1.1.2 Aspects of L2 Pragmatics

Learner corpus (LC)-based pragmatics studies, which are also called interlanguage pragmatics, tend to pay special attention to the investigation of L2 learners' development of the pragmatic abilities to "understand and perform action in a target language" (Kasper & Rose, 2002, p. 5) and "to communicate effectively and appropriately in specific social settings" (Vyatkina & Cunningham, 2015, p. 281).

Among many topics that can be discussed in the framework of pragmatics, some have attracted increasing attention. First, regarding modality, many studies suggest that learners overuse modal verbs in general (Ringbom, 1998), and especially directive modal verbs ("must," "should") (Maden-Weinberger, 2008), while they underuse epistemic modals ("may," "might"), though the tendency gradually disappears according to the increase in their L2 proficiency (Chen, 2010).

Second, as regards stance marking, Castello and Gesuato (2019) report that learners' L1 backgrounds influence their choice of backchannels (e.g., certainty marking, uncertainty marking, surprise marking, and confirmation request). Pérez-Paredes and Díez-Bedmar (2019) show that the use of certainty adverbs ("actually," "really," and "obviously") is influenced both by interview tasks and learners' proficiency levels. In dialogic tasks, "really" and "actually" are preferred, and advanced learners use "really" as a hedge and "actually" as a factualness marker.

Third, as regards intensification, the literature suggests that learners have a clear tendency to overuse a variety of intensifiers (Ringbom, 1998; Lorenz, 1998). Schweinberger (2020) focuses on the phrase "very" + adjectives and reports that "very" is overused by 9 of the 12 European learner groups. L1 Italian, Spanish, and Swedish learners overuse "very different," L1 Polish and Swedish learners underuse "very important," and non-native-speaker-like adjective choices are likely to be made by the latter group. Hong and Cao (2014) suggest that learners' L1 backgrounds influence their use of boosters, attitude markers, self-mentions, and engagement markers. The authors also mention that essay types (descriptive or argumentative) influence the use of hedges and self-mentions.

Fourth, regarding deictic references, many studies have mentioned learners' common tendency to overuse the first-person pronouns (Petch-Tyson, 1998; Callies, 2013) as well as the words referring directly to the situation of writing and speaking (e.g., "here" and "now") (Petch-Tyson, 1998). Recent studies reconsider such a tendency from the viewpoint of *origo* as a deictic centre (Rühlemann,

2019, p. 53). It seems that learners tend to overuse *origo*-nearer references ("I," "now," "this," "here") and underuse *origo*-farther references ("s/he," "then," "that," "there").

Fifth, regarding discourse markers, which do not add meanings but help control the flow of discourse (e.g., "yes," "oh," "well," and "you know"), many studies report that L2 learners underuse discourse markers in general (Romero-Trillo, 2002; Öztürk & Köse, 2021), the frequency of discourse markers correlates with speech fluency (Hasselgren, 2002), learners often make long pauses, while L1 English native speakers (ENS) adopt small words such as "like" and "well" as lexical hesitation markers solely or in combination with other words (Gilquin, 2008; Blanchard & Buysse, 2021), learners overuse referential type of discourse markers ("and," "but," "because," "so"), while they underuse interpersonal type of discourse markers ("yeah," "I see," "you know") (Fung & Carter, 2007), and leaners acquire different discourse markers at different timings, and they are influenced by their L1 backgrounds (Werner, 2017). The overuse/underuse of discourse markers, however, needs to be carefully checked. Jones et al. (2018) analyse an interview test corpus and report that "er" and "OK" are overused, while "you know" and "I mean" are underused by learners (p. 124). Aijmer (2011) points out that L1 Swedish advanced learners tend to overuse "well" in their speeches, but it is largely for fluency management, not for pragmatic attitude marking. Hong and Cao (2014) analyse interactional metadiscourse in young learner essays with a focus on the hedges ("could," "maybe"), boosters ("absolutely," " really"), attitude markers ("should," "must"), self-mentions ("I," "we"), and engagement markers ("you"), and they report that the frequencies of four groups of metadiscourse markers (boosters, attitude markers, self-mentions, and engagement markers) are significantly influenced by learners' L1 backgrounds, while the frequencies of two groups (hedges and self-mentions) are influenced by the essay types (i.e., descriptive or argumentative). Götz and Mukherjee (2019) analyse the data from LINDSEI and report that the number of discourse markers ("like," "you know") and small words ("sort of," "kind of"), which they regard as markers of "fluency enhancement strategies," increase as learners have longer study-abroad experiences.

Finally, politeness is also widely discussed in pragmatics research. It is usually defined as "a system of interpersonal relations designed to facilitate interaction by minimising the potential for conflict and confrontation inherent in all human interchange" (Lakoff, 1990, p. 34), and it concerns the protection of one's "face," that is, "the positive self-image or self-esteem that a person enjoys as a reflection of that person's estimation by others" (Leech, 2014, p. 25). A pragmatic face has two aspects. "Positive face" concerns "the positive consistent self-image or 'personality' (crucially including the desire that this self-image be appreciated and approved of) claimed by interactants," while "negative face" concerns "the basic claim to territories, personal preserves, rights to nondistraction i.e., to freedom of action and freedom from imposition" (Brown & Levinson, 1987, p. 61). Though the two faces often compete, good communication is realised only when these goals are well combined. Politeness control becomes more challenging when two participants have opposing stances. In such a situation, one may need to disagree with the collocutor (refusal, rebuttal) or require them to do something that they may not like to do (order, persuasion), which potentially leads to a face-threatening act (FTA). Regarding L2 learners' politeness control skills, Leech (2014) reviews previous studies and concludes that, despite the difference in their L1s, novice L2 learners tend to adopt shorter, more direct, and more impolite forms such as simple imperatives and direct requests, while advanced learners come to use longer, more indirect, and more polite forms, though they may not reach the level of ENS yet. Leech also says that "higher-level students are pragmatically more advanced in approximating to NS performance than lower-level students" (p. 271). Gablasova and Brezina (2018) analyse the data from an interview test corpus and report that advanced learners come to use "yes but" constructions, which are one of the pragmatic softener devices to avoid FTA in disagreement, more often and more frequently in combination with downtoners showing hesitation and delay than novice learners.

6.1.1.3 New Approaches

Recent LC-based pragmatics studies have come to explore the possibilities of new data, new taxonomy, new analytical viewpoint, and new application.

First, as new data, some researchers have begun to analyse multimodal corpora that include both texts and audio/videos, which enables them to discuss pragmatics not only at the textual level but also at the levels of phonology and gesture use. Especially, a speaker's gesture use has begun to attract much attention. As Barth and Schnell (2022) summarise, gestures, which are classified into manual/hand gestures, bodily gestures, and facial gestures (e.g., eye-brow raising), are closely connected with language. This is supported by the scientific fact that the same parts of the brain are used for processing symbolic gestures and speeches. Thus, "the study of gestures can help us understand language processing" (p. 64). The possibilities of corpus-based gestures analysis have already been explored in CL. For example, Adolphs and Carter (2013) collected 13 videos of English lectures and seminars and to develop the Nottingham Multimodal Corpus. They mention:

> Communication processes are multimodal in nature, and there is now a distinct need for the development of theories, analytical frameworks, and resources that enable the user to begin to carry out analyses of both the speech and gestures of the participants in a conversation[.]
>
> *(p. 1)*

They also present several case studies using their datasets, which include the analysis of the matching of phraseological and intonation boundaries concerning the target expression ("I don't know why"), the investigation of the pauses around the target expression ("I think"), and the descriptive analyses of head nods and iconic hand gestures. Regarding the functions of learners' gesture use in communication, there seem to exist an overlap with a language use. For example, Kosmala et al. (2019) compare learners' uses of non-verbal gestures and verbal disfluency markers (filled and unfilled pauses, repetitions, self-repairs, etc.) and suggest a coordination between speech/gesture suspensions. Meanwhile, Graziano and Gullberg (2013) showed that L2 speakers tend to produce more gestures when they speak more fluently, and they regard gestures as a kind of fluency marker. A gesture usually includes several motions in it. For a detailed analysis of a gesture, Kendon (2004) proposes the concept of a gesture unit (G-unit), which consists of four internal phases: preparation (e.g., moving an arm from a normal relaxed position), stroke (e.g., swing down an arm), hold (e.g., keep that arm position), and recovery/retraction (e.g., an arm goes back to a normal relaxed position).

Second, as regards taxonomy, many studies have developed a taxonomy to classify various types of pragmatic speech acts. When annotating the Michigan Corpus of Academic Spoken English (MICASE), Simpson-Vlach and Leicher (2006) identified 25 kinds of pragmatic features, which cover "advice/direction, giving or soliciting," "assigning homework," "definitions," "disagreement," and "discussion," for instance (pp. 68–69). Meanwhile, Weisser (2018), who points out that the traditional taxonomies are often loose and partial, proposes a new analytical taxonomy for his Dialogue Annotation and Research Tool (DART), which classifies more than 110 potential speech acts that cover "abandon," "accept," "acknowledge," "acknowledge Thanks," "agree," "answer," "apologize," "approve," and "attribute," for example.

Third, as regards an analytical viewpoint, more and more LC researchers have come to pay attention to the possible mixed effects of varied learner-related and task-related parameters on the learners' use of major pragmatic devices. For example, Götz (2019) examines how learners' usage of filled pauses in the interview tests can be influenced by their country of origin, proficiency level, age of L2 acquisition, as well as the examiner's experience. The analysis shows that L2 proficiency level significantly influences the number of filled fillers, but its effect is relatively more minor in comparison to the effects of other learning context variables. Castello and Gesuato (2019) examine lexical backchannels (convergence and confirmation request) and reveal that the frequency and function type of backchannels greatly vary according to learners' L1 backgrounds. Pérez-Paredes and Díez-Bedmar (2019) investigate L1 Spanish learners' use of certainty adverbs ("actually," "really," "obviously") in speeches and report that the frequency of each adverb is influenced not only by learner proficiency levels but also by task types.

Finally, regarding a pedagogical application, Lakew et al. (2021) conducted corpus-informed spoken grammar and pragmatics instruction to the students and teachers in Ethiopia for six weeks. It covers ellipsis (e.g., "[Do you have] Any questions?"), left-dislocation (i.e., presenting a topic at the head), right-dislocation (i.e., adding the comment at the end), fillers (e.g., "er," "well," "hmm"), backchannels (e.g., "uh-huh," "oh," "yeah," "I see"), and phrased chunks to create vagueness (e.g., "sort of"), modify and show politeness (e.g., "a bit"), and mark discourse structures (e.g., "you know" and "I mean"). Based on the questionnaire responses, the authors conclude that both the students and teachers welcomed such instruction.

6.1.2 ICNALE Case Studies

Among the many topics covered in pragmatics studies, we focus on Asian learners' use of major pragmatic devices (modality, intensification, and reference), politeness strategies, and gestures.

In Section 6.2, we analyse the essays by learners of English as a foreign language (EFL) taken from the ICNALE Written Essays and examine the frequencies of the words related to modality (non-epistemic/directive vs. epistemic), intensification (boosters vs. hedges), and anaphoric reference (*origo*-nearer vs. *origo*-farther). Then, we discuss whether advanced learners come to rely more on epistemic and non-directive modality, hedges, and *origo*-farther references.

In Section 6.3, we qualitatively analyse the speech transcripts of two learners of English as a second language (ESL) at an advanced level, which are taken from the ICNALE Spoken Dialogues. Our analytical focus is to be put on how two advanced learners try to control politeness in a persuasion task, where persuaders are requested to carefully consider the balance between respecting the collocutor's face and persuading the collocutor anyway.

Finally, in Section 6.4, we analyse the interview videos included in the ICNALE Spoken Dialogues and discuss how and to what extent EFL learners adopt three types of hand gestures in a picture description task: touching one's head, moving one's hand, and pointing to the picture. After surveying the quantity of each gesture and the relationship between learners' hand gesture use and their verbal fluency, we scrutinise the videos of three learners and qualitatively analyse what pragmatic functions are realised by their choice of each type of gesture.

6.2 Pragmatic Devices

6.2.1 Aim and RQs

Effective use of pragmatic devices is one of the keys to smooth and effective L2 communication. However, how Asian EFL learners use the words related to three kinds of basic pragmatic devices such as modality, intensification, and anaphoric reference in their essays, whether advanced learners really tend to use the epistemic modality more than the non-epistemic/directive modality, the hedges more than the boosters, and the *origo*-farther references more than the origo-nearer references as suggested in the previous literature, and to what degree the observed tendency is (not) influenced by the learner- and task-related variables, are not necessarily clear. Therefore, this study examines the following research questions:

RQ1 How do Asian EFL learners at four proficiency levels as well as ENS deal with three kinds of pragmatic devices in their essays?

RQ2 Do the learners' regions and essay topics influence the observed pattern of using three kinds of pragmatic devices?

6.2.2 Data and Method

In this study, we analyse essays written by Asian EFL learners at four proficiency levels (A2, B1_1, B1_2, and B2+) as well as ENS taken from the ICNALE Written Essays to examine how they deal with three aspects of pragmatics: modality, intensification, and anaphoric reference.

Though a variety of vocabulary may be related to the realisation of those pragmatic functions, we limit ourselves to examining the occurrences of the 52 words shown in Table 6.1. Based on the findings from the previous studies, we classify them into Type 1, which is expected to be used mainly by novice learners, and Type 2, which is expected to be used mainly by advanced learners and ENS.

Regarding modality, we pay attention to eight modal verbs. It is expected that learners come to use epistemic modals more often and non-epistemic/directive modals less often as their proficiency increases (Maden-Weinberger, 2008; Chen, 2010).

As regards intensification, previous studies have discussed a variety of lexical items, but we focus on 20 kinds of *-ly* adverbs, which are chosen from the list of boosters and hedges that Hyland (2004) introduces as the "items expressing doubt and certainty" (pp. 188–189). Considering the findings in the literature (Ringbom, 1998; Lorenz, 1998; Schweinberger, 2020), we could expect that learners come to use hedges more often, which help them write from a better-balanced viewpoint, and boosters less often.

Finally, as regards reference, we examine the occurrences of 24 words related to persons ("I" and "we" vs. "(s)he" and "they"), time ("now" vs. "then"), place ("here" vs. "there"), and anaphoric reference ("this" and "these," vs. "that" and "those"). It is expected that learners come to use *origo*-farther vocabulary more often, which makes their discourses more academic and professional, and *origo*-nearer vocabulary less often (Petch-Tyson, 1998; Callies, 2013).

We first analyse the whole data, compare the frequencies of Type 1 and Type 2 words adopted by each of the four proficiency groups as well as ENS, and identify

TABLE 6.1 Pragmatic items used for the analysis

Type	*Type 1*	*Type 2*
Modality	[Non-epistemic/Directive] will, can, may; must, should	[Epistemic] would, could, might
Intensification	[Boosters] actually, certainly, clearly, definitely, inevitably, necessarily, obviously, particularly, precisely, surely	[Hedges] basically, essentially, generally, largely, normally, partly, possibly, presumably, probably, relatively
Anaphoric reference	[*Origo*-nearer] I, my, me, mine, we, our, us; now, here; this, these	[*Origo*-farther] she, her, hers, he, his, him, they, their, them; then; there; that, those

which of the three kinds of pragmatic devices steadily increase or decreases according to the increase in learners' overall L2 proficiency. Next, we focus on the data of learners at A2 and B2+ levels to investigate whether the observed trends are stable and free from the possible influences of learners' regions (i.e., China: CHN, Indonesia: IDN, Japan: JPN, Korea: KOR, Taiwan: TWN, and Thailand: THA) and essay topics (i.e., a part-time job for college students and non-smoking at restaurants). When discussing frequency, we investigate the occurrence of word-forms, meaning that we do not consider their semantic functions realised in context. Also, when comparing the frequencies from the datasets of different sizes, we adjust the raw frequency per one million words (PMW).

6.2.3 Results and Discussions

6.2.3.1 RQ1 Pragmatic Device Use by Learners and ENS

The results of the investigation of the frequencies of Type 1 and Type 2 words related to modality, intensification, and reference adopted by Asian EFL learners at four proficiency levels as well as ENS are shown in Figures 6.1 to 6.3.

First, in terms of modality, Asian EFL learners, despite the difference in proficiency levels, tend to overuse non-epistemic modal verbs (30.5 to 45.2%) as well as directive modal verbs (22.5 to 38.2%), while they underuse epistemic modal verbs (−78.7 to −45.9%) in comparison to ENS, which underpins the findings from the previous studies. Then, from A2 to B2+, the frequency of epistemic modal verbs constantly increases by more than doubles (154.0%). Meanwhile, the pattern of change is not necessarily clear with the others: the frequency of non-epistemic modal verbs increases from A2 to B1_1 and then decreases by 10.2% from B1_1 to B2+, and that of directive modal verbs hardly changes. Thus, the hypothesis that advanced learners come to use epistemic modal verbs more often than novice learners has been confirmed, but the expected trend that

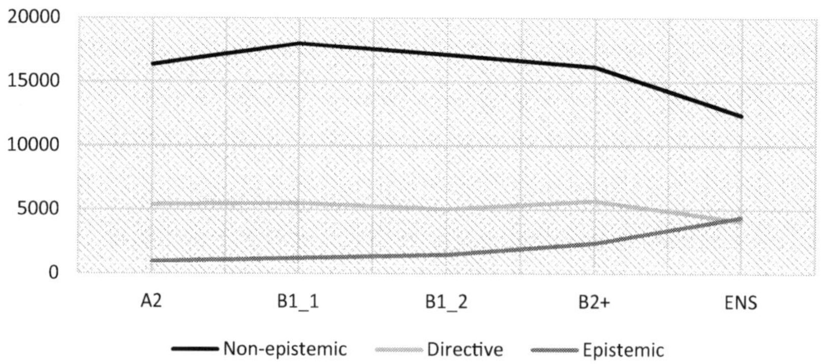

FIGURE 6.1 Frequencies of the modality-related words

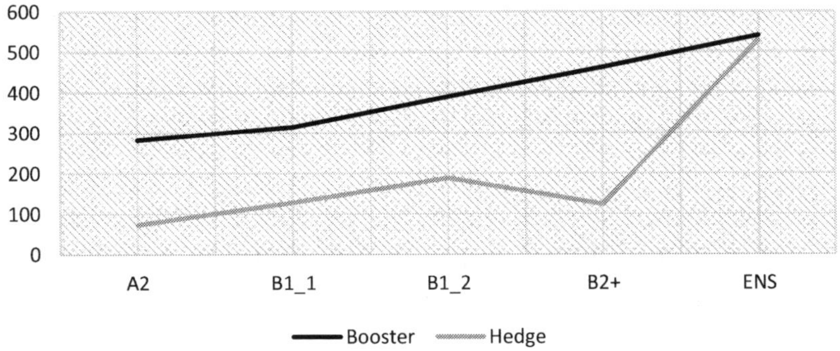

FIGURE 6.2 Frequencies of the intensification-related words

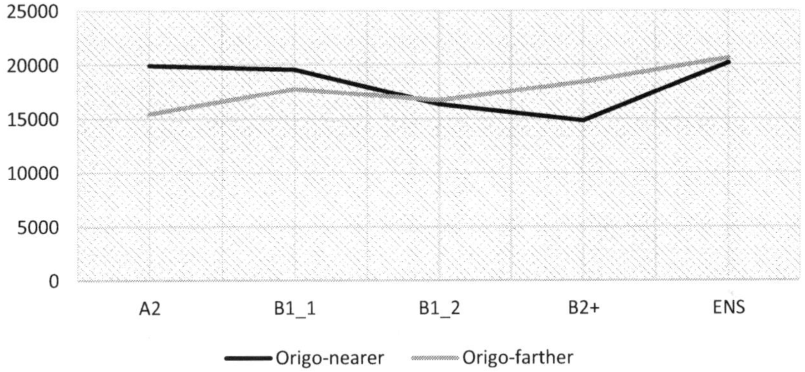

FIGURE 6.3 Frequencies of the anaphoric reference-related words

advanced learners come to use fewer non-epistemic and directive modal verbs has not been confirmed in a clear manner.

Next, in terms of intensification, learners tend to underuse both boosters (−47.8 to −14.5%) and hedges (−86.2 to −64.4%). The frequency of boosters constantly increases by 63.77% from A2 to B2+, while that of hedges increases from A2 to B1_2 by 157.8%, but it decreases by 34.5% from B1_2 to B2+. Thus, the hypothesis of learners' decreasing use of boosters has not been supported, while that of their increasing use of hedges has been confirmed only between A2 and B1_2.

Finally, in terms of anaphoric reference, learners tend to underuse both *origo*-nearer references (−26.7 to −1.3%) and *origo*-farther references (−10.8 to −25.1%). The frequency of the former constantly decreases by 25.72% from A2 to B2+, and the frequency of the latter increases by 19.12%, though we see a slight decrease between B1_1 and B1_2. The hypothesis of learners' decreasing use of *origo*-nearer references has been fully supported, and that of their increasing use of *origo*-farther references has been partly proven.

Thus, the data showed that Asian EFL learners come to use epistemic modal verbs, boosters, hedges, and *origo*-farther references more often as their proficiency levels go up, and they come to use *origo*-nearer references less often, though some are found to be only partial trends. These findings suggest that Asian EFL learners' pragmatic skills may develop at least in some aspects. Novice learners usually write about themselves and something immediately around them in a straightforward way. Meanwhile, advanced learners gradually come to adjust their stance by adopting epistemic modal verbs, boosters, and hedges and also by writing not about themselves but about someone else, though there still remains a wide gap between advanced learners and ENS in terms of the usage of pragmatic devices.

6.2.3.2 RQ2 Effects of Learner- and Task-related Variables

The analysis in the previous section presented that among the expected trends, only four were fully or partly proven: (i) increase of epistemic modal verbs, (ii) increase of hedges, (iii) decrease of *origo*-nearer references, and (iv) increase of *origo*-farther references. However, whether these trends are stable enough, in other words, whether they are seen commonly with learners from different regions and in both the part-time job essays and the non-smoking essays, is not clear yet.

First, the frequencies of epistemic modal verbs used by different learner groups in two kinds of essays are shown in Figure 6.4.

The increasing use of epistemic modal verbs is confirmed in five of the six region-based learner groups. The frequency increases by more than 120% for learners from Indonesia, Japan, Korea, and Taiwan, and by 41% for Chinese learners, though it slightly decreases for Thai learners. Also, the increasing trend is clearly seen in both types of essays. The frequency increases by 148.4% in the part-time job essays and by 159.4% in the non-smoking essays. The increase of epistemic modals seems to be a considerably stable trend.

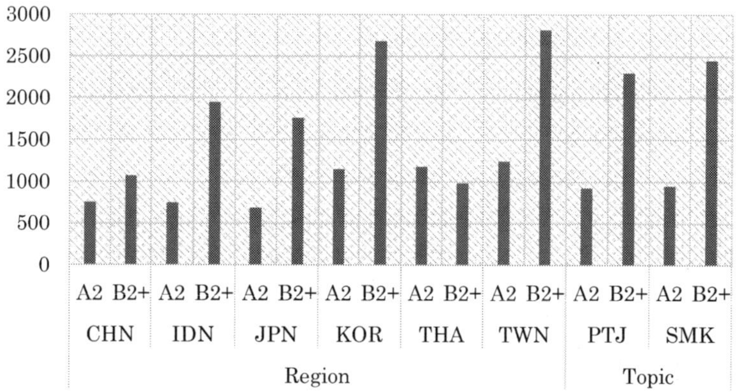

FIGURE 6.4 Region/topic effects on the frequencies of epistemic modal verbs

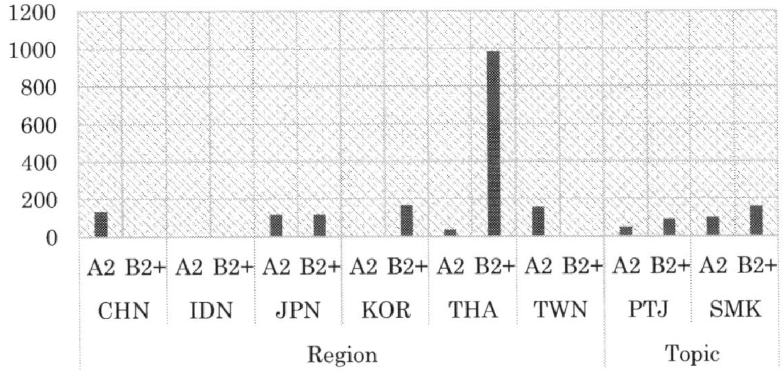

FIGURE 6.5 Region/topic effects on the frequencies of hedges

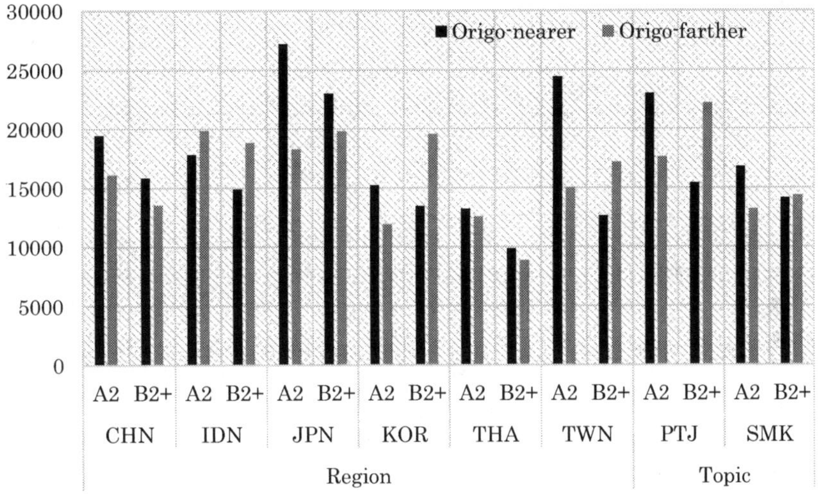

FIGURE 6.6 Region/topic effects on the frequencies of anaphoric references

Second, the frequencies of hedges used by different learner groups in two kinds of essays are shown in Figure 6.5.

The frequency of hedges is largely limited, and the trend of increasing use is seen only in only two of the six learner groups. The frequency increases only for Korean and Thai learners. Though a slight increase in frequency is seen in both types of essays, the increasing hedge use cannot be a stable trend applicable to a variety of EFL learners in Asia.

Finally, the frequencies of *origo*-nearer and *origo*-farther references adopted by different learner groups in two kinds of essays are shown in Figure 6.6.

The decreasing use of *origo*-nearer references is observed in all of the six learner groups. The frequency decreases by 11.4–48.2% for them. In addition, the same trend is confirmed in both types of essays. We could conclude that this is a highly stable trend for Asian EFL learners. Meanwhile, the increasing use of *origo*-farther references is seen only in three of the six learner groups. The frequency increases by 64.3% for Korean learners, by 13.9% for Taiwanese learners, and by 8.2% for Japanese learners, but it decreases for others. Though the increase is observed in both types of essays, the increasing use of *origo*-farther references is less likely to be a stable trend applicable to a majority of EFL learners in Asia.

Thus, the data analysis revealed that among the four trends, only two were stable across a variety of learner- and task-related variables: (i) increase of epistemic modals and (iii) decrease of *origo*-nearer references.

6.2.4 Summary

In this section, analysing the essays written by Asian EFL learners and ENS, we examined learners' use of three kinds of pragmatic devices: modality, intensification, and anaphoric reference. Major findings are summarised in Table 6.2, where "Match" represents the numbers of regions [R] (/6) and essay types [T] (/2) to which the overall increasing/decreasing trends are applicable.

We hypothesised that learners come to use more epistemic modal verbs and fewer non-epistemic/directive modal verbs, more hedges and fewer boosters, and more *origo*-farther references and fewer *origo*-nearer references as their proficiency increases. Our analyses, however, showed that only the two trends, increasing use of epistemic modals and decreasing use of *origo*-nearer references, were stable and applicable to a variety of Asian EFL learners as well as both essay types. Carefully considering our findings, it would be safer for us to conclude that Asian EFL learners' development in L2 pragmatic skills is more delicate and subtle than generally believed.

From a methodological viewpoint, the results of the current analysis strongly suggest the need to discuss learners' L2 outputs in combination with a variety of

TABLE 6.2 Summary of the findings: change in the use of three kinds of pragmatic devices

Type	*Sub-type*	*A2/B2+*	*B2+/ENS*	*Match*
Modality	Non-epistemic	Decreasing (B1_1/B2+)	> ENS	
	Directive	No change	> ENS	
	Epistemic	Increasing	< ENS	[R] 5/6 [T] 2/2
Intensification	Booster	Increasing	< ENS	
	Hedge	Increasing (A2/B1_2)	< ENS	[R] 2/6 [T] 2/2
Reference	*Origo*-nearer	Decreasing	< ENS	[R] 6/6 [T] 2/2
	Origo-farther	Increasing (B1_2/B2+)	< ENS	[R] 3/6 [T] 2/2

learner- and task-related variables. As demonstrated in recent studies such as Götz (2019), Castello and Gesuato (2019), and Pérez-Paredes and Díez-Bedmar (2019), learners' L2 use cannot be discussed meaningfully without considering learner-related variables (e.g., region of origin, L2 proficiency level, age of acquisition, learning context) as well as task-related variables (e.g., task type, the relation between a learner and an examiner). An integrative analytical approach paying due attention to these variables would be mainstream in future learner corpus research (LCR).

6.3 Politeness

6.3.1 Aim and RQs

It is said that "higher-level students are pragmatically more advanced" (Leech, 2014, p. 271), but whether this is applicable to Asian advanced learners has not been confirmed. Here we discuss how advanced ESL learners in Asia control politeness in persuasion roleplays. Unlike the other types of communication based on the cooperative principle between participants (Grice, 1975), persuasion is a unique speech act because a persuader and a receiver often have different goals and merits, and a persuader may need to fight with a receiver having a different opinion. Thus, a persuader is required to carefully choose their politeness strategy from promoting the receiver's positive face, protecting the receiver's negative face, and intentional face-threatening act (FTA). This study qualitatively analyses the utterances of two advanced learners from Hong Kong and the Philippines to examine the following research questions:

RQ1 How does a Hong Kong learner control politeness in a persuasion roleplay?
RQ2 How does a Philippine learner control politeness in a persuasion roleplay?

6.3.2 Data and Method

In this study, we analyse the utterances of a male learner at B2+ level from Hong Kong (HKG_003) and a female learner at the same level from the Philippines (PHL_002) in the non-smoking roleplays taken from the ICNALE Spoken Dialogues. In the task, a participant takes a role of a person who recently dined with their friend at a smoking-free restaurant. As the friend felt unwell during a meal because of too much smoke there, two had to stop eating and leave the restaurant. Therefore, a participant makes a phone call to the restaurant owner to request a refund. As the restaurant does not have a non-smoking policy, making a refund claim is highly challenging.

The analysis is based on the transcripts included in the dataset, where a serial code is given to each utterance. S1 and T2, for instance, represent the first turn for the student (interviewee) and the second turn for the teacher (interviewer).

6.3.3 Result and Discussion

6.3.3.1 RQ1 A Hong Kong Learner's Persuasion

The Hong Kong learner tries to present his refund request clearly and explicitly. His top priority seems to push the restaurant owner to agree with the refund, and he pays less attention to politeness.

The roleplay consists of 11 turns, 6 of which are learner turns. Each of them will be analysed from the viewpoint of politeness control.

(1) [S1] Earlier in this afternoon I have gone to—to your restaurant and have my lunch, um, and there are some people smoking in your restaurant and it is—the smell is not good. And we can't bear the smell and so that we go—we left your restaurant but we haven't finished our meal so please refund to us.

[T1] Uh, no, I don't think that's possible. Why—why would you want the refund?

[S2] Because your restaurant should mean—should be able to provide a comfortable atmosphere for us.

[T2] No, it was great and, um, I mean yes some people are smoking but they're enjoying themselves and the food was great, so you had the food and I don't understand why you need the refund.

[S3] Because we haven't finished our meals.

[T3] So that's really—I am sorry, but that's really your problem, you had the food, you didn't finish it.

[S4] But you can't provide a—a favorable, uh, atmosphere for us to have that food.

[T4] I am sure those people were smoking quite far away, it's a different table.

[S5] So, maybe, you can set up a smoke-king area, not—not, um, having them with us. And—and because of that smell we can't have our, uh, meal.

[T5] So, um, yes I will take that, um, suggestion, but I am really sorry, it's impossible for us to refund you and to repay you for the meal you had.

[S6] Maybe, you just have to, uh, refund to us because the—the environment is really, really dirty and smelly and if you don't, um, um, refund us we may, uh, tell this story to the news company.

In the S1 turn, the learner as a customer (LAC hereafter) skips any type of conventional greeting such as "Hi" or "Hello," and begins his phone call directly with an explanation about his uncomfortable experience and the explicit refund request. In conversations, information is often subdivided into pieces, and they are offered piecemeal through the repeated interactions between the participants, which helps the participants to reach co-understanding. However, LAC puts all of what he wants to say just in the first turn. As in many complaint speeches, consideration for the collocutor, in this case, the teacher as a restaurant owner (TAO hereafter), is hardly observed here.

In the S2 turn, responding to the question about the reason for the refund, LAC begins his answer with "Because" without any cushion expressions to soften the message. TAO's question here may violate the maxim of quantity (Grice, 1975) because LAC has already finished explaining the detailed background of his uncomfortable experience. Thus, LAC cannot help giving an abstract and off-focus explanation that the restaurant should offer a comfortable atmosphere for the customers. The use of a directive modal verb "should" exemplifies LAC's paying limited attention to the maintenance of politeness in the interaction.

Then, in the S3 turn, responding to the repeated questions from TAO, LAC begins with "Because" again, but what he says here is just a repetition of what he has already said in the S1 turn. No new information is added here.

In the S4 turn, following the TAO's rebuttal suggesting that the meals were offered anyway, LAC begins his counterclaim with "But," however, this is also just a repetition of what he said in the S2 turn.

In the S5 turn, LAC offers a compromising request, and he says the restaurant needs to create a smoking area (and presumably a non-smoking area as well). Realising that all the requests have been rejected, LAC may somewhat try to change his approach, which is reflected in the use of the hedging adverb "maybe" and choosing "can" instead of "should" or "must."

In the S6 turn, LAC tries his last persuasion by emphasising rationality in his refund claim by using amplifiers such as "just" and "really." He finally goes as far as to explicitly threaten TAO by suggesting that he may leak the incident to the mass media. Then, as the time is out, this roleplay is stopped by the interviewer. It is true that LAC tries his best to persuade TAO anyway, even at the risk of giving up the politeness control and conducting a face-threatening act, but his persuasion does not seem to end in success.

6.3.3.2 RQ2 A Philippine Learner's Persuasion

Contrary to the case of HKG_003, the Philippine learner (PHL_002) we discuss here tries to be polite and consistently pay due respect to the face of the collocutor. However, this consideration may make her wants less clear. The roleplay consists of 13 turns, seven of which are learner turns.

(2) [S1] So um, hello ma'am.

[T1] Hi, how may I help you?

[S2] So we would like to uh, so this call is uh, to inform you that we are—we want to have a refund from the restaurant from our earlier expense.

[T2] Why is that so, what happened?

[S3] Unfortunately, the restaurant not prohibit smoking, so lot of people smoke in there. And uh, me and my friend is not used to that kind of environment, so we left early and not finishing our food. So the restaurant didn't gave us the experience that we should have.

[T3] Alright.

[S4] And the value of our meal is not satisfied.

[T4] Uh-huh. But I do not like a no smoking policy and you understand that that's the situation in our restaurants. So I'm afraid I cannot give your refund for what—for the food that you weren't able to eat.

[S5] Uh, even you know maybe we can ask even if it's just half of the price of the payment.

[T5] Ah, I am really sorry, but we also have operational costs that yeah we have to buy food and we had to pay for the people in the restaurant, so I don't think that's possible, but yeah, feel free to come back to our restaurant.

[S6] Well, if possible, if you had this kind of restaurant, you should have an open area so that other people can also eat even if they smoke so that the air would circulate and won't disturb your customers.

[T6] Okay. Well, the comments of our customers are valuable, so yeah, I will take note of that. Thank you so much. I am sorry, but I cannot give in to your request.

[S7] Okay, thank you. Thank you.

First, in the S1 turn, the LAC begins her talk with a conventional conversation opener of "Hello" and further adds an honorific "ma'am." Even in persuasion, LAC tries to consider the face of the TAO.

In the S2 turn, LAC begins, "So we would like to uh ...." Presumably she intended to add "have a refund." However, as this may sound too abrupt, she stops the sentence halfway through and instead self-corrects her utterance by adopting a more formal construction of "this call is to inform you ...," which can be a kind of cushion to introduce what she really wants to say: "We want to have a refund." What should be noted here is that LAC combines the first-person plural pronoun "we" rather than "I" with an epistemic modal verb "would." These wordings strongly imply that LAC carefully tries to make her claim sound less impolite, less subjective, and less directive, all of which can be interpreted as a consideration for the negative face of the restaurant side.

Then, in the S3 turn, LAC begins an explanation about the reason for the refund request. Here LAC uses the resultative conjunction "so" three times. She tries to be logical rather than emotional. Although her true feeling is indirectly conveyed in the sentence adverb of "unfortunately," the conclusion of this remark that the restaurant did not give a good experience to the customer seems to be highly abstract and circumlocutionary. In addition, she says that she is not used to the smoking environment. This overly humble comment may make the hearer wrongly guess that she is admitting that the fault is hers instead.

In the S4 turn, LAC suggests that she and her friend could not be satisfied with the meal. However, by adopting a passive voice, she carefully deletes the subject, which also reflects her intention to make her claim less subjective.

Next, in the S5 turn, understanding that the restaurant does not intend to issue a refund, LAC proposes a new compromising request of a 50% refund. Even when mentioning this, LAC carefully avoids any directive connotation. A hedge-like filler of "Uh" as well as a combinatory use of the expressions such as "you know," "maybe," and "we can ask even if ..." contribute to the maintenance of high-level politeness.

Then, in the S6 turn, LAC proposes a different suggestion that the restaurant should have an open area for smokers so that the smoke does not enter the dining space inside. Here LAC uses a directive modal verb "should," but its strong effect is soon neutralised by the other wordings, including "if possible" and "if you had ...." The conditional *if* guarantees TAO "the basic claim to territories, personal preserves, rights to nondistraction" (Brown & Levinson, 1987, p. 61). Like the previous utterances, the S6 utterance is also highly verbose.

Finally, in the S7 turn, though LAC has not obtained any promise of a refund despite her efforts of persuasion, she says "Okay," and repeats "thank you" twice. Though we cannot say that LAC's persuasion succeeds, we see high-level politeness control through her speech.

6.3.4 Summary

In this section, we compared two kinds of persuasion speeches by two Asian ESL learners at B2+ advanced level. The developments of their discourses are summarised in Table 6.3.

TABLE 6.3 Summary of the findings: structures of the two persuasion speeches

Function	*HKG_003*	*PHL_002*
Opening	(Not stated)	hello ma'am (S1)
Reasons	(1) we haven't finished our meal (S1) (2) restaurant should ... provide a comfortable atmosphere (S2) (1′) we haven't finished our meals (S3) (2′) you can't [couldn't] provide a favorable atmosphere (S4) (1″) we can't [couldn't] have our meal (S5) (3) the environment is really, really dirty and smelly (S6)	(1) the restaurant [did] not prohibit smoking (S3) (2) the restaurant didn't gave [give] us the experience that we should have (S3) (3) the value of our meal is not satisfied (S4)
Request	(1) ... so please refund to us (S1) (1′) you just have to ... refund to us (S6)	we want to have a refund from the restaurant (S2)
Alternative requests	you can set up a smoking area (S5)	(1) we can ask even if it's just half of the price of the payment (S5) (2) you should have an open area (S6)
Closing	we may ... tell this story to the news company (S6)	Okay, thank you. Thank you. (S7)

Notes: (1′), (1″), and (2′) represent the repetition of the claims that have been made before.

Though the discourse structures are pretty similar for both, our analyses revealed many differences in terms of politeness control between the two learners. The Hong Kong learner frequently used shorter sentences and directive expressions, and he repeated his request and the reasons for it. He then went as far as to threaten the restaurant by suggesting the possibility that he may leak this incident to the media. Meanwhile, the Philippines learner used longer and verbose sentences and avoided making direct requests that might damage the negative face of the restaurant owner. She did not stick to her original request but flexibly presented an alternative request of a 50% refund.

As mentioned in Section 6.3.1, when persuading someone, one can choose from three politeness control strategies: promoting the receiver's positive face, protecting the receiver's negative face, and intentional FTA. The Hong Kong learner took an FTA-based approach, while the Philippines learner seemed to take an approach to respect the receiver's negative face. This shows that there exist various approaches to politeness control in persuasion. Leech (2014) suggests that novice learners tend to adopt less polite forms such as direct requests, while advanced learners tend to adopt more indirect and polite forms, but the persuasion speeches of these two advanced learners exemplify that the choice of politeness level in communication can be highly person-dependent.

6.4 Gestures

6.4.1 Aim and RQs

Due to the limited availability of multimodal LC that include video data, how Asian learners use gestures in L2 communication has hardly been explored yet. Therefore, this study focuses on learners' hand gesture use and examines the following research questions:

RQ1 *What types of gestures are used by Asian learners, and to what extent is the quantity of gestures correlated with their verbal fluency?*
RQ2 *What pragmatic functions are realised by the gestures adopted by Asian learners?*

6.4.2 Data and Method

In this study, expanding the scope of Ishikawa (2022), we analyse the videos recording the non-smoking picture description speeches (see Figure 3.6 for the prompt) of 30 Chinese learners (10 learners at each of B1_1, B1_2, and B2+ levels) and the same number of Japanese learners taken from the ICNALE Spoken Dialogues. The ratio of male learners to female learners is 6:4 for both groups.

Though innumerable forms of gestures occur in communication, we focus on the three types of hand gestures that are often observed in the picture description task—Type A: touching one's head (including a hair, a chin, a nose, and face parts), which usually suggest that a speaker has some communicative problems and

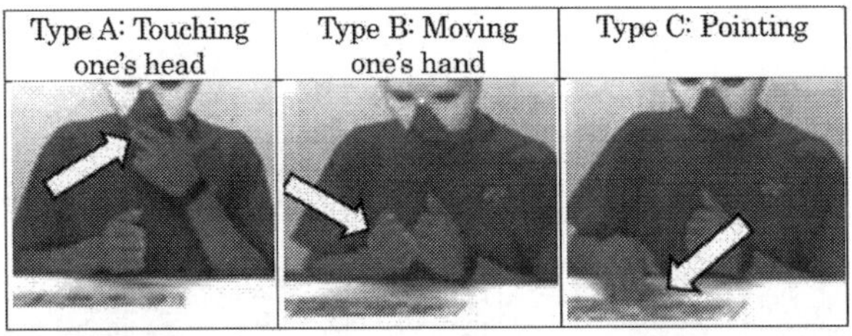

FIGURE 6.7 Typical hand gestures observed in the picture description task

feels nervous; Type B: moving one's hand (including fingers), which usually occurs when a speaker tries to control the rhythm of the speech; and Type C: pointing to the picture, which usually occurs when a speaker tries to confirm the sequence of the episodes to be described (Figure 6.7).

After manually checking the videos of 60 learners, we examine the quantity of each of the three kinds of gestures occurring during the task and decide the score from 0 (never), 1 (rarely), 2 (sometimes), and 3 (often). Minor accidental hand motions are not counted. These gesture scores are adjusted per one minute for mutual comparisons. Regarding RQ1, we compare the means of the three kinds of gesture scores obtained from different learner groups. Then, we examine the correlations between each of the gesture scores and the number of words uttered per minute. Next, regarding RQ2, we focus on three learners and examine what hand gestures are adopted and what pragmatic functions they play.

6.4.3 Results and Discussion

6.4.3.1 RQ1 Amount of Gesture Use

The results of the analyses of three kinds of gesture scores and their correlations with verbal fluencies are shown in Figure 6.8 and Table 6.4.

Figure 6.8 seems to suggest that (i) among three kinds of hand gestures, Type B (moving one's hand) occurs most often, Type A (touching one's head) comes next, and Type C (pointing) occurs the least; (ii) between two learner groups, Chinese learners use Type A gestures less and Type B gestures more than Japanese learners; and (iii) Type A increases from B1_1 to B1_2, but decreases from B1_2 to B2+, Type B consistently decreases from A2 to B2+, and Type C shows no clear patterns in change.

Regarding (i), a one-way ANOVA conducted on 60 learners' data revealed that the main effect of gesture types on their scores is significant (F (2, 118) = 6.277, p = .004, η_p^2 = .096) and the post-hoc test (Holm) suggested a significant difference between Type B scores (Mean: 0.715) and Type C scores (0.253) (p =.008, d=.489), though the difference between Type B scores and Type A scores (0.377) is not significant (d = .360). Thus, Asian EFL learners are found to use hand-moving gestures more often than the gestures of touching one's head or pointing to the pictures.

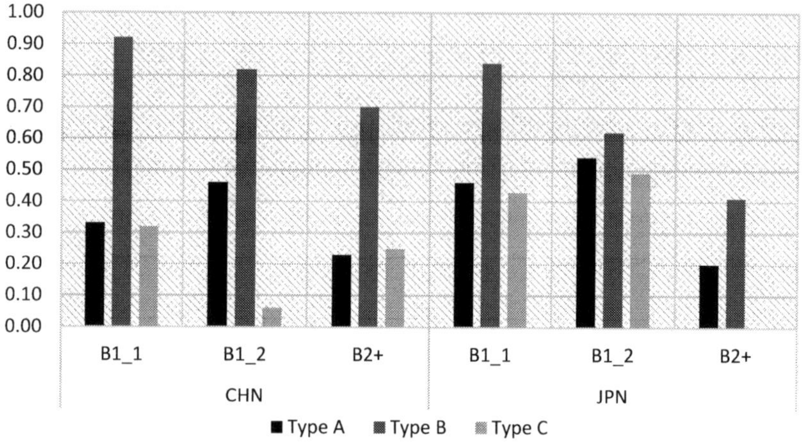

FIGURE 6.8 Gesture scores for Chinese and Japanese learners

TABLE 6.4 Correlations of gesture scores and the number of tokens

	Type A	*Type B*	*Type C*	*Tokens*
Type A	1.00			
Type B	0.24	1.00		
Type C	0.22	0.32	1.00	
Tokens	−0.06	0.24	−0.24	1.00

Meanwhile, regarding (ii) and (iii), a two-way ANOVA showed that the interaction of region and proficiency, as well as the main effect of each of them, on the three kinds of gesture scores are not significant: Type A (Interaction: F (2, 54) = 0.057, p = .945, η_p^2 = .002, Region: F (1,54) = 0.084, p = .773, η_p^2 = .002, Proficiency: F (2, 54) = 1.101, p = .340, η_p^2 = .039); Type B (Interaction: F (2, 54) = 0.046, p = .955, η_p^2 = .002, Region: F (1,54) = 0.343, p = .561, η_p^2 = .006, Proficiency: F (2, 54) =0.338, p = .715, η_p^2 = .012); and Type C (Interaction: F (2, 54) = 1.511, p = .230, η_p^2 = .053, Region: F (1,54) = 0.443, p = .509, η_p^2 = .008, Proficiency: F (2, 54) = 0.735, p = .484, η_p^2 = .026). These results suggest that the differences in the patterns of three kinds of hand gesture use largely belong to individual learners rather than to learner groups based on region and/or proficiency. What should be noted here is that, despite the regions and proficiency levels, a certain number of learners never use gestures. In the current data, hand gesture use was not observed with 25 out of 60 learners.

Then, to what extent are the quantities of hand gestures adopted by learners correlated with their verbal fluency? As seen in Table 6.4, the number of tokens shows weak positive correlations with Type B gesture scores (r = 0.24) and equally weak negative correlations with Type C gesture scores (r = −0.24), while the meaningful correlation with Type A gesture score was not observed. Thus, three types of hand gestures are related to verbal fluency in different ways. When learners fluently speak, they naturally use more hand-moving gestures, which sets the tempo of the speech and facilitates fluency. Meanwhile, when they have language problems during the picture description task, they often adopt pointing gestures and confirm the flow of the story to be described. In this sense, hand-moving gestures and pointing gestures seem to concern the positive and negative sides of speech fluency.

6.4.3.2 RQ2 Functions of Hand Gestures

In the previous section, we discussed the quantities of three kinds of hand gestures and how they are related to verbal fluency. What pragmatic functions does each gesture perform in the learner speeches? Here we qualitatively analyse the videos of three learners: JPN_001 (B1_1, female), JPN_024 (B1_1, female), and CHN_016 (B2+, male). We discuss six still images taken from each video, which present characteristic hand gestures adopted by each learner.

First, we discuss significant hand gestures adopted by a female learner at B1_1 level from Japan (JPN_001) (Figure 6.9). The number of tokens per one minute was 61.1 for this student. As this is far below the mean value (83.6 tokens) of 60 learners, she is classified as a relatively disfluent speaker.

JPN_001 puts both hands on the table at the beginning (Figure 6.9a). After describing the first picture by saying, "[a] mother and children play in the park" (she wrongly uses the word "children" to refer to a child), she stops for a while as she cannot decide how to describe a smoker appearing in the second picture. Then, she naturally moves her left hand to her chin (Figure 6.9b). Though she does not use any verbal fillers such as "well" and "uh," this gesture functions as a non-verbal filler, with which a hearer (in this case, an interviewer) can understand

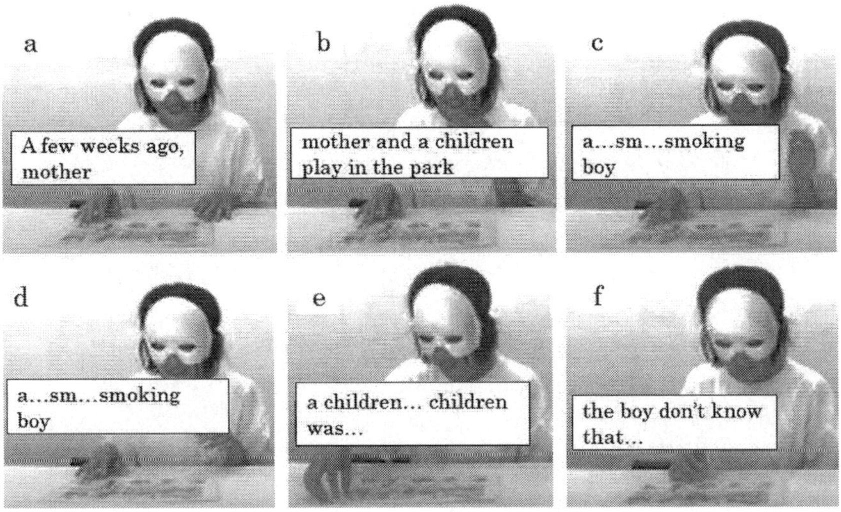

FIGURE 6.9 Hand gestures of JPN_001

that she has a problem in expression and now she is thinking of it. Next, she begins to say "a boy ..." to refer to a male smoker. However, she soon realises that it is not appropriate, and she self-corrects by saying "a ... sm ... smoking ... boy" with her hand moving up (Figure 6.9c) and then down (Figure 6.9d). This hand motion seems to help her self-correct and come up with a better expression. Then, she tries to describe the third picture, which depicts a child coughing due to the smoke, and begins to say, "a children ... children was ...." However, she cannot remember the verb "cough" and therefore points to the third picture (Figure 6.9e). With this pointing action, she self-corrects and begins a new sentence by saying, "[a child] feel not his smoking" presumably to mean "[a child] does not like his smoking." Such pointing gestures occur frequently, and when she says, "the boy don't [doesn't] know that this park prohibits smoking," she also puts her hand on the picture (Figure 6.9f).

These gesture uses adopted by JPN_001 would tell us that hand gestures often appear when a speaker faces some expressive problem. Hand gestures help the speaker to come up with an appropriate word or expression and to overcome the current problems.

Next, we will discuss the case of another female learner at B1_1 level from Japan (JPN_024) (Figure 6.10). The number of tokens per one minute was 64.2 for this student. Though the value is slightly higher than that for JPN_001, she is also classified as a relatively disfluent speaker.

Unlike JPN_001, who uses hand gestures mainly when having expressive problems, this student consistently moves her hands. At first, when she begins her sentence with "A mother ...," she moves both of her hands upward and makes a hands-opening gesture (Figure 6.10a), which iconically represents the beginning of something. Then, when she pronounces the following words: "and," "her," and "son," she moves

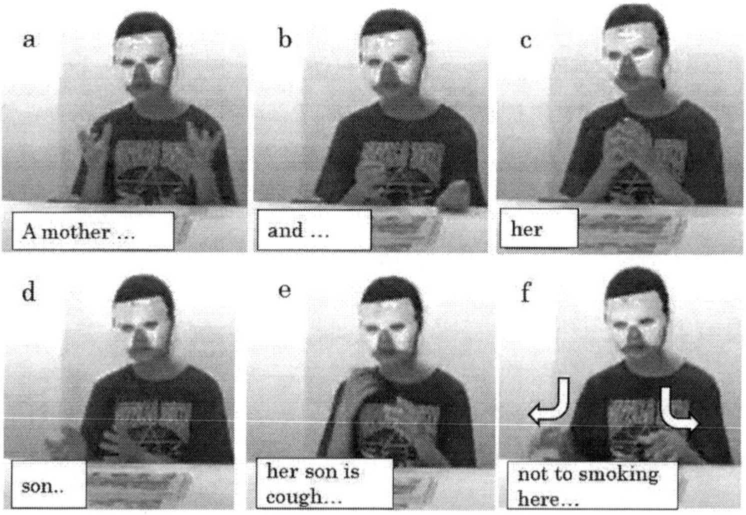

FIGURE 6.10 Hand gestures of JPN_024

her hands down to the table (Figure 6.10b), then moves them upward to clasp her hands (Figure 6.10c), and moves them down to the table again to make another hands-opening gesture (Figure 6.10d). In this case, each gesture marks the boundary between the words rather than between the phrases or sentences. She also uses hand gestures to emphasise what she verbally says. For example, when she says, "her son is cough [coughing] …," she unconsciously moves her right hand toward her throat (Figure 6.10e), which supplements and emphasises the meaning of the verb "cough." Also, when saying the word "here," she first moves both of her hands down, then moves each to the opposite sides as if she tried to cover her nearby space (Figure 6.10f), which clearly supplements the meaning of "here." She often tries to convey the meaning through the dual means of words and gestures.

This gesture use of JPN_024 tells us that some speakers adopt hand gestures not only when facing expressive problems but almost consistently. For these speakers, gestures, which often supplement and emphasise the meaning of what they verbally say, are inseparably integrated into their language.

Finally, we discuss the gesture use of a male learner at B2+ level from China (CHN_016) (Figure 6.11). The number of tokens per one minute was 117.0 for this student. As this value is much higher than the mean (83.6 words/minute), he could be classified as a highly fluent speaker.

In comparison to the two Japanese learners, CHN_016 uses hand gestures only occasionally. In the beginning, he puts his right hand on the table (Figure 6.11a). When he refers to a smoker depicted in the second picture, he first says, "a man with a smoking." However, he soon realises that this is not correct, and he tilts his head and self-corrects by saying "a man smoking" with opening his hand (Figure 6.11b) and continues "carrying a cigarette." Next, seeing the third picture, he

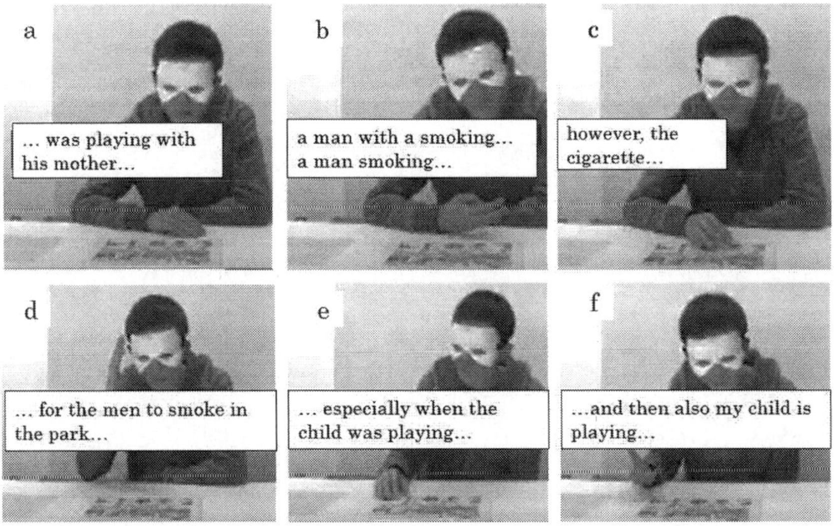

FIGURE 6.11 Hand gestures of CHN_016

begins saying, "However, the cigarette ..." then stops a while, presumably because he cannot immediately remember the verb "cough" when he points to the picture (Figure 6.11c). Thus, he adjusts himself, comes up with another expression, and continues saying, "(The cigarette) is obviously affecting the little child." He continues, "and the mother ... thought it is quite ... it is quite ... a bad behavior for the men to smoke in the park ...," but this is too wordy and ambiguous a description. Presumably realising this, he touches his head lightly (Figure 6.11d), which may help him reconsider his utterances, and he continues, "especially when the child was playing." Thus, overcoming the small expressive problem, he moves his hand down to the table again (Figure 6.11e), and says, "in the ... in the sand ...." Next, he says, "then the mother ... came to the men and say ... well, sir, you are not allowed to smoke cigarettes here and then also my child is playing ...." As he is a very fluent speaker, he can continue speaking as long as he likes, but maybe noticing that he has spoken too much in a sequence, he opens his hand (Figure 6.11f), which functions as a kind of visual punctuation mark. And he adds, "... in this field ...."

The gesture uses of CHN_016 exemplifies how hand gestures also play an important role for fluent speakers. They often help the speaker to self-correct, mark the boundaries of the meaning units, and restructure their utterances.

6.4.4 Summary

In this section, we first analysed the quantities of three kinds of hand gestures: Type A (touching one's head), Type B (moving one's hand), and Type C (pointing to the picture), which 60 learners from China and Japan adopted during the picture description task. Then, we examined the correlations between learners' three types of gesture use and their verbal fluency. Finally, by analysing three learner videos, we discussed the primary functions of each hand gesture. Major findings are summarised in Table 6.5, where the tendencies that were not proven to be statistically significant appear in the round brackets.

TABLE 6.5 Summary of the findings: features of three kinds of hand gestures

	A: Touching one's head	*B: Moving one's hand*	*C: Pointing to the pictures*
Quantity	(++)	+++	(+)
Region	(JPN)	(CHN)	N/A
Proficiency	(Increase, then decrease)	(Consistently decrease)	No clear patterns
Correlation with fluency	No clear correlations	Weak positive correlations	Weak negative correlations
Functions	(1) To suggest an expressive trouble (2) To fill the pauses (3) To reconsider the utterance	(1) To self-correct (2) To remember a word (3) To mark the boundary (4) To emphasise the meaning	(1) To self-correct (2) To confirm the sequence (3) To come up with what to say

These results show that (i) hand gestures play important pragmatic roles not only for novice learners who have expressive problems but also for more advanced learners who can speak fluently; (ii) functions of hand gestures are complex and overlapping and therefore difficult to clarify neatly; (iii) the pattern of hand gesture use greatly varies between individual learners, rather than between some learner groups; and (iv) hand gestures, which sometimes mark a speaker's disfluency but at the same time helps them to overcome it, can be the indices of both disfluency and fluency.

Our analyses also suggested that the investigation of learners' use of varied pragmatic devices based on the multimodal learner corpora could be an extremely promising field. In this study, we focused only on the hand gestures adopted by learners, but discussing learners' hand gestures, head gestures, as well as varied acoustic features of their utterances in combination, could offer a new angle to the LC-based pragmatics studies.

7

INDIVIDUAL DIFFERENCES

7.1 Introduction

7.1.1 Individual Differences in LCR

7.1.1.1 Background

Previous chapters, which focused on three aspects of learners' L2 skills—vocabulary, grammar, and pragmatics—revealed interesting facts about Asian learners' L2 English use, but they simultaneously suggested that the possibility that learners' L2 usage patterns may be influenced by the differences in learners' individual backgrounds.

Noting that "many of the variables that affect the nature of interlanguage concern the learners themselves," Gilquin (2015) lists the variables causing individual differences, which include age, gender, country/area, mother tongue, parents' L1, languages spoken at home, proficiency, L2 exposure inside and outside the classroom, motivation, prosodic knowledge, attitudes toward L2, self-attributed importance to competence in pronunciation, and experience and ability in related fields such as music and acting (p. 17, 27).

These can be classified into several groups, including basic attributes (e.g., age, gender, country/area), L1 type (e.g., mother tongue, parents' language, language used at home), proficiency (e.g., overall proficiency, skill-based proficiency), attitudes (e.g., motivation, positive/negative attitudes toward L2 and its culture), and learning history (e.g., curriculums, teachers, materials, instruction, and exams at schools, L2 exposure outside classrooms, staying in L2-speaking countries). Among these, we pay attention to gender as well as motivation and learning history in this chapter.

DOI: 10.4324/9781003252528-9

If considering various types of individual differences in quantitative analysis, we may need a new statistical framework. Regarding the correlation and regression analysis, recent statistics recommend the use not of a traditional linear model but of a linear mixed model. A mixed model, which focuses both on fixed and random effects, can deal with non-independent, multilevel, hierarchical, longitudinal data in a more appropriate manner. For example, when discussing the relationship between the frequencies of "I" used by 20 Chinese learners and their proficiency test scores, we usually calculate the coefficients by regarding 20 learners as a set of independent samples. However, females and males, high/middle/low-motivated learners, or learners from X/Y/Z universities in it, may show different correlation patterns. Instead of calculating the coefficients for each level of such a grouping factor (fixed effects), a mixed model regards it as a normally distributed random variable (random effects) (Schäfer, 2020). Wulff and Gries (2021) suggest that corpus linguistics (CL) and learner corpus research (LCR) have not contributed enough to the studies of learners' individual differences in second language acquisition (SLA), and they introduce a new statistical method called multifactorial prediction and deviation analysis using regression/random forests (MuPDAR(F)), which typically consists of three steps: creating a model to predict the linguistic choice of an L1 English native speaker (ENS) from a set of linguistic variables, applying the model to learner data to predict what ENS would have done in their places, and creating another model to explain the ENS/learner gap. Though these new approaches are not necessarily common yet, they are expected to spread more widely in the future LCR.

7.1.1.2 Aspects of Learner Differences

LCR in the early days paid attention mainly to learners' L1 type, and it aimed to identify the aspects of L1 interference seen in learners' L2 performance. This direction seems to be in line with that of contrastive analysis (CA), which aims to clarify the structural differences and similarities between a pair of languages. CA became popular in the 1960s, but since then, it has gradually lost its popularity. Granger (1996) once mentioned that learner corpora (LC) would help CA to revive in the modern days, and she emphasised the importance of shifting from CA to LC-based contrastive interlanguage analysis (CIA) and then back to CA again. Presumably reflecting such a principle, two pioneer LC, namely, International Corpus of Learner English (ICLE) and Louvain Interlanguage Database of Spoken English Interlanguage (LINDSEI), collect the data from learners with a variety of L1 backgrounds, while they collect the data basically from advanced learners alone and exclude an L2 proficiency variable from the target of analysis.

However, when discussing the L2 acquisition process of a broader range of learners, it would be difficult not to take L2 proficiency into consideration. Thanks to the release of the Trinity Lancaster Corpus (TLC) (Brezina et al., 2019) (see Section 1.2.2), which includes reliable learner proficiency data from the Graded Examinations in Spoken English, some recent studies have tried to clarify the complex interaction of learners' L1, L2 proficiency, and task/test-related parameters (e.g., Götz, 2019; Pérez-Paredes & Díez-Bedmar, 2019).

In comparison to L1 backgrounds and L2 proficiency surveyed above, other variables have hardly been investigated, which is primarily due to the limited availability of LC that include detailed learner background data. This may seem to be somewhat strange when considering that learner variables such as gender, motivation, and learning history have been widely discussed in the fields of sociolinguistics and applied linguistics.

7.1.1.3 Gender

Gender differences in language have been discussed mainly in the field of sociolinguistics, which usually analyses L1 speeches.

Lakoff (1975) observes female college students' speeches and identifies the linguistic features characterising "women's language," which she claims causes the women to be given a lower status in society. Lakoff's model is called a deficit model. According to Lakoff, women's language is characterised by the frequent use of hedges (e.g., "kind of"), qualifiers (e.g., "I think that ..."), empty adjectives (e.g., "lovely," "cute"), polite or super-polite forms (e.g., "would you mind if ...?"), apologies (e.g., "I'm sorry, but ..."), tag questions (e.g., "... don't you?"), hyper-correct prestige grammar and articulation, direct quotation, intonational emphasis, raising pitch at the end of a statement, *wh*-imperatives (e.g., "Why don't you ...?"), modal verbs, indirect requests, intensifiers (e.g., "so," "very"), and colour-related vocabulary, and also by the limited use of coarse language and jokes. In addition, women are also characterised by a limited amount of speech.

Lakoff's deficit model has influenced many following researchers, but O'Barr and Atkins (1980), who analyse courtroom conversations, suggest that the differences outlined by Lakoff may be caused not by the gap in gender but by the gap in social class, status, and power. When being placed in lower social status, male speakers also use "deficit" language.

Among many features listed in Lakoff (1975), speech quantity has attracted much attention. Conventionally, people have believed that women are more talkative and verbose than men. However, Lakoff (1975) suggests that female speakers speak less than male speakers. Tannen (1990) also reports that men talk quite a great deal when with their male friends, even if they may not talk much with their wives. Speech quantity may be related to the number of turn-takings in the conversations. Zimmerman and West (1975) report that female speakers do not try to take turns by interrupting the speech of male collocutors. A similar tendency is also reported in Coates (1986), who concludes that female speakers avoid violating male speakers' turns and choose to wait until they finish their speeches. Speech quantity may also be related to the occurrence of fillers. Tottie (2011) analyses L1 spoken corpora and reveals that filled pauses ("er/uh" and "erm/um") function as an important sociolinguistic marker and their occurrence patterns significantly vary according to text types as well as speakers' gender, age, and social class. The analysis shows that older, male, and educated speakers use more fillers, while younger, female, and less educated speakers use fewer fillers. The author concludes that fillers as planning signals or planners should be re-examined from a new viewpoint.

Recent studies have tried to establish a more sophisticated taxonomy to classify the features of women's language. Summarising the major literature, Voegeli (2005) develops a list of gender differences that may appear in the language, which the author used for her analysis of gender identity in the community of drag kings, transgender, and gender activists. According to Voegeli's list, female speeches are characterised by particular types of lexis (differentiated vocabulary in trivial areas, weaker swear words, adjectives evoking frivolity and triviality, and intensifying adverbs), syntax (tag questions, hedges, subordinate clauses, mean length of sentences, introductory adverbial clauses, and standard language norms), and stance (politeness, minimal reactions to show interest, cooperative conversational style, and personal and emotional style); while male speeches are characterised by the other types of lexis (stronger swear words and "neutral" adjectives), syntax (colloquial expressions, dialects, elliptic sentences, directives), and stance (factual [locatives and quantity-related expressions], *I*-focused language, and judgement-related vocabulary).

Gender has become one of the important research topics in CL, which often pays attention to "how men and women interact by means of language" in various discourse situations and the questions such as "Who speaks most? Who interrupts most frequently? Who gives more supportive feedback? Who laughs most often?" are discussed on the basis of a "close analysis of recorded or transcribed speech" (Lindquist, 2009, p. 150). Murphy (2010) analyses an age-based L1 English adult speaker corpus and discusses how female speakers of different age groups use hedging devices, vague category markers (e.g., "and everything," "or whatever/something"), amplifiers (e.g., "very," "really," "so"), boosters ("must," "absolutely," "altogether"), and taboo language (e.g., expletives, religious references, animal/sex-related abusives") (p. 43). Though the gender comparison is not the main target of her study, Murphy also mentions that female speakers may underuse several amplifiers (e.g., "fairly," "fierce," "well", "pretty," "right") (pp. 122–133) and insulting devices (p. 201), while they may overuse hedging adverbials (p. 83), many amplifiers (e.g., "really") (p. 132), and boosters (pp. 159 160).

In LCR, a few studies discuss gender as a key topic. For example, Stormbom (2018) reports that when referring to a gender-indefinite person, learners tend to use "he," while ENS often use "they." The author also adds that the overuse of "he" may be related to learners' L1 backgrounds. Excluding these exceptions, however, gender seems to be discussed less often in LCR. This may be due to the gender imbalance existing in many LC, where the number of male participants is often considerably smaller than that of female participants. Gilquin (2015) notes that "some variables are less likely to be kept constant in a learner corpus, for example gender" (p. 16). In the case of ICLE Version 3.0, the proportion of male participants is 22%, and it is only 4% in some of the national subcorpora. This reflects the gender imbalance in the demography of the students majoring in English at colleges, mainly in Europe. Regarding this point, the ICLE development team explains, "[a]s the humanities tend to attract more female than male students, it has not been possible to collect a well-balanced corpus in terms of gender" (Granger et al., 2020, p. 6), but we must note the possibility that such an imbalance in gender representation in major LC may have led to limited attention to gender in general in LCR. In addition, it may also be influenced by the researchers' overall tendency to make little of the metadata included in LC. Ädel (2015) points out that "so few learner corpus studies actually draw on corpus metadata" and adds, "researchers need to integrate metadata to a much greater extent than has been the case to date" (p. 419).

Despite these limitations, some of the recent LC studies discuss the possible influence of gender on learners' L2 outputs. Babanoğlu (2015) analyses learner essays and reports that, in contrast to the conventional view, male learners use more feeling/emotion-related vocabulary than female learners, which the author says is a stable trend seen across different L1 groups. Ballesteros Chica and Fernández-Cruz (2020) analyse a small set of learner essays and report that male learners are more like to make grammatical errors in general, especially the errors related to nouns, verbs, and articles. Signell (2012) analyses the essays of L1 Swedish secondary students and reports that the degree of syntactic accuracy is higher for female students at the junior high school level but for male students at the senior high school level, and female students tend to focus on personalised accounts in their writing, while male students in junior high school have a sparse and concise writing style. Sulistyaningrum (2018) analyses the essay data from the ICNALE Written Essays and reports that male learners' essays are characterised by the overuse of quantifiers, locatives, and determiners, while female learners' essays are by intensifiers, additive connectives, and adversative connectives. Yuka Ishikawa (2014) analyses speeches of Japanese and Philippine learners as well as ENS, which are taken from the ICNALE Spoken Monologues, and reports that female British speakers use hesitators ("um," "mmm") more often than male counterparts, while they are seldom used by learners, despite the difference in gender. Ishikawa (2020a) also analyses the utterances of Japanese learners in the persuasion roleplays extracted from the ICNALE Spoken Dialogues and reports that female learners speak less and use hedges and response markers more often than their male counterparts. This study also suggests that the frequency of high-frequency vocabulary is influenced more strongly by the gap in gender rather than the gap in proficiency.

7.1.1.4 Motivation

Motivation has attracted much attention in the field of applied linguistics since the 1960s. Based on the analysis of Canadian speakers of English who learn French, Gardner and Lambert (1972) classify motivation into two types: instrumental motivation and integrative motivation. The former concerns a "practical need to communicate in the second language"—in other words, a "carrot-and-stick" principle—while the latter concerns "an interest in the second language and its culture" as well as "the intention to become part of the culture." Sometimes it also entails attitudinal factors such as "language anxiety" and "parental encouragement" (De Bot et al., 2005, p. 72). Gardner and Macintyre (1991) show that the former type of motivation, tied to awards, may lead to better performance in the short term, while the latter tends to become "eternal influence and incentives" and leads to better performance in the long term. These two kinds of motivations are also conceptualised as extrinsic (caused by something outside of a learner) and intrinsic (caused by something inside a learner) motivations (Deci & Ryan, 1985).

Influenced by a dynamic system theory (Smith & Thelen, 1993) or, more recently, by a complex dynamic systems theory (CDST) (Larsen-Freeman & Cameron, 2008), motivation studies have come to pay more attention to the dynamic status of L2 learners' motivations. The level of motivation is not always the same, but it can "constantly change due to a wide range of interrelated factors" during the short-term or long-term acquisition processes (De Bot et al., 2005, p. 74). Thus, motivations come to be redefined as:

> the dynamically changing cumulative arousal in a person that initiates, directs, coordinates, amplifies, terminates, and evaluates the cognitive and motor processes whereby initial wishes and desires are selected, prioritised, operationalised, and (successfully or unsuccessfully) acted out.
>
> *(Dörnyei & Ottó, 1998, p. 64)*

Dörnyei (2005) discusses how learners' motivation is based on one's future possible self (an ideal future image about oneself), which is a composite of L2 learning experiences, an ideal L2 self (the type of an L2 speaker one hopes to become), and an ought-to L2 self (the types of an L2 speaker one believes they should become). In this framework, one's learning history is integrated into their motivation.

Motivation is expected to influence the process of L2 acquisition to some degree. Dörnyei and Skehan (2003) note that correlations of "aptitude or motivation with language achievement range (mostly) between 0.20 and 0.60, with a median value a little above 0.40" (p. 589). This means that approximately 16% of the success in L2 acquisition may be explained by motivation-related variables.

In spite of its potential influence on the L2 acquisition process, motivation is rarely included in the metadata of existing LC, many of which collect the data only from advanced and highly-motivated learners. However, there are several exceptions. For example, the PAROLE corpus (Hilton et al., 2008; Hilton, 2009), which includes speeches of young adult learners studying English, French, and Italian, collects data on motivation as well as two kinds of L2 learning aptitudes (i.e., skills in nonword repetition and morphosyntactic analysis). More recently, the PELEC corpus (Blanco Suárez et al., 2020), which includes spoken and written outputs of primary school students in Spain, also collects data on motivation. The PELEC's learner survey includes questions about intrinsic and extrinsic motivation as well as effort and self-efficacy, willingness to integrate into the L2 community, anxiety levels, and parental support. These corpora are of importance, but the numbers of participants are relatively smaller: the PAROLE includes the data of only 32 learners of English, and the PELEC includes that of 252 students in total. In both cases, it would be rather difficult to compare the outputs of learners with different types and/or different strengths of L2 motivation.

Limited attention to motivation could be a weak point of LCR. The analysis of the relationship between learners' motivation and their L2 outputs would be a new promising research topic for LCR.

7.1.1.5 Learning History

Among many variables related to L2 learning history, to what extent and in what manner L2 learners have practised each of the four basic language skills—listening, reading, speaking, and writing—inside and outside classrooms is of paramount importance. Such metadata is particularly important when analysing the L2 output of Asian learners, especially in the regions of English as a foreign language (EFL) because they tend to pay exclusive attention to the acquisition of L2 receptive skills, which are required in many of the locally administered English proficiency tests, and they seldom have opportunities to use L2 outside classrooms.

Earlier SLA studies emphasised the importance of receptive skills such as listening and reading. Krashen (1985) claims that "humans acquire language in only one way—by understanding messages, or by receiving 'comprehensible input'" (p. 2). Thus, "early theoretical accounts of SLA are premised on the centrality of (oral) input processing" (Manchón & Polio, 2022, p. 1). Even now, both of the two major approaches in SLA, namely, behaviouristic and usage-based approaches, commonly put the greatest emphasis on input (Ädel, 2015, p. 405).

Krashen (1982) thought that "input is responsible for progress in language acquisition," while "[o]utput is possible as a result of acquired competence" (p. 61). However, Krashen's disrespect for speaking and writing is rebutted by the other researchers. Swain (1985) claims that output has three key functions indispensable in L2 acquisition: noticing (triggering), hypothesis testing, and metalinguistic reflection, and she says, "producing the target language may be the trigger that forces the learner to pay attention to the means of expression needed in order to successfully convey his or her own intended meaning" (p. 249). By taking a risk to speak and write in L2, learners can notice the gap between what they like to say and what they can say in L2, as well as that between their interlanguage and the target language, then test and correct their L2 hypothesis by checking it against the obtained feedbacks, and consciously reflect on their L2 knowledge, all of which helps them to smoothly move from input-based semantic processing to output-based syntactic processing in L2. The importance of output and the cognitive processing it activates has also been mentioned in the recent acquisition theories (Leow & Suh, 2022, p. 11), including Focus-on-Form (Long & Robinson, 1998), Second Language Acquisition Model (Gass, 1988), Noticing Hypothesis (Schmidt, 1990), Skill Acquisition Theory (DeKeyser, 2015), and L2 Learning Process in Instructed SLA Model (Leow, 2015).

Recent L2 teaching methodologies have emphasised the importance of a well-balanced combination of input, output, and interaction. Hendrikx et al. (2019) discuss how learners' L1 and the method of L2 teaching (a traditional class vs. a content and language integrated learning [CLIL] class) influence their acquisition of intensifying constructions. The data analysis suggests that CLIL students, who have more chances to use the target language, tend to produce intensifying constructions in a more target-like way.

Metadata about learners' previous practice of each of the four skills inside and outside classrooms, however, has been scarcely covered in the learner profiles offered in the existing LC. The ICLE team fully realises that "the learners' exposure to the English language may be quite limited in some countries and quite extensive in others" (Granger et al., 2020, p. 10), but they collect the metadata only about the time spent in an English-speaking country and the years of studying English at schools as elements regarding L2 learning history. Meanwhile, some of the recent LC have begun to collect a broader range of learning-history metadata. For instance, the SCooLE corpus (Möller 2017), which is a dataset that the author compiled for her analysis of the effects of the CLIL-based instructions, surveys how often learners have spoken English, read English books and magazines, watched English films and TV programs, and visited English websites when they have free time outside schools, in addition to what English textbooks they have used at schools (p. 95).

Incorporating such detailed learning-history metadata into the output text analysis would undoubtedly lead to expanding the scope and reliability of LCR.

7.1.2 ICNALE Case Studies

Among the many variables that may cause individual differences in L2 outputs, we focus on gender and motivation/learning history.

In Section 7.2, we analyse the utterances of female and male participants (both learners and ENS) during the interviews, which are taken from the ICNALE Spoken Dialogues. Then, we quantitatively discuss whether there exists a significant difference between female and male participants in terms of the total number of tokens as well as the usages of high-frequency words and lexicogrammatical features.

In Section 7.3, we analyse the monologue speeches and essays by EFL learners taken from the ICNALE Spoken Monologues and the ICNALE Written Essays to discuss the relationship between 16 kinds of learner variables, which are related to motivation and L2 learning history, and three kinds of text variables.

7.2 Gender

7.2.1 Aim and RQs

As briefly summarised in Section 7.1.1.3, previous studies have shed light on various types of gender differences in L1 English use, but whether they are commonly observed in L2 English speeches by Asian learners and L1 English speeches by ENS largely remains uncertain. Therefore, this study examines the following research questions:

RQ1 Do female speakers speak less than male speakers?
RQ2 Is gender difference a staple factor in classifying different speaker groups?
RQ3 What words, lexicogrammatical features, and dimensions characterise female and male speakers?

Before examining these research questions, we would like to clarify what "gender" means in this case study. When collecting learners' background data, the ICNALE team asked participants about their sex and told them to choose between female and male. In this sense, the gender gap we discuss here encapsulates the biological sex gap.

7.2.2 Data and Method

In this study, we analyse all the utterances of learners in English as a second language (ESL) and English as a foreign language (EFL) regions at B1 level (including B1_1 and B1_2) as well as ENS in the interviews, which are taken from the ICNALE Spoken Dialogues. The participants analysed here include 28 Chinese learners (20 females and 8 males), 22 Indonesian learners (15 and 7), 57 Japanese learners (30 and 27), 10 Korean learners (7 and 3), 31 Thai learners (20 and 11), 23 Taiwanese learners (13 and 10), 19 Hong Kong learners (12 and 7), 18 Malay learners (10 and 8), 19 Pakistani learners (6 and 13), 35 Philippine learners (15 and 20), and 20 ENS (3 and 17).

For RQ1, we examine the number of words uttered by each speaker. Then, we compare the mean values of females and males.

For RQ2, we first tag the whole dataset with the MAT (see Section 5.1.1.4) and choose the top 50 frequent words and lexicogrammatical tags (Table 7.1), which are used as samples for a comparison between genders.

Next, based on the contingency table with 50 words as cases and 22 speaker groups as variables and the other table with 50 tags as cases and 22 speaker groups as

TABLE 7.1 Words and lexicogrammatical tags used for the analysis

Word	I, the, to, and, a, it, is, in, so, you, that, my, yes, because, 's, think, can, like, have, of, 't, for, yeah, but, not, we, he, with, time, they, there, or, okay, don, me, if, very, are, just, more, this, was, smoking, do, when, job, some, restaurant...
Tag	AWL, TTR, NN, VPRT, FPP1, PIN, RB, JJ, VBD, TO, PRIV, TPP3, BEMA, PIT, SPP2, EMPH, POMD, CAUS, XX0, PRED, ANDC, DEMO, GER, NOMZ, CONT, THATD, DEMP, PUBV, PRMD, AMP, COND, SUAV, EX, HDG, PROD, TIME, PHC, PLACE, NEMD, THVC, PASS, SPAU, DPAR, DWNT, STPR, OSUB, TOBJ, WZPRES, WHCL, WHSUB

Notes: The top 50 words do not include the fillers ("uh," "umm," and "um"), and the top 50 tags include two kinds of indices related to the overall vocabulary use: Average word length (AWL) and Type/token ratio (TTR).

variables, we conduct hierarchical cluster analyses to examine whether the variables are classified in terms of gender.

Cluster analysis (see Section 1.3.3) is one of the multivariate statistical methods. This method "arranges data objects into a hierarchy of relative similarities" (Moisl, 2020, p. 402), and as such, it enables us to see how a set of cases or variables can be clustered. The results of the analysis are usually presented in a dendrogram (tree diagram), where similar cases or variables are agglomerated first, and less similar cases or variables are agglomerated later. By examining the dendrogram, we see which cases or variables are (not) alike in quality. Here the initial distance is defined as the square root of $(2-2r)$, and the distance after agglomeration is calculated by the Ward method.

Finally, for RQ3, we merge all the data into female speeches and male speeches and identify keywords and key lexicogrammatical tags overused or underused by female speakers on the basis of log-likelihood ratios (LLR). Here we focus only on the items with 15.03 or higher LLR values ($p < .0001$). Then, we compare the mean values of six kinds of text-type dimensions proposed by Biber (see Section 5.1.1.4).

7.2.3 Results and Discussion

7.2.3.1 RQ1 Speech Quantity

First, the comparison of all the female speakers and all the male speakers showed that the mean number of tokens uttered during an interview is 1850.55 for a female group and 2066.939 for a male group. Two-way ANOVA showed that the interaction of region and gender is not significant (F (10, 260) = 0.651, p = .769, η_p^2 = .024), but the main effects of region (F (10, 260) = 7.539, p < .001, η_p^2 = .225) and gender (F (1, 260) = 6.605, p = .011, η_p^2 = .025) are both significant. Thus, the speech quantity of female speakers was proven to be approximately 10% smaller than that of male speakers.

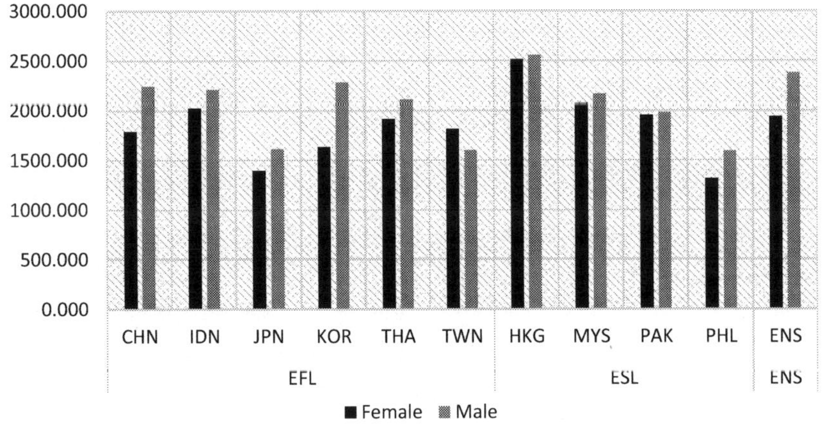

FIGURE 7.1 Mean number of words uttered by female/male speakers

Next, the results of the region-based comparisons are summarised in Figure 7.1. According to the graph, female speakers seem to speak less than male speakers in all the groups except for Taiwanese learners. However, the post-hoc test (Holm) showed a marginally significant difference only for Chinese learners (t (260) = 1.846, p= .066, d= 1.069), and the difference was not significant for the remaining groups, which may be influenced by the relatively limited number of participants in each group.

Thus, our data suggested that female speakers may speak less than male speakers, though the results of statistical significance tests presented a somewhat mixed picture. This broadly supports the findings of Lakoff (1975) and Tannen (1990) based on the observation of L1 English speeches.

7.2.3.2 RQ2 Classification

The results of cluster analyses based on the top 50 words and the top 50 lexicogrammatical tags as cases are shown in Figures 7.2 and 7.3.

In Figure 7.2, when drawing a cutting point between 0.8 and 0.9, we can see the 22 speaker groups classified into two large clusters. If gender were a more influential factor than a region, each of the two clusters would represent female and male speakers, respectively, but the diagram shows that the upper cluster includes EFL learners of both genders while the lower cluster includes ESL learners of both genders, though ENS belong to both. Figure 7.3 also presents a broadly similar

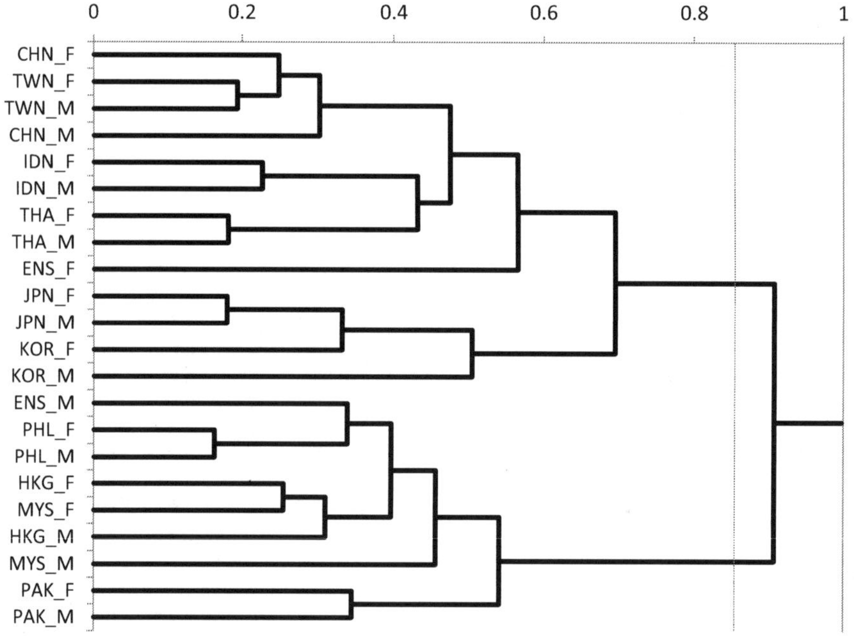

FIGURE 7.2 Word-based clustering of female/male speakers

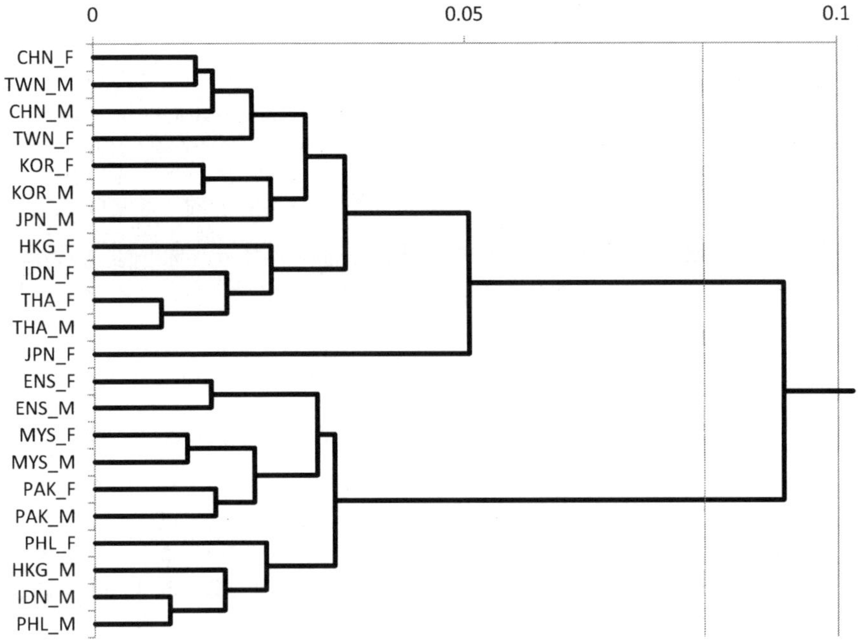

FIGURE 7.3 Lexicogrammatical tag-based clustering of female/male speakers

pattern, though the upper EFL cluster includes female Hong Kong learners, and the lower ESL cluster includes male Indonesian learners and ENS of both genders. These results show that the ESL/EFL gap may be a more decisive factor than the gender gap in group classification.

Figures 7.2 and 7.3 also suggest that the effect of the gender gap varies between different groups. The gap is relatively more significant for ENS participants in Figure 7.2 and for learners from Indonesia and Hong Kong in Figure 7.3, for whom males and females belong to a different cluster. It should be noted that the vocabulary of female ENS and male Korean learners and the lexicogrammar of Japanese female learners are markedly different from those of the other participants. The latter may partly explain the reason for the gender gap of Japanese learners observed in Ishikawa (2020a).

7.2.3.3 RQ3 Keywords, Key Tags, and Dimensions

The results of the keyword and key lexicogrammatical feature tag analyses are shown in Table 7.2.

Regarding the items characterising female speakers' speeches, what attracts our attention first is that as many as seven out of 33 keywords are non-lexical fillers ("um," "mm," "eh," "mmm," "hmm," "ummm," "huh"), which proves that they tend to hesitate to take turns in the conversations (Coates, 1986) or to avoid beginning their statements clearly and immediately. Such a passive attitude

TABLE 7.2 Gender-related keywords and key lexicogrammatical features

	Overused by females	*Overused by males*
Words	um, mm, eh, mmm, hmm, she, yes, umm, like, because, many, I, we, huh, can, my, sometimes, it, brave, will, handle, and, sea, but, think, too, want, he, need, courage, friends, afraid, sad	sir, ah, probably, of, well, that, be, sort, as, much, gonna, basically, should, where, tend, right, alright, get, would, here, able, was, over, a, from, you, pretty, girlfriend, games, operating, totally, mobile, desktop, ahh, number, fine, efficiently, step, terms, 'd, point, 've, cigarette, same, on, basketball, getting, seen
Features	FPP1, TPP3, CAUS, ANDC, POMD, NN, PIT	DPAR, PIN, RB, DEMO, PASS, NOMZ, JJ, STPR, AMP, NEMD, SPP2, TOBJ, PHC, DEMP

of female speakers in the interactions may also be reflected in their overuse of an interjection of "yes." They seem to choose to be "polite" and "cooperative" (Voegeli, 2005) rather than to make ardent claims.

Second, female speakers use a few limited types of hedges, including vague quantifiers ("many," "sometimes") and possibility modals (POMD: "can"), which implies that female speakers pay less attention to controlling their stance in the discourses. Both Lakoff (1975) and Voegeli (2005) mention women's preference for using hedges, which, however, was not clearly confirmed in our data. This is presumably because female speakers' limited speech quantity and their overall passive attitudes lead to a decreasing frequency of hedges.

Third, female speakers may have a tendency to focus on themselves and someone very close to them, which is reflected in their overuse of first-person pronouns (FPP1: "I," "my," "we") as well as the expression "my friends." Voegeli (2005) says that men's language tends to be "I-focused," but our data showed that it might also characterise women's language. When referring to themselves or someone close to them, female speakers often dwell upon their affective aspects such as feelings, emotions, wants, and personal thoughts. Thus, they overuse expressions such as "I + like/think/want/need" and "I'm afraid/sad." They also show strong sympathy for the mother depicted in the non-smoking picture prompt, who publicly criticises a man smoking near her son in the park. As a result, the third-person pronoun (TPP3: "she") is often used in combination with the words praising the mother's character ("she is brave," "she has the courage"). These are roughly in accordance with the view that women's language is characterised by "personal and emotional style" (Voegeli, 2005).

Finally, female speakers tend to extend the sentences by using independent clause coordination (ANDC: "and"), conjunctions like "but," causative adverbial subordinators (CAUS: "because"), and "it is … to do" constructions that include a pronoun "it" (PIT). Thus, their sentence length tends to be relatively longer (Voegeli, 2005), though complex syntactic patterns such as subordinations are hardly observed.

Next, we examine the features of male speakers' speeches. First, male speakers use a few types of fillers ("ah," "ahh") and discourse particles (DPAR: "well"), but they are not so much in quantity and variety in comparison to the case of female speakers. This suggests that male speakers feel less hesitant to take turns in conversations with the interviewers and develop their own claims.

Second, male speakers use a much wider range of hedges ("sort [of]," "probably," "would," "basically," "tend [to do]," "pretty [bad/good]") in comparison to female speakers. Male speakers seem to pay more attention to controlling their own stance in their discourses. Previous studies have suggested that hedge use is one of the staple features of women's language, but our data showed that it also characterises male speakers, who try to control their own stance intentionally and strategically to make their claims more effective.

Third, unlike female speakers focusing mainly on the personal feelings and emotions of themselves and the people around them, male speakers show more interest in a variety of things around them, which explains the reason for their overuse of a variety of nouns ("games," "desktop," "terms," "cigarette," "basketball"), many of which concern the fields of computers and sports. They also show interest in abstract concepts, which is reflected in their use of nominalisations (NOMZ)—nouns with nominalising suffixes—such as "ability," "application," and "advertisement," for instance.

Fourth, regarding grammatical complexity, unlike female speakers, who extend the sentences by combining clauses with "and," "but," and "because," male speakers often try to enhance phrase-level complexity with (i) noun-modifiers such as attributive adjectives (JJ), demonstratives (DEMO: "that [man]"), *that*-relative clauses on object position (TOBJ: "[the experience] that [I had]"), and stranded prepositions (STPR: "[my family I came] from"), (ii) verb-modifiers such as amplifiers (AMP: "totally") and adverbs (RB: "efficiently"), as well as (iii) various types of phrasal coordination (PHC) including total prepositional phrases (PIN: "of/on/in/from [X]"). They also use (iv) a wider range of verb aspects ("[be] getting," "[be] seen"), (v) expressions related to "factual," especially "locative and quantity" (Voegeli, 2005) aspects of things ("here," "where," "over," "point," "as much as"), and (vi) demonstrative pronouns (DEMP: "that [is correct]") enhancing cohesion in a discourse. These features lead male speakers' speeches to sound more syntactically complex and elaborated.

Finally, male speakers have a clear tendency to speak more actively and interactively with their collocutors, which is reflected in their overuse of second-person pronouns (SPP2: "you"), which often collocate with necessity modals (NEMD: "should") in persuasion roleplays, and an honorific "sir," as well as varied "colloquial expressions" (Voegeli, 2005) ("gonna," "right," "alright," "fine," and contraction markers of "'d" and "'ve").

As summarised, many of the high-frequency words and lexicogrammatical features overused or underused by female speakers can be related to the features of women's or men's language that have been discussed to date.

TABLE 7.3 Six dimension scores for female and male speakers

	D1 Involved	*D2 Narrative*	*D3 Explicit*	*D4 Overt*	*D5 Abstract*	*D6 Online*
Female	***23.55***	−3.34	−0.33	1.02	−2.03	−1.10
Male	22.09	***−3.30***	***−0.15***	***1.17***	***−1.83***	***−0.99***

Note: A larger value appears in bold italics.

At the end of this section, we have a look at the six kinds of text-type dimension scores for female and male speakers (Table 7.3), which Biber (1988) regarded as key factors in determining the features of varied spoken and written text types.

As shown in the table, the D1 value is slightly larger for female speakers, while other values are lower for them. Thus, we could say that female speakers' speeches tend to be relatively more involved (D1), non-narrative or explanatory (D2), situation-dependent (D3), covert in persuasion (D4), concrete (and trivial) (D5), and less elaborated informationally (D6), while male speakers' speeches tend to be more informational (D1′), narrative (D2′), explicit (D3′), overt in persuasion (D4′), abstract (and formal) (D5′), and informationally elaborated online (D6′). The dimension features for female speakers are also broadly in line with the typical aspects of "women's language," which Lakoff (1975) and Voegeli (2005) say is trivial, norm-based, polite, indirect, cooperative, personal, and emotional.

Our analyses suggested that many of the gender differences seen in L1 English are also observed in L2 English use. As mentioned in Section 7.1.1.3, O'Barr and Atkins (1980) suggest that the aspects of women's "deficit" language may be caused not by the gap in gender but by the gap in social power and status, but our findings from the same controlled interview datasets show that they can still be related to the difference in gender, though they may be influenced more strongly by other variables including regional background.

7.2.4 Summary

In this section, we first analysed the speech quantities in the interviews of female and male speakers from different regions. Next, we classified female and male speaker groups in terms of the frequencies of the top 50 high-frequency words and the same number of high-frequency lexicogrammatical features to investigate whether the groups are divided according to gender differences or not. Finally, we compared the speech data of all the female speakers and all the male speakers to identify the words and lexicogrammatical features significantly overused or underused by female speakers. Major findings are summarised in Table 7.4.

Many of the aspects of the so-called "women's language" seen in L1 English were also observed in L2 English use, but our data revealed several new findings: hedges are used more often, and in a greater variety, not by female speakers but by male speakers; "*I*-centred" style may characterise female speakers rather than

TABLE 7.4 Summary of the findings: gender-related speech features

Features	*Female speakers*	*Male speakers*
Speech quantity	Approx. 10% less	Approx. 10% more
Speech style	Passive, polite, cooperative, and less interactive	Affirmative, active, interactive, and colloquial
Stance control	Limited stance control	Intentional stance control
Focus	Emotions and feelings of the speakers and the people around them	A variety of things around the speakers and some abstract concepts
Sentence structure	Extending the sentence length by combining clauses	Enhancing phrase complexity
Effect	Gender gap < ESL/EFL gap	

male speakers; and the gender difference is not a solely influential factor determining the speech features.

The interpretation of these findings, however, is not easy. As Lindquist (2009) says:

> [M]any things regarding men's and women's language can be described by means of corpora, and ongoing changes can be documented, but how this knowledge should be related to the situation of males and females in society and possible reforms in that era are a matter of opinion.
>
> *(p. 165)*

Also, we may need to remember the warning by Johnson (1997), who writes that "many linguists have become so preoccupied with the need to uncover statistically significant gender differences that they frequently seem to overlook one important fact: the two sexes are still drawing on the same linguistic resources" (p. 11). Regarding this, Baker (2014) carefully re-examines the occurrences of the female/male keywords in the spoken data from the British National Corpus and concludes that "[w]hen males and females are compared in similar settings, the amount of difference reduces and is only slightly larger than comparisons of single-sex groups" (p. 41).

Finally, we would like to mention the limitation of the current study. Here we focused on the difference between female speakers and male speakers, but the construct of gender can be more comprehensive. It includes not only cisgender but also non-binary (transgender, genderqueer, agender, dual-gender, gender expansive, gender fluid, and so on). The ICNALE team had realised the importance of dealing with each participant's gender identity from such a wider framework, but we avoided asking them to choose their gender identity from many options, which is because we worried that such a question might give unexpected pressure on some participants.

This kind of ad hoc approach, however, may need to be critically reconsidered in the future compilation of LC. For example, the ICLE team has already allowed the participants to choose their gender from three options: female, male, and unknown. It is reported that approximately 0.4% of the participants chose "unknown." In addition, the ICLE team mentions that "the learners will also have the option of selecting the 'non-binary' category" in future data collection (Granger et al., 2020, p. 6). A similar approach will also be considered in the future expansion of ICNALE.

7.3 Motivation and Learning History

7.3.1 Aim and RQs

As summarised in Sections 7.1.1.4 and 7.1.1.5, motivation and L2 learning history are expected to influence learners' L2 use. Considering that highly motivated students often use L2 outside classrooms, these two factors should be discussed in combination. Due to the lack of LC that includes detailed learner-related metadata, how these factors influence (or do not influence) the aspects of the spoken and written L2 outputs of Asian EFL learners remains ambiguous. Therefore, this study examines the following research questions:

RQ1 *To what extent are the learner variables related to motivation and learning history and the output lexical variables correlated?*
RQ2 *How are these variables classified?*

7.3.2 Data and Method

In this section, we analyse the monologue speeches and essays produced by EFL learners at B1 level (including B1_1 and B1_2) from six regions, which are taken from the ICNALE Spoken Monologues and the ICNALE Written Essays. We aimed to examine roughly the same amount of data from each of the two corpus modules. The number of learners finally included in the analyses was 454 speakers (54 from Japan and 80 sampled from each of the remaining five regions) and 449 writers (125 from China, 70 from Indonesia, 89 from Japan, 58 from Korea, 43 from Thailand, and 64 from Taiwan). The data of learners who had not completed the learner background survey were excluded from the analysis.

To explore the possible effects of a variety of learner variables on output variables, we examine 16 learner variables (three on motivation and 13 on learning history), which are obtained from the ICNALE Learner Background Survey Sheet (see Section 2.2.4 for the definition of each category), and three output variables about vocabulary (see Section 4.2) (Table 7.5). All the learner-related indices are based on the means of the students' responses to the related questions, and each value ranges between 1 and 6.

Regarding RQ1, we conduct a correlation analysis to see to what extent learner and output variables are related. Then, as regards RQ2, we conduct correspondence

TABLE 7.5 Learner and output variables used for the analysis

Type	*Category*	*Content*
Learner variables (motivation)		
Motivation	IntMot	Strength of integrative motivation
	InsMot	Strength of instrumental motivation
	OvlMot	Strength of overall motivations (sum of the above)
Learner variables (L2 learning history)		
Learning at schools and inside/ outside classrooms	Prm	Quantity of L2 learning in primary school
	Sec	Quantity of L2 learning in secondary school
	Col	Quantity of L2 learning in college
	InC	Quantity of L2 learning inside a classroom
	OutC	Quantity of L2 learning outside a classroom
Learning of the four skills	L	Quantity of L2 listening practice
	S	Quantity of L2 speaking practice
	R	Quantity of L2 reading practice
	W	Quantity of L2 writing practice
Additional learning experience	ENS	Experience in learning with ENS-teachers
	Pron	Experience in learning pronunciation
	SPres	Experience in learning speech presentation
	EsW	Experience in learning essay writing
Output variables		
Lexical indices	TKN	Number of tokens (quantity/fluency)
	STTR	Mean segmental type/token ratio (lexical diversity)
	MWL	Mean word length (lexical sophistication)

analyses based on the contingency tables with 19 learner and output indices as variables (Item 1) and 454 speakers or 449 writers as cases (Item 2). Like a cluster analysis (Section 1.3.3), correspondence analysis, which is also called optimal scaling or homogeneity analysis (Brezina, 2018, p. 200), is a kind of multivariate statistical method and as "a graphical technique for representing the information in a two-way contingency table," it enables us to "construct a plot that shows the interaction of the two categorical variables along with the relationship of the rows to each other and the columns to each other" (Rencher & Christensen, 2012, p. 565). On the scatter plot, samples are classified horizontally and vertically, and similar samples are positioned in the vicinity.

7.3.3 Results and Discussions

7.3.3.1 RQ1 Correlations

Strengths of correlations (r) between learner and output variables are summarised in Table 7.6, where "*ns*" represents that the r value is not significant at $\alpha = .05$.

There are three significant findings from the correlation table. First, among 16 learner variables, overall motivation and three variables related to additional learning

TABLE 7.6 Correlations between output variables and learner variables

	Speeches			*Essays*		
	TKN	*STTR*	*MWL*	*TKN*	*STTR*	*MWL*
Learner variables (motivation)						
IntMot	0.19	*ns*	*ns*	0.11	0.13	*ns*
InsMot	0.10	*ns*	*ns*	*ns*	*ns*	0.09
OvlMot	0.18	0.10	*ns*	0.10	0.13	*ns*
Learner variables (L2 learning history)						
Prm	0.11	0.11	*ns*	*ns*	*ns*	0.11
Sec	0.19	0.10	*ns*	*ns*	0.13	*ns*
Col	0.35	0.21	*ns*	*ns*	*ns*	0.11
InC	0.31	0.18	*ns*	*ns*	*ns*	*ns*
OutC	0.29	0.17	*ns*	*ns*	0.11	*ns*
L	0.35	0.18	*ns*	*ns*	*ns*	*ns*
R	0.27	0.16	*ns*	*ns*	0.12	*ns*
S	0.32	0.19	*ns*	*ns*	*ns*	*ns*
W	0.28	0.17	*ns*	*ns*	0.11	*ns*
ENS	0.10	0.10	*ns*	*ns*	*ns*	*ns*
Pron	0.29	0.24	*ns*	0.09	0.10	*ns*
SPres	0.29	0.22	*ns*	0.17	0.15	*ns*
EsW	0.35	0.27	*ns*	0.13	0.13	*ns*

Note: When the values are higher than 0.12, they are significant at $\alpha = .01$ level.

experiences (pronunciation, speech presentation, and essay writing) are correlated with four of the six output variables. Then, the integrative motivation and variables of L2 learning at three school types and outside classrooms, as well as learning of the reading and writing skills, are correlated with three of them. We can say that these learner variables influence the lexical quality of learners' spoken and written outputs relatively more strongly than the others. It may seem somewhat strange that additional learning experiences are correlated most strongly with the output quality, but this is presumably because learners with such special learning experiences have been consistently offered more exposure to L2.

Second, among six output variables, the number of tokens in speeches, which represents speech fluency, is influenced by all the 16 learner variables. Then, the segmental type/token ratio, which represents the lexical diversity of the outputs, is influenced by 14 variables in speeches and nine variables in essays. This means that learners who are highly motivated and have had sufficient L2 exposure in the past speak more and use a wider range of vocabulary both in speeches and essays. Meanwhile, the number of tokens in essays are affected only by a part of the learner variables, and the mean word length as an index of lexical sophistication is least likely to be influenced both in speeches and essays. It should be noted here that speeches are generally more likely to be influenced than essays.

Third, we compare the correlation strengths in each subset of related variables. Regarding motivation, integrative motivation is correlated with three output variables, while instrumental motivation is only with two. Also, the correlation values are generally higher for the former. This may support the conventional view that integrative motivation based on a pure interest in L2 itself or its culture can be more lasting and therefore more effective than instrumental motivation based on short-term practical needs, such as passing a term test and getting a better score in the proficiency tests. Then, as regards school types, L2 learning in college shows higher scores than the others. Also, L2 learning outside classrooms is correlated with more output variables than in-classroom learning, which may support the importance of spontaneous contact with the target language. Next, as regards skill types, the practice of oral skills (listening and speaking) shows a correlation with speech variables only, while the practice of written skills (reading and writing) correlates with speech variables as well as lexical diversity in essays. Finally, as regards additional learning experiences, the experiences of learning pronunciation, speech presentation, and essay writing are correlated with both speech and essay variables, while the effect of the experience of learning with an ENS teacher is the smallest. It is often suggested that an ENS teacher can develop students' oral skills more effectively than a non-native teacher, but such a gap is not clearly observed in our metadata survey.

Thus, we have observed that learners' L2 learning motivation and L2 learning history may influence the lexical quality of their spoken and written outputs to some extent, though we must note that the correlation values are generally low. Also, we have confirmed that the effects of learner variables tend to be larger in speeches than in essays, and among three kinds of output variables, the mean word length is hardly influenced by any variable and therefore may be qualitatively different from the other two output variables.

7.3.3.2 RQ2 Classification

The results of the correspondence analyses are shown in the scatter plots below (Figures 7.4 and 7.5).

In Figure 7.4, which represents the relationship between learner variables and speech variables, the horizontal axis (DIM 1) and the vertical axis (DIM 2) explain 51.2% and 18.4% of the variance, respectively, meaning that approximately 70% of the variance is summarised in this plot. On the horizontal axis, the number of tokens and the other variables are divided into the right and left halves, suggesting a unique status of speech fluency, which can be influenced by any learner variable. Then, on the vertical axis, the learner variables related to the past L2 learning (at schools, inside/outside classes, four skills, and additional learning experiences) are in the upper half, while motivation variables and the output variables related to lexical diversity and difficulty are both in the lower half, which proves a relatively stronger tie between motivation and lexical quality in speeches. A greater contribution to L2 output of motivation rather than the past L2 learning history seems to support many of the previous studies claiming the paramount importance of motivation in L2 acquisition (e.g., Dörnyei & Skehan, 2003, p. 589).

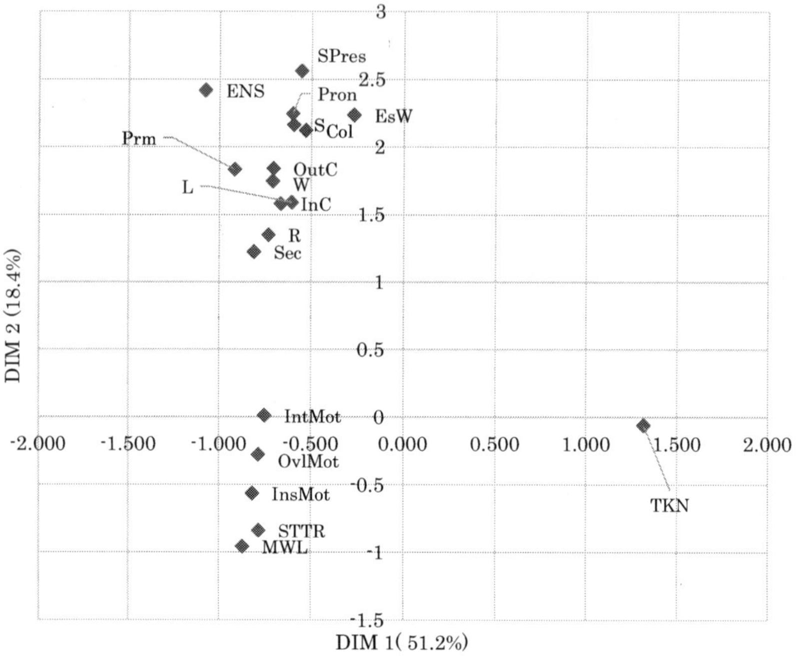

FIGURE 7.4 Positioning of learner/output variables in speeches

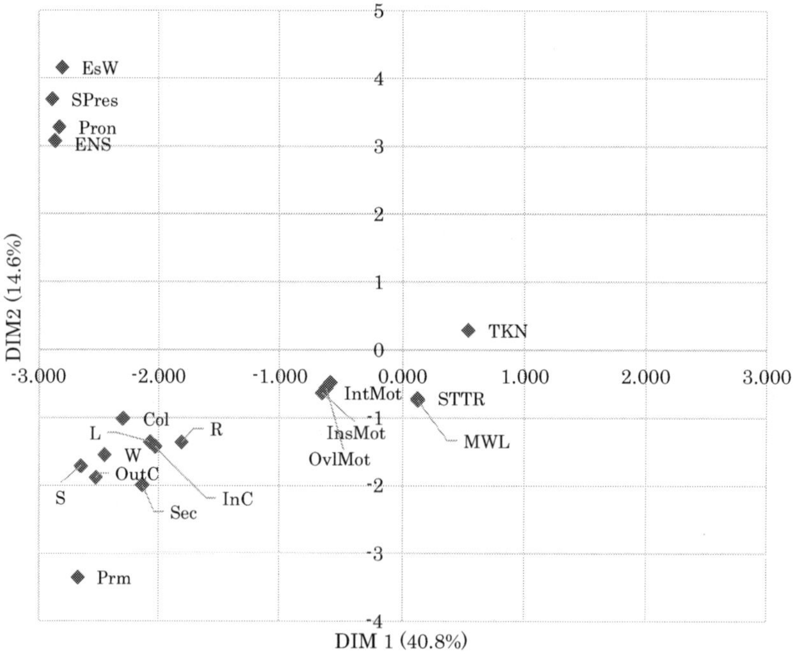

FIGURE 7.5 Positioning of learner/output variables in essays

Next, in Figure 7.5, which shows the relationship between learner variables and essay variables, the horizontal axis explains 40.8%, and the vertical axis explains 14.6% of the variance. On the horizontal axis, learner variables on the left and output variables on the right are neatly divided, which suggests that, unlike in the case of speeches, the influence of learner variables is more negligible in essays, though motivation is positioned relatively closer to the output variables. Then, on the vertical axis, additional learning experiences in the upper half and the others (motivation, L2 learning at schools or inside/outside classes, and four-skills learning) in the lower half are divided. Though the links are not strong, the former may be related to the essay length, while the latter to the vocabulary sophistication.

7.3.4 Summary

In this section, we analysed the ICNALE Learner Background Survey Sheet to examine the relationship between learner variables and L2 spoken and written output variables. Major findings from correlation analysis and correspondence analyses are summarised in Table 7.7, where [Cor] [Str] [Pos] represent correlated output variables, strength of the correlations, and closely positioned output variables; and the output variables correlated with only a part of the target learner variables appear in the round brackets.

The analysis in this section has proven that learners' background variables, especially motivation variables, are likely to influence learners' L2 outputs to some extent. This result may bring into question the traditional analytical methods used in LCR. As mentioned in Section 7.1.1.2, LCR in the early days focused almost exclusively on the analysis of L1 influence, and then it has gradually widened its scope by paying more attention to L2 proficiency and task influences. However, in future studies, we would be required to consider a much wider range of learner variables, which should include motivation and learning history, when discussing the aspects of learners' L2 output data.

TABLE 7.7 Summary of the findings: effects of learner variables on the outputs

Learner variables	*Related output variables (spoken)*	*Related output variables (written)*
Motivation	[Cor] TKN, (STTR) [Str] Int > Ins [Pos] STTR, MWL	[Cor] (TKN) (STTR) (MWL) [Str] Int > Ins
L2 learning at schools and inside/outside classrooms	[Cor] TKN, STTR [Str] Col > Sec > Prm; InC ≈ OutC	[Cor] (STTR) (MWL) [Str] Sec > Prm/ Col; OutC > InC
Learning of the four skills	[Cor] TKN, STTR [Str] L/S > W/R	[Cor] (STTR) [Str] R/W > L/S
Additional learning experiences	[Cor] TKN, STTR [Str] EsW > SPres ≈ Pron > ENS	[Cor] (TKN) (STTR) [Str] SPres > EsW >Pron > ENS

This direction seems promising, but we must realise that it also has demerits. Stratifying learners in terms of numberless learner variables that may (or may not) influence their outputs would inevitably lead to a drastic decrease in the number of learners that we can analyse together. According to Barker et al. (2015), who list the types of information that LC should offer, the most important types of information are L1 and nationality/region, language-learning background (private/state schools, private lessons, number of years, intensity, tutors, self-study), performance level, age and stage of learning, and task specification; and the other important types of information are sex, intensity of language learning, and reason for taking a test (when the data is collected from a test) (pp. 517–518). If we pay equal attention to each of these parameters, we could never analyse a sufficient amount of learner data. Even when we have the data of 100 Chinese learners, for example, we may not be able to find a learner who is female, at B1 upper level, of high integrative motivation, and with the experiences of studying English at primary schools and attending courses of essay writing and presentations at colleges. LC researchers and LC developers should continue to reflect on the dilemma between the SLA-based need to consider more learner variables and the CL-based need to analyse a more extensive amount of data.

8

ASSESSMENT

8.1 Introduction

8.1.1 Assessment in LCR

8.1.1.1 Background

Language assessment or language testing "intersects almost all language-related issues that applied linguists study" (Chapelle & Plakans, 2013). Assessing learners' L2 proficiency to monitor their learning and give guided feedback (i.e., formative assessment) or to grade them (i.e., summative assessment) is a crucial part of language teaching. However, reliable proficiency assessment is a demanding task because proficiency can be a highly elusive concept. In second language acquisition (SLA) and applied linguistics, it has been defined as "the ability to function effectively in the language in real-life contexts" (Higgs, 1984), "a person's overall competence and ability to perform in L2" (Thomas, 1994), "the extent to which an individual possesses the linguistic cognition necessary to function in a given communicative situation, in a given modality (listening, speaking, reading, or writing)" (Hulstijn, 2011), and "a multicomponent phenomenon underlying one's knowledge of and ability to use a language" (Leclercq & Edmonds, 2014), for instance. As such, proficiency may include a great variety of elements.

For proficiency measurement, teachers often conduct an objective multiple-choice test, but assessing learners' L2 speeches and essays, which directly reflect their L2 performance in the actual contexts, is another practical approach. In this sense, learner corpus (LC), a large-scale collection of spoken and written L2 outputs of

DOI: 10.4324/9781003252528-10

learners with varied backgrounds, can be one of the indispensable datasets for L2 assessment studies. Gablasova (2021) emphasises that a "robust analysis of patterns in learner production makes corpora and corpus methods a valuable resource in language testing" (p. 45).

Despite its potential values, LC have not been used so widely in L2 assessment studies. This is because many of the existing LC do not include the output assessment data, and therefore LC users have no other ways to discuss the quality of learner outputs than to compare them with the outputs of L1 English native speakers (ENS) as a yardstick. However, a few of the recently compiled LC have come to include not only learners' outputs but also the assessment data on them (e.g., NICT-JLE Corpus, Trinity Lancaster Corpus, ICNALE, etc.) (see Sections 1.2.2 and 1.2.3). These datasets are expected to bring new possibilities to learner corpus research (LCR).

First, they may help LCR respond to the "social turn" that characterises the recent SLA (McNamara, 1996; Block, 2003). Objective test-based assessment illustrates learners' decontextualised L2 knowledge, that is, what learners know about L2, while output-based or performance-based assessment can show learners' L2 performance in a context, that is, how they deal with a variety of communicative tasks related to real society and the real world.

Second, they may contribute to the enhancement of the quality of English language teaching (ELT). By analysing a large amount of assessment data, teachers could develop reliable "rating scales," which describe the aspects of learners' speaking and writing skills "across the proficiency continuum." They could also identify "critical features" distinguishing one proficiency level from another level (Barker et al., 2015, p. 512). These would enable teachers to give more effective feedback to learners.

Third, they may contribute to the future development of automated assessment, that is, the automated scoring of learner speeches and essays (see Section 8.1.1.3). Studies of automated assessment, which aim to "predict human scores for a given task and population of test takers," are now rapidly spreading in the field of natural language processing (NLP) and speech processing, where researchers train or "calibrate" a scoring engine on the basis of a set of prescored samples taken from learners with different score levels (Higgins et al., 2015, pp. 589–590).

Finally, they may present a new model to follow in ELT and LCR. Traditionally, teachers have used ENS output samples as a model that learners need to follow. Also, under the framework of contrastive interlanguage analysis (CIA) (Granger, 1996, 2015), LC researchers have discussed the aspects of learner outputs in reference to the ENS output samples as a yardstick. These may eventually lead to the imposition of ENS centrism on learners (see Section 2.2.6). However, if we identify a set of learners' benchmark speeches and essays whose quality is guaranteed from a large-size assessment dataset and use them as an alternative to conventional ENS model samples, we might be able to establish a new form of ELT and LCR that is not bound by an ENS view (see Section 8.1.1.4).

TABLE 8.1 Six qualities of test usefulness

Criteria	*Content*
Reliability	A result is consistent between different test conditions.
Construct validity	A test measures what it should measure.
Authenticity	A test reflects real-life experiences.
Interactiveness	A test measures a wide range of aspects of ability.
Impact	A test has a positive washback effect.
Practicality	A test can be administered under various constraints.

8.1.1.2 Reliability in Assessment

When collecting output assessment data, we need to pay attention to its quality. Bachman and Palmer (1996) suggest that the usefulness of language testing should be discussed in terms of six qualities (p. 18) (Table 8.1), which also applies to the assessment of learners' L2 speeches and essays.

Among the six elements, a special emphasis should be put on reliability because the other five requirements tend to be met relatively easily in performance-based assessment, unlike in the case of a multiple-choice test. Bachman and Palmer (1996) say that reliability is "an essential quality of test scores, for unless test scores are relatively consistent, they cannot provide us with any information at all about the ability we want to measure" (p. 20).

How can we collect reliable assessment data? There are two different approaches. One is to increase the number of rating categories included in a rubric, which leads to examining the quality of L2 outputs from a broader range of viewpoints. The other is to increase the number of raters working on the assessment of each of the output samples, which makes a rating score more stable.

According to Chiang et al. (2015), the construct of reliability can be classified into three subsets: consistency over time (test-retest reliability), consistency across items (internal consistency), and consistency across different researchers (inter-rater reliability) (p. 96). When assessing learner outputs, which is usually conducted only once, we should naturally pay attention to internal consistency among rating categories and inter-rater consistency among different assessors.

Internal consistency, or "the consistency of people's responses across the items on a multiple-item measure," is related to the similarity of the scores given to different categories adopted in a rubric. As all the categories are theoretically linked to the single underlying construct, "people's scores on those items should be correlated with each other." Meanwhile, inter-rater reliability, or "the extent to which different observers are consistent in their judgments" (p. 98), is related to the similarities of the scores given by different raters. If a learner has some kind of skills and they can be detected by a careful observer, "different observers' ratings should be highly correlated with each other" (p. 99).

Two kinds of reliability are usually measured by Cronbach's alpha (α), which is conceptually equivalent to "the mean of all possible split-half correlations for a set of items" (Chiang et al., 2015, pp. 97–98). A value of +.80 (or + .70 in some literature) is regarded as an indicator of good consistency. Cronbach's α is mathematically identical to the interclass correlation coefficient (3, *k*) (Shrout & Fleiss, 1979), which is calculated by subtracting the error mean square from the between-subjects mean square (BMS) and dividing the difference with the BMS.

As summarised above, a rubric (or rating categories in it) and a rater are the keys to a collection of reliable output assessment data. Here we like to survey some of the related studies.

First, regarding a rubric, many studies discuss the difference between a holistic assessment (a rater gives a single score to the whole of a learner output) and an analytical assessment (a rater gives a score to each of the plural aspects of a learner output). The former is "fast and easy to use, and practical for decision-making" (Kuiken & Vedder, 2021, p. 126), but it depends mainly on a rater's intuition and may not guarantee the construct validity (Weigle, 2002; Jönsson et al., 2021). Meanwhile, the latter is usually based on a few categories, with which a rater can assess the learner outputs from multiple angles. Thus, it provides "more specific information about learners' language proficiency" (Kuiken & Vedder, 2021, p. 127). However, how many and what kind of categories should be adopted is not clear, which is confirmed by the fact that different rubrics adopt different categories. For speech assessment, the IELTS rubric includes four categories: fluency and coherence, lexical resource, grammatical range and accuracy, and pronunciation; while the *TOEFL iBT* rubric includes the same number but different types of categories: general description (task completion), delivery, language use, and topic development. For essay assessment, the ESL Composition Profile (Jacobs et al., 1981) (see Section 3.5.3 and 3.3.4) adopts five categories: content, organisation, vocabulary, language use (grammar), and mechanics (word spelling and punctuation); the IELTS rubric includes four categories: task response, coherence and cohesion, lexical resource, and grammatical range and accuracy; and the *TOEFL iBT* rubric adopts only one category of a task description.

Next, regarding a rater, previous studies have discussed to what extent a rater's background, such as L1, experience or training, and occupations, may influence the rating output. First, as regards L1 influence, we tend to believe that reliable assessment can be done solely by experienced ENS teachers. However, this may not always be the case. Shi (2001) compares the assessment scores that ENS and Chinese raters gave to Chinese learners' English essays and reports that their scores are largely similar, though ENS raters attend more positively to content and language, and Chinese raters attend more negatively to the organisation and the length. Hijikata-Someya et al. (2015) compare the holistic assessment scores that ENS and non-ENS raters gave to Japanese students' English summaries and reveal that the former found the assessment of content and language difficult, while the latter found that of vocabulary use and paraphrasing difficult. Also, inter-rater reliability was higher for ENS raters. Second, as regards experience and training influence, Weigle (1994) compares the assessments that non-experienced raters conducted before and after a rater training session and reports that training experiences help them understand the characteristics of learners, tasks, and rating criteria more deeply. Third, as regards occupation influence, Brown (1995) analyses the rating data from the Japanese Language Test for Tour Guides and reports that in terms of the overall scores, there is "little evidence that native speakers are more suitable than nonnative speakers or that raters with teaching background are more suitable than those with an industry background."

8.1.1.3 Automated Assessment

Among possible applications of LC-linked output assessment data (see Section 8.1.1.1), we focus on the automated assessment and benchmark sample identification. This section surveys the studies on the former topic.

L2 output assessment seems to be possible only by "skilled instructors armed with rubrics and domain knowledge and a lot of time," but a good amount of human assessment data allows a computer to "extract and transform relevant evidence from student output" and "make useful inferences about the students' abilities" (Foltz et al., 2020, pp. 1–2). Thus, many researchers have endeavoured to develop an engine to "predict human scores for a given task and population of test takers" from a set of prescored learner speeches and essays (Higgins et al., 2015, pp. 589–590).

When developing such an engine, we need to collect good rating data, choose appropriate linguistics features for score prediction, and finally test the accuracy rate of the developed engine or algorithm.

First, regarding the data collection, DiCerbo et al. (2020) emphasise, "[w]ithout reliable human scores, the machine-learning algorithm will not be able to create reliable prediction models to approximate those scores," because "automated essay scoring [...] can only approximate the scoring of the constructs that human themselves can score" (p. 36). This shows that human rating data used for the training of a scoring engine should be of a high level of internal and inter-rater reliability.

Second, regarding the features, we are required to choose a set of linguistic features closely related to the scores or levels given by human raters. However, which features to focus on has not been sufficiently clarified yet. Thus, just as in the case of rating rubrics (see Section 8.1.1.1), various scoring engines adopt different types of features. For example, E-rater 2.0, an essay scoring engine developed by Educational Testing Service (ETS), investigates 12 features, which include lexical indices (total number of words, type/token ratio, frequency of least common words, word length), error indices (grammar errors, usage errors, mechanics errors), and so on (Burstein et al., 2004). Also, TOEFL SpeechRater, a spontaneous speech scoring engine developed by ETS, adopts 13 features, which include acoustic model score (pronunciation), speech articulation rate, unique words, frequency of long pauses, and so on (Xi et al., 2008).

In addition, many individual researchers have tried to identify developmental features, that is, lexicogrammatical features whose frequency significantly changes between good outputs and poor outputs or between novice learners and advanced learners. According to Kojima and Kaneta (2020), who conducted a meta-analysis of 52 studies focusing on essay assessment, essay quality can be determined primarily by fluency (e.g., the number of words) and then by accuracy (e.g., error-ratio per unit) and lexical complexity, which can be subdivided into lexical diversity (e.g., type/token ratio), lexical density (e.g., content-word ratio), and lexical sophistication (e.g., difficult-word ratio). Meanwhile, the effect of syntactic complexity (e.g., length of a clause, number of clauses, frequency of subordination, passive forms, prepositional phrases, etc.) is found to be the smallest. Kobayashi (2013) analyses L1 Japanese learners' speeches and essays and reports that the speeches of advanced learners are characterised by the use of "well," "so," "maybe," and coordinate conjunctions; and those of novice learners are by the use of nouns, present-*be* verbs, and "yes/no," while the essays of advanced learners are characterised by the use of past-tense verbs, subordinate/coordinate conjunctions, and "we," and those of novice learners are by the use of nouns, present-tense verbs, and "I." Kobayashi and Abe (2016) analyse the frequency of Biber's (1988) lexicogrammatical features in L1 Japanese learners' speeches and report that the top ten most important features include tokens, types, other total nouns, past tense, emphatics, infinitives, possibility modals, analytical negations, causative adverbials, subordinators, and contractions. Kobayashi et al. (2011) analyse the relationship between the language quality of around 781 science journal articles, which were rated by professional language editors, and the frequencies of major meta-discourse markers (Hyland, 2005), and report that "good" papers include transition markers (e.g., "but"), frame markers (e.g., "subsequently"), code glosses (e.g., "or"), hedges (e.g., "could"), boosters (e.g., "evident"), and engagement markers (e.g., "allow"). LaFlair et al. (2020) assign Biber's lexicogrammatical tags to learners' outputs taken from the spoken and written exam corpora and reveal that speakers gradually increase their colloquiality and fluency, and writers increase their literateness and lexical variety as their proficiency levels increase.

Third, regarding the accuracy in score prediction, several studies test the existing engines. The correlation coefficients with human ratings are reported to be 0.81 for SpeechRater and 0.83 for E-Rater (Evanini et al., 2015), though the exact agreement rate on single test items remains 58% for the former (Zechner et al., 2009). The performance of speech-scoring engines tends to be inferior to that of essay-scoring engines. This is because speech score prediction requires an additional process of speech recognition. Zechner et al. (2009) report that its accuracy rate remains only around 50%. Also, Brezina et al. (2019), who used the latest speech recognition system to transcribe learner speeches for compilation of the Trinity Lancaster Corpus (TLC), report that as the system ignores fillers and speech fragments, it identified only 6 of the 17 turns that occurred in the interaction. Next, regarding the accuracy in score/level prediction algorithms, Kobayashi and Abe (2016) report that the accuracy rate in predicting learners' speech proficiency levels from the frequencies of selected lexicogrammatical features was around 60%, though it varied according to the level of learners: 0% for Level 1 (novice), 60% for Level 2, 65% for Level 3, 84% for Level 4, 50% for Level 5, 30% for Level 6, 27% for Level 7, 7% for Level 8, and 35% for Level 9 (advanced). Also, Kobayashi et al. (2011) report that the accuracy rate in classifying journal articles into either of the two levels (good and poor) from the frequencies of discourse markers was around 80% for good articles, 83% for poor articles, and 82% for both.

As surveyed above, an increasing number of studies have paid attention to the topics such as rating data collection, proficiency-linked linguistic feature selection, and verification of score predicting engines and algorithms. The techniques developed in these studies can be applied to other LC-related research purposes. For example, Kyle et al. (2015) conduct a multinomial logistic regression to predict writers' L1s from their usages of particular lexical and phrasal items in the essays. The analysis shows that accuracy in prediction decreases when processing advanced learner essays. Such a study is called native language identification or NLI.

Automated assessment of L2 outputs is a highly interdisciplinary research field, where collaboration between LC experts and NLP experts would become more and more critical. Ballier et al. (2020) introduce a recent NLP competition, whose aim was to produce a machine learning model to predict learners' levels based on the Common European Framework of Reference for Languages (CEFR) from the LC essay data. After summarising a variety of methods reported at the competition, they insist that such competitions potentially contribute to the further development of LCR.

8.1.1.4 Benchmark Sample Identification

ENS outputs have often been regarded as a referential model that learners need to follow and imitate both in the fields of LCR and English language teaching (ELT). Such an attitude, however, may need to be critically reconsidered.

First, regarding the use of ENS outputs as a reference or a yardstick for LCR, especially in CIA as its staple analytical framework, many have criticised (i) the CIA's dependence on a comparative technique, which might marginalise learners' interlanguage, (ii) its use of a narrow range of ENS outputs, which might not represent the status of the English language, and (iii)its negative backwash effects such as the imposition of ENS centrism on learners and teachers, as we discussed in Section 2.2.6. Surveying the discussions surrounding a yardstick, Gilquin (2022) mentions the importance of the shift from "one norm to rule them all" toward diversified "corpus-derived rules." Gilquin does not necessarily protest the use of an ENS yardstick if it is appropriately chosen, but she also suggests that LC researchers can use non-native expert outputs (e.g., academic papers) in addition to institutionalised "new Englishes" as new references. Though non-native expert outputs seem to be a promising alternative to the ENS yardstick, comparing students' L2 essays with the authentic academic papers written by non-native professional scholars would be problematic because they are essentially different in terms of linguistic sophistication, contents, and expected readers. This implies the need for us to look for a different type of non-native reference.

Next, regarding an ELT model, Kachru (1991) insists that a British and American English model, which inevitably reflects British and American cultures and values, would be inappropriate for learners in other regions, and he emphasises the importance of accepting a variety of "Englishes." Meanwhile, Quirk (1990) touches upon the importance of Standard English as a reliable model and adds, "[i]t is neither liberal nor liberating to permit learners to settle for lower standards than the best, and it is a travesty of liberalism to tolerate low standards which will lock the least fortunate into the least rewarding careers" (p. 9). In spite of the criticism, Quirk's views are still widely supported (Cunningham, 2009). As Jones et al. (2018) note, an ENS model has been chosen and supported not only by teachers but also by learners themselves, who tend to "aspire towards a native or native-like proficiency in English" and "overlook the fact that they can still be successful in their use of English without achieving such a level" (p. 2). However, continuing to present L2 learners with ENS speeches and essays as a sole model in classes entails several theoretical and practical problems. First, it does not reflect the actual status of the English language in the current world. According to a report by Crystal (2003), the ratio of ENS belonging to the "inner circle" to all the English speakers in the world is only 20–30% (p. 61), and the current ratio is expected to be lower than that. Second, it does not respond to a recent view of English as a lingua franca (ELF) as a type of "communication in English between speakers with different first languages" (Seidlhofer, 2005). Third, even if there are no such intentions on a teacher's side, it may eventually impose dogmatic ENS centrism on learners. As Timmis (2013) warns, teaching the features of ENS' authentic outputs means "imposing a false identity on the learners" (p. 84). Finally, ENS outputs are not necessarily good in language quality. Leech (1998) notes that "when we come to examine a reference corpus of native-speaker speech, the less admirable features of the native speaker's performance can show up especially clearly" (p. xix). These problems also require us to look for another referential model to be introduced in L2 classes, which should help learners establish their own English rather than the English of someone else.

When reconsidering these issues common to LCR/CIA and ELT, we may be tempted to explore the new possibility of analysing LC-linked output assessment data, identifying benchmark learner output samples that represent different levels, and using high-quality benchmark samples as a new yardstick for CIA and also as a new model to be presented in L2 classrooms.

8.1.2 ICNALE Case Studies

We first discuss the reliability of the rating data collected in the ICNALE project. Then, among several applications of LC-linked output assessment data, we focus on automated assessment of learner proficiency as well as benchmark sample identification.

In Section 8.2, we analyse the rating data from the ICNALE Global Rating Archives and examine both internal consistency among rating categories and inter-rater reliability among assessors. We also discuss how different rating categories are interrelated and whether varied rater backgrounds influence their rating scores.

In Section 8.3, we analyse the same rating data and aim to develop a regression model to predict the rating scores from the frequencies of particular lexical items.

In Section 8.4, we aim to identify a set of learner samples representing different proficiency levels. The high-quality learner outputs are expected to be used as one of the alternatives to the ENS outputs as a yardstick for CIA.

8.2 Reliability

8.2.1 Aim and RQs

As outlined in Section 3.6, the ICNALE Global Rating Archives is a unique rating dataset, but the reliability of the collected rating data, the validity of the rating categories adopted in the rubric, and the possible influences of rater backgrounds on the rating scores have not been thoroughly investigated yet. Therefore, this study examines the following research questions:

RQ1 *What level of internal consistency and inter-rater reliability is attained in the collected rating data?*
RQ2 *How are the rating categories interrelated?*
RQ3 *To what extent do rater backgrounds influence the rating scores?*

8.2.2 Data and Method

In this study, we use a part of the rating data collected in the ICNALE Global Rating Archives. The number of raters that we examine here is 120 in total: 60 raters were in charge of speech assessment, and the remaining 60 were in charge of essay assessment. Among these, 48 raters rated both speeches and essays, and 24 did either of them. They rated the same set of 140 speeches or essays. The backgrounds of speakers/writers, who included both learners of English as a second language (ESL) and English as a foreign language (EFL) as well as ENS, were kept secret. Table 8.2 summarises the backgrounds of 120 raters.

The dataset we use here consists of 12 kinds of rating scores that 60 raters assigned to 140 spoken samples or the same number of written samples, which include 10 kinds of analytical scores (intelligibility/INT, complexity/CLX, accuracy/ACC, fluency/FLU, comprehensibility/CPH, logicality/LGC, sophistication/SPH, purposefulness/PPS, willingness to communicate/WIL, and involvement/INV), the analytical score sums (ANAS), and the overall holistic rating scores (HOL).

For RQ1, we examine the degrees of consistency between 11 kinds of scores (i.e., 10 analytical scores and a holistic score), each of which is based on the mean

TABLE 8.2 Backgrounds of 120 raters

Background	*Speech raters*	*Essay raters*
Gender	Female (29), male (31)	Female (34), male (26)
Proficiency	B2 (18), C1 (20), C2 (14), (near-) ENS (8)	B2 (15), C1 (24), C2 (12), (near-) ENS (9)
Occupation	Business (6), English teacher (32), other teacher (7), others (15)	Business (7), English teacher (35), other teacher (8), others (10)
Rating experiences	Never (7), 1–5 times (17), 6+ times (36)	Never (7), 1–5 times (13), 6+ times (40)
L1	Chinese (10), English (2), Filipino (15), Indonesian (3), Japanese (9), Korean (3), Lao (6), Thai (5), others (7)	Chinese (5), English (4), Filipino (14), Indonesian (3), Japanese (11), Korean (3), Lao (6), Thai (6), others (8)

Note: Proficiency levels are based on the raters' self-reports.

TABLE 8.3 Scores assigned to 11 rating categories

	Analytical holistic rating scores				
Rater	*INT*	*CLX*	*ACC*	...	*HOL*
SR_001	5.49	4.73	5.11	...	51.59
SR_002	5.03	5.09	4.46	...	47.41
...	...	...	...	...	...
SR_060	5.11	5.36	5.29	...	54.09

TABLE 8.4 Scores assigned by 60 raters

	Sums of the 10 analytical scores				
Sample	*SR_001*	*SR_002*	*SR_003*	...	*SR_060*
SS_001	43	70	74	...	33
SS_002	42	42	80	...	66
...	...	...	...	...	...
SS_140	67	65	51	...	79

of the scores assigned to 140 samples, as well as between the analytical score sums assigned by 60 raters. In both cases, we calculate Cronbach's α (see Section 8.1.1.2) as a reliability index. Tables 8.3 and 8.4 introduce parts of the data used for the analysis of speech assessment scores. SR and SS represent "speech rater" and "speech sample," respectively.

Next, for RQ2, we conduct hierarchical cluster analyses on the contingency tables based on speech assessment scores (Table 8.3) and essay assessment scores, both of which include 60 raters as cases and 12 kinds of scores as variables. The initial

TABLE 8.5 Two kinds of reliability values

Reliability types	*Output types*	*Cronbach's α*	*CI (95%)*
Internal consistency	Speech	0.810	(0.730, 0.874)
	Essay	0.792	(0.705, 0.862)
Inter-rater reliability	Speech	0.983	(0.979, 0.987)
	Essay	0.964	(0.955, 0.972)

Note: "CI" stands for confidence intervals.

distance is defined as the square root of $(2-2r)$, and the distance after agglomeration is calculated by the Ward method.

Finally, for RQ3, we compare the mean values of the analytical score sums assigned by different subgroups of raters, which are classified in terms of gender, proficiency, occupation, rating experience, and L1 (Table 8.2). When analysing the effects of occupation and L1, we focus only on the major subcategories.

8.2.3 Results and Discussions

8.2.3.1 RQ1 Reliability in the Rating Data

The results of the analysis of internal consistency among 11 rating scores and inter-rater reliability among 60 raters in speech and essay assessments are shown in Table 8.5.

Regarding internal consistency, the coefficients are significant both for speech assessment (F (59, 590) = 5.26, $p < .001$) and essay assessment (F (59,590) = 4.81, $p <.001$), meaning that 11 kinds of rating categories all measure the same construct. Also, regarding inter-rater reliability, the coefficients are significant both for speech assessment (F (139, 8201) = 58.77, $p < .001$) and essay assessment (F (139, 8201) = 28.00, $p <.001$), meaning that there exists a satisfactory level of reliability among the assessment by 60 raters.

8.2.3.2 RQ2 Classification of Rating Categories

We have confirmed that different rating categories adopted in the rubric are most likely to measure the same single construct when seen as a set. How are they internally structured? The results of hierarchical cluster analyses based on the scores of ten analytical categories, which include four language-related indices (L), four content-related indices (C), and two attitude-related indices (A), as well as the analytical score sums (ANAS) and overall holistic rating scores (HOL), are summarised in the two dendrograms below (Figures 8.1 and 8.2), where we place the cutting points at around 1.0.

In both dendrograms, 12 categories seem to be classified into four clusters, though the variables included in each cluster are not consistent between the two kinds of assessments. When evaluating speeches, raters seem to pay attention to four

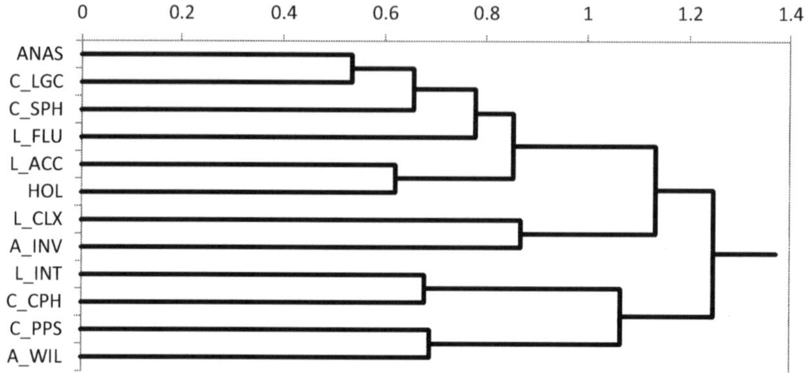

FIGURE 8.1 Clustering of the rating categories in speech assessment

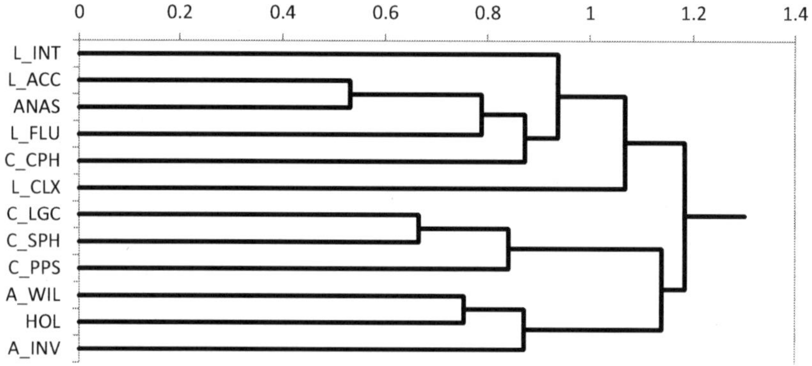

FIGURE 8.2 Clustering of the rating categories in essay assessment

aspects: language/content (logicality, sophistication, fluency, accuracy), interactiveness (complexity, involvement), understandability (intelligibility, comprehensibility), and persuasiveness (purposefulness, willingness). Meanwhile, when evaluating essays, raters seem to pay attention to the same number but somewhat different types of aspects: language/understandability (intelligibility, accuracy, fluency, comprehensibility), language quality (complexity), content (logicality, sophistication, purposefulness), and attitude (willingness, involvement). Three category types (content, language, and attitude) that the ICNALE team assumed at the time of a rubric development are classified relatively neatly in essay assessment, but they are instead mixed up in speech assessment.

Regarding the two umbrella categories, an analytical score sum is included in the language/content cluster, and it is the closest to logicality in speech assessment, while it is included in the language/understandability cluster, and it is the closest to accuracy in essay assessment. A holistic score is included in the language/content cluster, and it is the closest to accuracy in speech assessment, while it is included in the attitude cluster, and it is the closest to willingness to communicate in essay assessment. These findings suggest that raters tend to put the top priority on language quality (accuracy in particular), and they also pay attention to a writer's attitude to appeal to the readers when assessing essays.

8.2.3.3 RQ3 The Effect of Rater Backgrounds

The results of the analysis of the mean values of the analytical score sums assigned by groups of raters classified in terms of gender, L2 proficiency, occupation, rating experiences, and L1 are shown in Figures 8.3 to 8.7.

FIGURE 8.3 Gender effects on rating scores

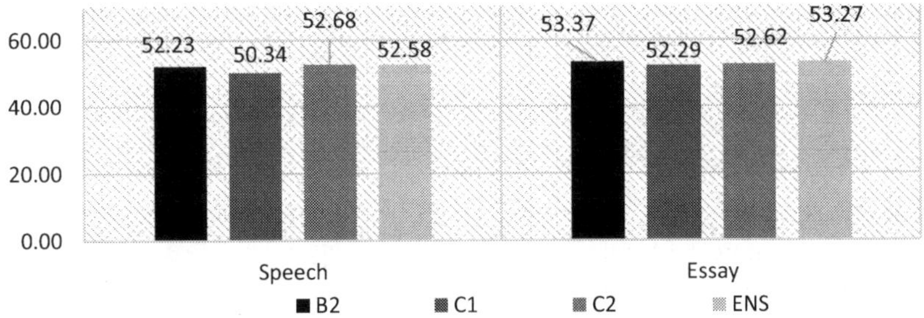

FIGURE 8.4 L2 proficiency effects on rating scores

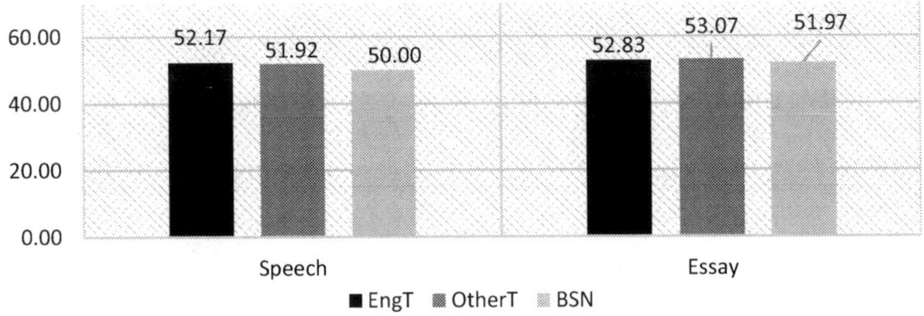

FIGURE 8.5 Occupation effects on rating scores

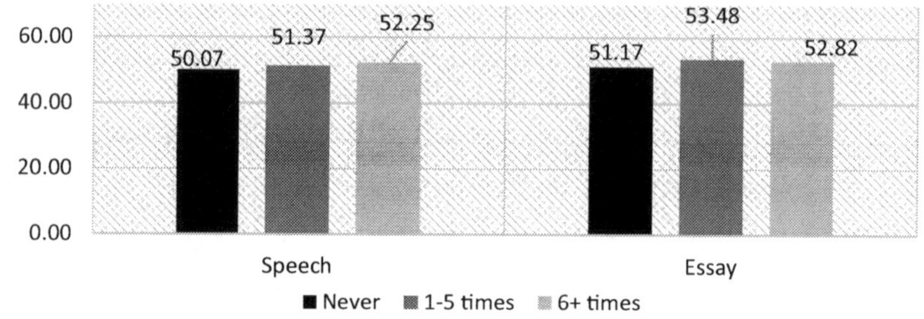

FIGURE 8.6 Experience effects on rating scores

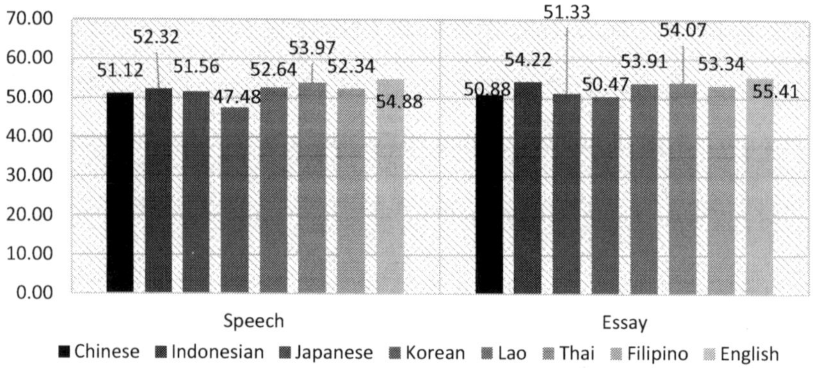

FIGURE 8.7 L1 effects on rating scores

The graphs above suggest the possibilities that female raters (Figure 8.3), C2 or B2 raters (Figure 8.4), raters teaching English or other subjects (Figure 8.5), raters with rating experiences (Figure 8.6), and ENS as well as L1 Thai and Indonesian raters (Figure 8.7), may give somewhat higher scores than the others. When based on these findings, we might say that female raters with the highest or the lowest L2 proficiency and with sufficient teaching and rating experiences are more accustomed to hearing or reading the outputs of learners, and therefore they are often more generous in assessment.

However, these gaps are not statistically significant. The main effects of gender (speeches: Welch's t (56.27) = 0.558, p=.458; essays: Welch's t (53.86) = 1.423, p = .238), proficiency (F (3, 56) = 1.432, η_p^2= .071, p = .243; F (3, 56) = 0.346, η_p^2= .018, p = .792), occupation (F (2, 42) = 0.776, η_p^2= .036, p = .467; F (2, 45) = 0.202, η_p^2= .009, p = .818), experience (F (2,57) = 1.070, η_p^2= .036, p = .350; F (2, 57) = 0.978, η_p^2= .033, p = .382), and L1 (F (7, 45) = 1.103, η_p^2= .146, p = .378; F (7, 44) = 1.60, η_p^2 = .203, p= .161) do not reach the significance levels.

The current analysis shows that the effect of rater backgrounds on the rating scores can be smaller than usually expected, though this result may be influenced by

TABLE 8.6 Summary of the findings: aspects of speech/essay assessment data

	Speech assessment	*Essay assessment*
Internal consistency (11 rating categories)		
Cronbach's α	.810	.792
Clustering	Language/content, interactiveness, understandability, persuasiveness	Language/understandability, language quality, content, attitude
Key variables	Logicality/ accuracy	Accuracy/ willingness to communicate
Inter-rater reliability (60 raters)		
Cronbach's α	.983	.964
Gender effect	(Female > Male)	(Female > Male)
Proficiency effect	(C2 … > … C1)	(B2 … > … C1)
Occupation effect	(English Teacher > Teacher> Business)	(Teacher > English Teacher > Business)
Experience effect	(6+ > 1–5 > 0)	(1–5 > 6+ > 0)
L1 effect	(ENS > THA …. > KOR)	(ENS > IDN … > KOR)

two factors specific to the ICNALE project, where all raters were required to read a detailed rater handbook, take a check test, and make the mean rating scores and their standard deviation fall precisely between the preset range (see Section 3.6.4).

8.2.4 Summary

In this section, we examined the reliability of the rating data collected in the ICNALE Global Rating Archives from two viewpoints: internal consistency among 11 rating categories and inter-rater reliability among 60 raters. Regarding the former, we discussed the internal structures of the categories, and regarding the latter, we investigated the effects of rater backgrounds on the rating scores. Our findings are summarised in Table 8.6, where the round brackets represent that the differences were not statistically significant.

These results show that the assessment data collected in the project are of a certain level of reliability. Also, we confirmed that the gaps in the rating scores given by ENS raters and non-ENS raters, and also raters with and without teaching experiences, were not statistically significant, which supports the conclusion of Brown (1995), who emphasises that "there is little evidence that native speakers are more suitable than nonnative speakers or that raters with teaching backgrounds are more suitable than those with an industry background."

Though many non-native teachers and researchers tend to assume that the assessment of L2 learners' outputs is challenging and can be conducted reliably only by professional ENS raters, our data does not support such a common view. Our findings may help performance-based assessments spread more widely in English language teaching in Asian EFL regions. They also illuminate the need to collect more output assessment data from a variety of raters, including both non-native speakers and ENS, which leads to the further contribution of LCR to L2 assessment studies.

8.3 Automated Assessment

8.3.1 Aim and RQ

As noted in Section 8.1.1.3, the topic of automated assessment has been discussed mainly in the NLP field, and the applicability of automated score prediction to English language teaching in Asia has not been fully confirmed yet. Therefore, this study aims to obtain the regression models to predict human rating scores for Asian learners' speeches and essays from the simple lexical indices. The study examines the following research questions:

RQ1 What models predict human rating scores for Asian learners' speeches and essays?
RQ2 To what extent are the obtained models applicable to new data?

8.3.2 Data and Method

In this study, we analyse the dataset from the ICNALE Global Rating Archives, which includes analytical and holistic rating scores that 120 raters in total assigned to 140 spoken or written output samples (see Section 8.2.2).

When conducting regression modelling, we need to be careful about the risk of the model's overfitting. Therefore, we divide a set of 140 samples into Set A and Set B, each of which includes 70 samples. First, we develop a model on Set A data (RQ1), and then we test its validity with Set B data (RQ2). This is an ordinary procedure for the development of any type of scoring algorithm. Yan and Bridgeman (2020) say whenever "a new model is trained, its performance is evaluated on a separate cross-validation sample at the overall level, individual prompt level, and subgroup level" (p. 303).

For RQ1, we first calculate the overall rating score (ORS) by averaging the analytical score sum (/100) and the holistic score (/100), which we aim to predict from the basic lexical indices: the total number of tokens and the frequencies of the top 30 words (Table 8.7). If using a text analytical concordancer, one can easily obtain these values from the raw learner texts, which is of importance when considering the practicality of the obtained models for L2 teaching.

TABLE 8.7 Words used for the regression modelling

Speeches	*Essays*
I, to, my, and, the, time, so, can, have, job, part, a, is, you, in, it, but, that, think, for, me, 't, because, yeah, do, study, this, work, yes, want	to, time, the, a, part, job, is, and, for, students, in, they, have, of, it, I, can, college, their, that, money, you, are, we, not, work, important, will, do, so

Note: Two kinds of fillers ("uh," and "um") that frequently occur in speeches are excluded from the current analysis.

Next, based on the contingency table with 31 indices (the total number of words and the frequency of 30 words) as variables and 70 spoken or written samples (Set A) as cases, we conduct a stepwise multiple linear regression analysis, which aims to obtain a model to predict a dependent variable from a set of independent variables. As "a traditional *ordinary least-squares* regression (OLS) model," it has been adopted by many automated scoring engines (Yan & Bridgeman, 2020, p. 303). We adopt a hybrid (forward and backward combination) stepwise method, which begins with a zero-predictor model and adds a new predictor step by step. Such a procedure is said to be suitable for "exploratory analyses where no clear theoretical grounds for variable inclusion are available" (Brezina, 2018, p. 123).

Then, for RQ2, we test the validity of the obtained models by applying them to the Set B data. Here we investigate how accurately each model predicts the ORS as well as the six proficiency levels based on ORS values: A (70%+), B (60%+), C (50%+), D (40%+), E (30%+), and F (<30%).

8.3.3 Results and Discussions

8.3.3.1 RQ1 Score Prediction Modelling

Multiple linear regression models for predicting the ORS in speeches (parts of persuasion roleplays) and essays and their goodness-of-fit values (adjusted r squared and the Akaike information criterion: AIC) are shown in Table 8.8.

The r squared values represent the proportion of the variance in the dependent variable as explained by a set of independent variables. As they naturally increase according to the model complexity (i.e., the number of independent variables adopted in the model), we usually pay attention to the adjusted r squared values when comparing two or more models. Meanwhile, AIC evaluates model fitness by penalising the model complexity. Thus, a model showing a higher adjusted r squared value and a lower AIC value is usually interpreted as a better model.

Significant findings are discussed. First, the analyses show that it is possible to predict the ORS in speeches and essays at around 35–55% accuracy from the number of tokens and the frequencies of just six to ten words. Though we also examined the residuals, they did not show any stable patterns, meaning that the models obtained here are of a certain level of reliability.

TABLE 8.8 Regression models for predicting overall rating scores

Type	*Speech ORS prediction*	*Essay ORS prediction*
Formula	y = 0.16 [TOKEN] +1.63 [work] + 1.25 [that] + 1.21 [in] + 0.58 [my] −2.09 [do] −1.21 [yeah]−1.07 [to] −1.01 [you] −0.98 [t] −0.79 [time] + 34.81	y = 0.19 [TOKEN] +0.55 [a] +1.02 [it] +1.12 [that] +2.15 [so]−1.47 [job]−1.39 [not] +8.11
Adj. r^2	.550	.347
AIC	331.02	325.83

Second, in terms of *r* squared values, the speech ORS prediction model is better, while in terms of AIC, the essay ORS prediction model is better. This is because the former includes 11 predictors, and the latter includes only seven predictors.

Third, a set of the variables selected in the models show that the ORS tends to increase when speakers refer more directly to the topic ("my" continuing to "work" part-time) and use more formal constructions that include function words ("that" as a complementiser and "in" as a preposition), while it tends to decrease when speakers refer more to the hearers ("you"), use interrogative or negative forms ("do" you …?, I "do" not …), and speak more casually ("yeah," and "t" as a contraction marker). Raters pay attention to whether a speaker firmly grips the purpose of the persuasion task and whether they can produce sociolinguistically appropriate utterances, in addition to how much they speak in the interaction. Meanwhile, regarding essays, it was suggested that ORS tends to increase when writers use more formal and grammatically sophisticated sentences, especially when they present a reasonable control of the number of nouns ("a"), textual cohesion ("it"), and structural embeddings (V + "that," "so" +SV), and it decreases when they simply repeat the topic (part-time "job" for college students) without appropriately developing it. These words, which are chosen for the regression models, can be a key to a good speech or a good essay.

Next, we pay attention to the scatter plots, which show the relationships between prediction (estimation) and observation (Figures 8.8 and 8.9).

As shown in the two scatter plots, the range of the predicted values is narrower for essays (most fall between 40 and 60) than for speeches (most fall between 30 and 70), which leads to a relatively greater discrepancy between the observed and the predicted values for essays. This may suggest that the quality of essays is a more complex construct in comparison to that of speeches, and therefore the essay score prediction from the lexical cues is more difficult.

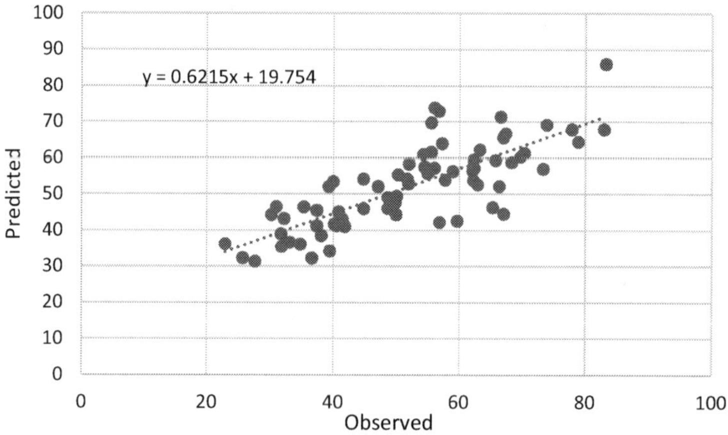

FIGURE 8.8 Observed/predicted ORS in speeches (Set A)

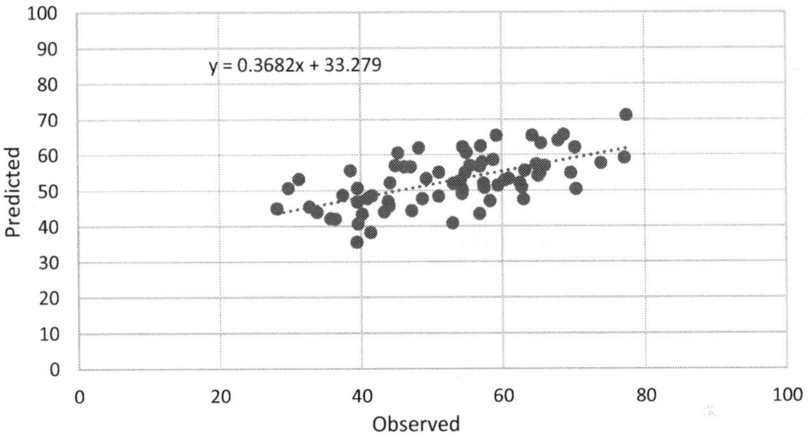

FIGURE 8.9 Observed/predicted ORS in essays (Set A)

8.3.3.2 RQ2 Applicability of the Models

Then, how accurately do these models predict the ORS when applied to new datasets (Set B)? The relationships between prediction (estimation) and observation, as well as the linear regression models explaining them, are shown in Figures 8.10 and 8.11.

The adjusted *r* squared values are 0.222 for speeches and 0.102 for essays, meaning that the models developed from the Set A data explain approximately 10 to 22% of the variance of the ORS values in the Set B data. Then, the AIC values are 336.57 for the former and 301.69 for the latter. These values may not be so high, though it is natural that they lower when models are applied to new datasets.

Seen from the practical viewpoint, however, not only the exact matches but also the near-matches are of some use. Therefore, we examine the degree of the gap between observation and prediction both in terms of the ORS values and the six proficiency levels (A–F) (Tables 8.9 and 8.10).

Regarding the ORS, the gap is smaller than 11 points for 36 of the 70 speech samples (51.4%) and 35 of the 70 essay samples (50.0%). The mean difference is 11.3 points for the former and 10.7 points for the latter, suggesting that the obtained models predict the human rating scores (/100) with only a 10-point prediction error on average.

Regarding proficiency levels, the number of the samples whose levels are exactly predicted (i.e., 0-level difference) is 18 for speeches (25.7%) and 22 for essays (31.4%), but if including the samples with the one-level difference, it increases to 51 for the former (72.8%) and 48 for the latter (68.5%). The mean differences are 1.09 and 1.04, showing that the models predict the learners' performance levels based on human ratings with only a one-level prediction error on average.

The accuracy of the prediction based on the two regression models is largely close to the accuracy level reported in the previous automated assessment studies (e.g., Kobayashi & Abe, 2016). This proves that the obtained models are of a certain level of applicability to new data.

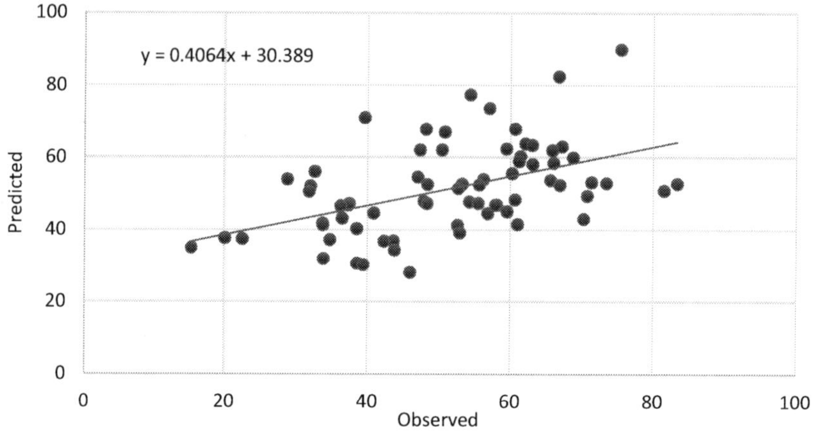

FIGURE 8.10 Observed/predicted ORS in speeches (Set B)

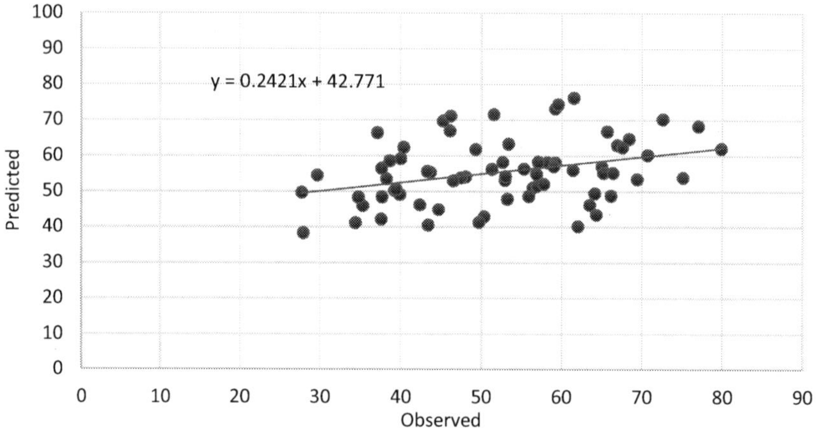

FIGURE 8.11 Observed/predicted ORS in essays (Set B)

TABLE 8.9 Gap in score prediction

Type	*Difference in scores*				*Mean difference*
	0–5 points	*6–10 points*	*11–20 points*	*21+ points*	
Speeches	19 (27.1%)	17 (24.3%)	25 (35.7%)	9 (12.9%)	11.3
Essays	17 (24.3%)	18 (25.7%)	24 (34.3%)	11 (15.7%)	10.7

TABLE 8.10 Gap in level prediction

Type	*Difference in proficiency levels*				*Mean difference*
	0 level	*1 level*	*2 levels*	*3+ levels*	
Speeches	18 (25.7%)	33 (47.1%)	15 (21.4%)	4 (5.7%)	1.09
Essays	22 (31.4%)	26 (37.1%)	19 (27.1%)	3 (4.3%)	1.04

TABLE 8.11 Summary of the findings: output quality prediction

	Speeches	*Essays*
Regression	y = 0.16 [TOKEN] +1.63 [work] + 1.25 [that] + 1.21 [in] + 0.58 [my] −2.09 [do] −1.21 [yeah]−1.07 [to] −1.01 [you] −0.98 [t] −0.79 [time] + 34.81 (Adjusted r^2= .550)	y = 0.19 [TOKEN] +0.55 [a] +1.02 [it] +1.12 [that] +2.15 [so]−1.47 [job]−1.39 [not] +8.11 (Adjusted r^2= .347)
Features of high-ORS outputs	(1) direct reference to the topic (2) use of the formal constructions	(1) use of formal and grammatically sophisticated constructions (2) control of the number of nouns, textual cohesion, and structural embeddings
Features of low-ORS outputs	(1) reference to the hearers (2) use of the interrogative or negative forms (3) casual speech	(1) simple repletion of the topic
Accuracy in prediction (Set B)	Model fit: Adjusted r^2= .222 ORS gap: 11.3 (/100-point) Level gap: 1.09 (/6-level)	Model fit: Adjusted r^2= .102 ORS gap: 10.7 (/100-point) Level gap: 1.04 (/6-level)

8.3.4 Summary

In this section, we made multiple regression models to predict the mean ORS given by 60 raters from the total number of words and the frequencies of several basic words. Then, we tested their validity on new datasets. Major findings are summarised in Table 8.11.

By creating regression models, we identified a small set of words directly influencing the rating scores. They suggest that raters tend to evaluate the speeches in which a speaker focuses on the completion of their communicative mission and the essays in which a writer pays due attention to formality and grammatical accuracy.

Also, the obtained models, when applied to new datasets, were proven to explain approximately 22 % of the variance of the speech scores and 10 % of the variance of the essay scores. The expected gaps were only 10.7–11.3 in ORS prediction and

1.04–1.09 in level prediction. This suggests that even if it cannot substitute human raters, an automated assessment may help L2 teachers quickly grasp the rough quality of learner outputs. In this sense, LC-based automated assessment studies, which have been sporadic due to the lack of appropriate output-based assessment data, seem to be an up-and-coming field of research.

8.4 Benchmark Sample Identification

8.4.1 Aim and RQ

In Section 8.1.1.4, we noted that using the ENS outputs as a reference for CIA and as a model for L2 teaching can be problematic because the linguistic quality of the ENS outputs is not necessarily guaranteed (Leech, 1998), and it may lead to the imposition of ENS centrism on learners and teachers (Timmis, 2013). This suggests the potential merits of using high-quality learner outputs whose values are accepted by a majority of raters as a new reference. However, whether low-quality ENS outputs and high-quality learner outputs are really found, how conventional CIA changes when adopting learner outputs as a yardstick, and how we can utilise high-quality learner outputs in classes are all unclear. Therefore, expanding the analysis in Ishikawa (forthcoming), this study examines the following research questions:

RQ1 Are all the ENS outputs rated as a top-level sample?
RQ2 Are there any learner outputs rated as a top-level sample?
RQ3 How does the choice of a different yardstick influence the result of the CIA-based keyword analysis?
RQ4 What learner samples are chosen as a benchmark representing different levels?
RQ5 How can we use the benchmark samples in L2 classes?

8.4.2 Data and Method

Here again, we analyse the 120 raters' assessment data taken from the ICNALE Global Rating Archives. The target samples include 140 speech clips from the part-time job roleplays and the same number of part-time job essays, both of which were produced by 136 learners and 4 ENS.

First, following the procedure presented in Section 8.3, we calculate the overall rating scores (ORS), which is an average of the 100-point analytical score sum and the 100-point holistic score, and classify the output samples into six levels: A (70%+), B (60%+), C (50%+), D (40%+), E (30%+), and F (<30%). Also, when identifying benchmark samples, we pay attention to the coefficient of variance (CV) of the ORS values. CV is calculated by dividing standard deviation with the mean, and it represents the degree of variance after normalising the difference in the means. Speeches and essays with lower CV values could be better candidates for the benchmark samples of different quality levels.

For RQ1, we examine the ORS values and the ORS-based levels of four ENS speeches and the same number of ENS essays.

For RQ2, we identify learners' speeches and essays whose ORS values reach 70% or above.

For RQ3, we compare the roleplay speeches (8,079 words) and essays (103,825 words) about the part-time job topic produced by all the EFL learners at A2 level with various yardsticks. First, regarding the speeches, as the ICNALE Spoken Dialogues collects the ENS outputs only from the teachers, we use two kinds of yardsticks: the outputs of ENS teachers (ENS_2) and the Level A learner outputs. Then, regarding the essays, as the ICNALE Written Essays collect the ENS outputs from three occupational groups, we use five kinds of yardsticks: the outputs of ENS students (ENS_1: a peer reference), ENS teachers (ENS_2: a pedagogical reference), ENS business people (ENS_3: a business reference), and all the ENS participants (ENS_1–3: a general reference) (see Section 2.2.1), as well as Level A learner outputs. We conduct keyword analyses based on the log-likelihood ratios (LLR) and identify the top-ten words overused most significantly by A2 learners (see Section 4.3.2). Finally, we examine to what degree an ENS yardstick and a new learner yardstick yield different keywords.

Next, for RQ4, among all the samples classified into each of the six levels (A–F), we choose the four samples with the lowest CV values. These samples, whose quality is unanimously accepted by a variety of raters, can be regarded as a benchmark representing each level.

Finally, for RQ5, choosing a pair of high/low-quality benchmark outputs produced by learners with the same L1 backgrounds as a sample, we illustrate how an L2 teacher can apply a CIA technique to L2 teaching by encouraging the students to critically compare a pair of the peer learner outputs. This will outline the possibility of CIA and L2 teaching free from the conventional ENS references and the ENS centrism that they may bring.

8.4.3 Results and Discussions

8.4.3.1 RQ1 ENS Output Quality

To what degree are the ENS speeches and essays appropriate as a reference and also a model? The ORS values and ORS-based levels of the eight ENS output samples (four speeches and four essays) are shown in Table 8.12.

Among four ENS teacher speeches, three are classified as Level A, and the mean ORS value reaches 78.64, while among four student essays, only one is classified as Level A, and the mean ORS value is only 64.66. This means that the ENS outputs, especially students outputs, are not always the best in quality, which reminds us of the warning in Leech (1998).

Here we like to examine the ENS outputs showing relatively lower ORS values. Table 8.13 shows the beginning parts of the speech of ENS_003 (interviewee turns only) and the essay of ENS_002.

TABLE 8.12 ORS and ORS-based levels of ENS output samples

	Code	*Region*	*Occupation*	*ORS*	*SD*	*CV*	*Level*
Speech	ENS_003	US	Teacher	66.76	14.63	0.22	B
	ENS_004	UK	Teacher	81.50	18.27	0.22	A
	ENS_011	CAN	Teacher	83.34	18.00	0.22	A
	ENS_019	AUS	Teacher	82.94	15.02	0.18	A
	Mean	—	—	78.64	16.48	0.21	[A]
Essay	ENS_001	AUS	Student	68.69	22.05	0.32	B
	ENS_002	UK	Student	57.03	26.35	0.46	C
	ENS_003	NZL	Student	72.57	18.31	0.25	A
	ENS_006	US	Student	60.35	20.70	0.34	B
	Mean	—	—	64.66	21.85	0.34	[B]

TABLE 8.13 ENS speeches and essays with the low ORS values

Speech of ENS_003 (Male) (ORS= 66.76)	*Essay of ENS_002 (Female) (ORS= 57.03)*
[S1] Well, I need the money for my social life and our – as you know, my paying the tuitions and college life is not easy. [S2] That's right. That part I understand, but I try my best to balance my ah … studying as well as my working hours. [S3] I agree with that, studying is my first priority, but at the meantime as in the life that we live, we do need some extra income. As long as I can keep up with my studies and make the extra time to do my study and do a good job, doing my homework and study, I can also put some hours [Overlapping]….	It's not. But it never ceases to amaze me how many ordinary people believe that it is and then they regurgitate an awful lot of these boring old wives tales like; character building, responsibility, work experience etc. What a load of bollocks. It is quite simply a case by case scenario really and that's all it is. Those that need a few extra quid for university fees, college fees, books, party cash or living expenses, work part-time jobs and those who are cashed up, don't. That's it in a nutshell really and end of story …

Note: S1, S2, and S3 represent the first, second, and third turn for the interviewee.

The speech of the ENS_003 is sophisticated in terms of lexis and grammar, but the speaker tends to keep his turns for a longer time rather than increasing the interactions with the interviewer, and he speaks quite slowly with many pauses and hesitations, all of which makes his speech sound passive and responsive rather than persuasive. It is true that he sufficiently speaks, but he just repeats the same content ("I need the money") without developing his claim, and most of what he says is highly abstract ("college life is not easy," "try my best to balance my … studying as well as my working hours," "studying is my first propriety"). Considering these points, this speech, though it is made by an ENS teacher, is less likely to be a good model for others to follow.

On the contrary, the ENS_002 is a passionate and eloquent writer. She presents a unique discussion, where her good sense of irony often stands out. Her claim is interesting and reasonable, but her consistent use of colloquial vocabulary ("an awful lot of ...," "these boring old wives tales," "What a load of bollocks") and the colloquial grammar ("It's not" ➔ "A part-time job is not important for college students," "It is quite simply a case by case scenario really ..." ➔ "It is (quite) simply a case-by-case scenario," "Those that ..." ➔ "Those who, ..." "work part-time jobs" ➔ "work part-time" or "do/have a part-time job") makes her text less academic and even less readable, which presumably explains why relatively lower rating scores are assigned to this essay. As in the case of the speech of ENS_003, it would be difficult for us to regard this essay as a model for students.

CIA researchers and L2 teachers have a general tendency to believe in the outstanding value of the ENS outputs as an example of "standard" English, but the assessment data suggests that the ENS outputs may not always be a good referential yardstick for CIA and a good model for L2 learners to follow.

8.4.3.2 RQ2 Level A Learner Outputs

In the last section, we confirmed that some of the ENS outputs are not classified as Level A. Then, are there any learner outputs classified as Level A? The analysis of the assessment data identified 11 speeches and 9 essays belonging to the top level, which are shown in Table 8.14.

TABLE 8.14 Level A learner samples

	Code	*Proficiency*	*ORS*	*SD*	*CV*
Speech	THA_021	B1_2	83.21	16.08	0.19
	KOR_013	B2+	78.84	13.67	0.17
	CHN_038	B2+	77.86	14.87	0.19
	HKG_012	B2+	75.47	14.93	0.20
	TWN_001	B2+	73.89	15.09	0.20
	KOR_016	B1_2	73.46	17.1	0.23
	TWN_034	B1_2	73.33	12.06	0.16
	HKG_005	B2+	71.38	15.17	0.21
	CHN_035	B2+	70.79	17.53	0.25
	IDN_012	B1_2	70.36	16.12	0.23
	CHN_032	B2+	70.28	14.45	0.21
Essay	SIN_006	B2+	79.87	16.90	0.21
	PHL_064	B2+	77.42	14.90	0.19
	SIN_005	B2+	77.13	15.89	0.21
	SIN_014	B2+	76.98	19.12	0.25
	HKG_008	B2+	75.04	17.45	0.23
	CHN_009	B1_2	73.87	16.74	0.23
	IDN_177	B2+	70.68	18.62	0.26
	CHN_160	B2+	70.38	18.15	0.26
	KOR_004	B2+	70.24	20.07	0.29

Table 8.14 exemplifies that not only ENS but also learners can produce top-quality outputs, which is a natural but important finding to be noted. Most of the Level A samples are produced by ESL earners at B2+ level, but some of them are produced by EFL learners and also learners at B1 level. These learner samples can be a candidate for a new non-ENS reference for CIA and also as a new model in L2 teaching.

8.4.3.3 RQ3 Effects of a Yardstick Choice

To what extent do Level A learner samples stand as a new yardstick for CIA? Tables 8.15 and 8.16 summarise the sets of the top-ten overused keywords of Asian EFL learners at A2 level, when compared to the ENS and learner yardsticks. All the keywords are significant at α=.05 level. Among the keywords chosen from the learner yardstick, the items overlapping with those from the ENS yardsticks appear in italics.

Regarding the speech keywords, seven of the ten items chosen from the learner yardstick overlap with those from the most canonical ENS-teacher

TABLE 8.15 Top-ten speech keywords chosen from two kinds of yardsticks

ENS_2	*Learner*
uh	*umm*
umm	*uh*
study	*money*
want	*college*
money	hmm
college	yes
yeah	*yeah*
eh	*eh*
borrow	*I*
I	want

TABLE 8.16 Top-ten essay keywords chosen from five kinds of yardsticks

ENS_1	*ENS_2*	*ENS_3*	*ENS_1–3*	*Learner*
we	we	we	we	*we*
money	you	money	money	I
society	part	part	part	*money*
study	money	you	job	*think*
must	job	time	time	*can*
job	time	can	can	lot
free	can	job	society	know
agree	think	our	you	don
earn	our	society	must	*because*
because	so	think	our	't

yardstick ("umm," "uh," "money," "college," "yeah," "eh," "I"). Regarding the essay keywords, five of the ten items from the learner yardstick overlap with those from some of the four kinds of ENS yardsticks ("we," "money," "think," "can," "because"). Though the number of overlapping keywords seems to be somewhat smaller in essays, it is also small even between the ENS yardsticks (e.g., three between ENS_1 and ENS_2, and four between ENS_1 and ENS_3).

Considering these points, we could safely conclude that a learner yardstick is qualified to be considered as one of the new yardsticks for CIA. As avoiding any type of ENS reference in CIA seems to be extreme and even unreal, using a learner yardstick in addition to the ENS yardsticks would be a reasonable option. It helps researchers see the learner interlanguage from a more diversified and balanced viewpoint, and it also contributes to neutralising the ENS centrism inherent in the traditional L1 and L2 comparisons.

8.4.3.4 RQ4 Learners' Benchmark Samples

We already identified Level A learner outputs (RQ2), but Table 8.14 exemplifies that some samples show relatively higher CV values. Also, it would be more desirable for us to have not only the top-level samples but also a set of samples representing different output quality levels. Thus, we chose four learner samples showing the lowest CV values for each of the six levels (Table 8.17), which we regard as the candidates for new non-ENS benchmark samples.

These benchmark samples can be utilised for various types of research aiming to clarify the aspects of L2 outputs of Asian learners of English. As the quality level of each of these outputs is determined not by the judgement of someone but by the collective knowledge of raters with varied L1 and occupational backgrounds, these samples would expand the possibility of CIA independent from the ENS reference.

8.4.3.5 RQ5 Comparison of Benchmark Samples

These benchmark samples can also be utilised for L2 teaching. In this section, we would like to propose a task making Asian students qualitatively compare a pair of high/low-quality outputs produced by learners with the same regional backgrounds. This is an attempt to combine CIA with discovery learning (DL) (Bruner, 1961), more specifically, data-driven learning (DDL) (Johns, 1991). As the proposed task needs no ENS models, it is least likely to impose ENS centrism on Asian learners.

DL focuses on the act of "rearranging or transforming evidence in such a way that one is enabled to go beyond the evidence so reassembled to additional new insights" (Bruner, 1961). It is often characterised by the 4E principles—"elicit, engage, experience, explore" (Bicknell-Holmes & Hoffman, 2000). DL usually entails the elements such as (1) exploration and problem-solving, which lead to creating, integrating, and generalising knowledge; (2) student-driven and interest-based activities, in which the student should be given the right to determine the sequence and frequency of learning; and (3) activities to encourage the integration of new knowledge into the learner's existing knowledge base (Bicknell-Holmes & Hoffman, 2000).

TABLE 8.17 Candidates for the non-ENS benchmark samples

Lev	*Speech*				*Essay*			
	Learner	*Profic.*	*ORS*	*CV*	*Learner*	*Profic.*	*ORS*	*CV*
A	THA_021	B1_2	83.21	0.19	SIN_006	B2+	79.87	0.21
	KOR_013	B2+	78.84	0.17	PHL_064	B2+	77.42	0.19
	CHN_038	B2+	77.86	0.19	SIN_005	B2+	77.13	0.21
	TWN_034	B1_2	73.33	0.16	HKG_008	B2+	75.04	0.23
B	TWN_002	B2+	69.78	0.21	TWN_007	B2+	69.65	0.19
	KOR_008	B2+	67.22	0.21	IDN_178	B2+	69.42	0.21
	CHN_037	B1_2	67.09	0.21	IDN_161	B2+	67.89	0.22
	CHN_046	B2+	62.93	0.19	JPN_014	B1_1	66.92	0.22
C	CHN_047	B1_1	58.96	0.22	JPN_008	B1_1	59.58	0.24
	THA_002	B1_2	57.72	0.22	TWN_012	B2+	59.46	0.24
	MYS_015	B1_2	55.54	0.22	KOR_030	B1_2	58.24	0.24
	KOR_018	B2+	54.22	0.21	TWN_010	A2	55.94	0.23
D	IDN_026	A2	48.29	0.27	IDN_009	B1_2	49.72	0.30
	KOR_005	B2+	45.94	0.28	IDN_027	B1_2	49.31	0.31
	CHN_027	B1_1	44.78	0.27	KOR_013	B2+	48.27	0.30
	JPN_004	B1_1	43.63	0.26	THA_001	B1_2	45.24	0.27
E	THA_013	B1_1	39.97	0.34	THA_003	A2	39.90	0.44
	THA_003	B1_2	39.43	0.33	IDN_020	B1_2	39.54	0.41
	CHN_036	B1_1	39.27	0.32	IDN_004	B1_1	38.65	0.39
	KOR_001	B1_1	38.14	0.32	KOR_010	B1_2	37.59	0.39
F	TWN_025	A2	28.80	0.53	THA_012	A2	29.76	0.60
	JPN_010	B1_2	27.68	0.65	PAK_114	B2+	29.70	0.61
	THA_009	A2	25.72	0.48	TWN_016	A2	28.14	0.55
	THA_006	B1_1	22.50	0.60	TWN_013	A2	27.96	0.60

Note: "Profic." represents the proficiency levels. As the ICNALE Global Rating Archives is still under construction, these are the tentative candidates for benchmark samples.

DDL is one of the applications of a DL principle to L2 learning. It is defined as a "microcomputer-based approach to foreign language learning," where the task of a student is to "'discover' the foreign language" rather than to memorise it, and that of a teacher is to provide "a context in which the learner can develop strategies for discovery—strategies through which he or she can 'learn how to learn" (Johns, 1991). In its original definition, DDL is based on the students' hands-on corpus analysis on their computers. However, many scholars also suggest the merits of "paper-based" DDL (Boulton, 2010), in which the students analyse the materials printed on the worksheet (e.g., concordance lines, text extracts, a list of the keywords) and answer the guided questions prepared by a teacher. The twin foundations of DDL, "authenticity and autonomy," are maintained in both types of DDL (Timmis, 2015, p. 135).

The proposed task can be conducted with and without computers, in other words, both as a hard and a soft version of DDL (Gabrielatos, 2005). In each case, the comparison of peer Asian student outputs of different quality levels will help the students discover and grasp what a good speech/essay is, how it is different from a less good speech/essay, and how they can come closer to a good model, through their own interaction with the text data. So long as a good output model is taken from learner outputs rather than ENS outputs, this task can be free from the risk of imposing a false identity on learners.

Meaningful text comparison might be somewhat difficult for those who have never experienced that. In that case, prior to the student task, a teacher can demonstrate how to analyse and compare the texts. Here we would like to present sample analyses of the speeches of THA_021 (Male, B1_2, ORS: 83.2, Level: A) and THA_006 (Male, B1_1, ORS: 22.5, Level: F) as well as the essays of KOR_004 (Female, B2+, ORS: 70.2, Level A) and KOR_003 (Female, B1_1, ORS: 31.3, Level: E).

First, two Thai learners' persuasion speeches are shown in Table 8.18.

Though there are many differences to be mentioned, it would be better for a teacher to focus just on a few points. Here we pay attention to the four points: speech quantity, reasons for a claim, respect for the collocutor, and flexibility in a claim.

First, regarding the quantity, THA_021 speaks 189 words, while THA_006 speaks only 58 words in the same roleplay task, which suggests that the former is more fluent and more willing to persuade the interviewer. This is also suggested by the occurrence of overlapping in the speech of THA_021. A teacher could make the students confirm that speaking enough is a prerequisite for a good speech.

Then, regarding the reason for a claim, THA_021 says that he needs to continue working part-time because his mother is sick and his family cannot afford to take care of her. Presenting such concrete reasons makes his claim more reasonable and persuasive. Meanwhile, THA_006 just says that he needs to work because he wants money and experience. His explanation is largely abstract, and he never explains why he wants money and what experiences he wants to have. Thus, THA_006's claim may sound somewhat selfish and unreasonable. Through such analysis, a teacher could suggest that a good claim always has good reasons.

Next, regarding the respect for the collocutor, THA_021 consistently pays respect to the interviewer as a college supervisor, who is concerned about the decrease in his school grade. Thus, he says "I understand" as many as four times, and he explicitly says that he really appreciates the teacher's advice, which helps to maintain the teacher's "face" (see Section 6.1.1.2). Meanwhile, THA_006 almost always talks about his own wants and needs and shows no respect for the collocutor's standpoint. By pointing out this difference, a teacher could help the students understand that even when persuading someone, one needs to respect the collocutor's face, and pragmatic and sociolinguistic appropriateness is a key to a good speech.

Finally, regarding flexibility in a claim, THA_021 faces a disagreement of opinions during the interaction, and he tries to reconcile the opposing standpoints by flexibly suggesting a new option to continue working and study more, which is a more acceptable option from the collocutor's viewpoint. Such flexibility is not seen in the speech of THA_006. Here a teacher could show that what matters in conversation is not to stick to one's claim but to create a co-understanding and a new solution through the exchange of opinions.

As surveyed above, THA_021's speech can be one of the good models to follow for Asian learners. It is true that there remain a few minor grammatical problems in his speech, but this should be regarded as a merit rather than as a demerit in using a

TABLE 8.18 Benchmark speeches of A/F levels (THA_021 and THA_006)

Speech of THA_021 (male) *(ORS= 83.2, Level= A)*	*Speech of THA_006 (male)* *(ORS=22.5, Level= F)*
[S1] Okay, I—I understand it, like recently my grade is really low. Uh, I will try my best in order to get a higher grade, but for now I really—I really necessary to use the money from this part time job because my mom is sick, and actually like my family doesn't really have much money for those. So I try to save money as much as I can in order to save my mom, and I understand that like learning is also important for me, but I feel like I—now as I really need to do something instead. [T1] Okay, so there is one thing that you can do, apart from working. So you can ask for scholarships, you know. [S2] Right, I understand. [T2] So, why don't you do that and you—you don't need to work and you can have more time to concentrate on your study only. I think it's much better. What do you think? [S3] I understand what you saying but my—my—my mother case real kind of urgent. If I have to wait for scholarships, that gonna take quite long. But that's a really good idea from you. I really appreciate from you, from your idea. So, I'm just gonna try to work hard in order to gain a better grade and also I really have to learn. [Overlapping] [T3] Oo, oo, you said work hard, right? So, it means you gonna spend more hours on working? [S4] No, in this case, in working hard I mean like study harder. [T4] Uh-huh, I see. You have to make yourself clear. [S5] Okay. [T5] Okay, you gonna study harder. [S6] Yeah, study harder. [T6] And how? Can you tell me some example, how you gonna deal with them? [S7] Like how I'm gonna …	[S1] I is—I is want to—I want to work part time continue, because I, uh, want some money and, uh, experience in me. [T1] You mean, uh, work experience. [S2] Yeah. [T2] And why do you need it now? I think you need to finish your study first. [S3] Uh, I think part time—part time, uh, is less time in the day, uh, when, uh, after me—uh, after—after me learn—me—me can—hmm, we can work part time. [T3] But why don't you spend a few hours to study instead of working? Because I think you need to spend more time to study, not for working, to in—to get the better grade. Your grade is low, see …

Note: [S] and [T] represent an interviewee (student) and an interviewer (teacher), respectively.

learner output as a model. By lightly mentioning the problems in a class, a teacher can naturally encourage the students to focus on form (Long & Robinson, 1998). Also, the students will understand that even the most highly rated speeches may sometimes include small mistakes, but they do not cause a problem in communication, and they do not influence the rating. This seems to be an important lesson for Asian students, who tend to pay attention only to grammatical accuracy when speaking and writing in L2.

Next, two Korean learners' essays are shown in Table 8.19.

TABLE 8.19 Benchmark essays of A/E levels (KOR_004 and KOR_003)

Essay of KOR_004 (female) (ORS= 70.2, Level= A)	*Essay of KOR_003 (female) (ORS=31.3, Level= E)*
I disagree with the statement that it is important for college students to have a part time job. While it is true that college tuition fees are high these days, there have also been scholarships and loans being offered too. I believe that this has to take into account the idea of "opportunity cost." Take for example the case of a student who is deciding whether or not to work to support his studies or to spend more time studying to obtain a better result. The student has the option of working harder and spending more time to study to obtain scholarship for his studies. The scholarship could solve the student's financial problems in addition to getting excellent results. I believe that this is an issue of investment of time. Students who do part time job are generally tired when they attend classes. This could affect their studies indirectly. A person could choose to instead invest his or her time on studies instead while applying for a loan to support the tuition fees. Being able to pay the tuition fees by working part time and being tired or sleepy in classes is not a good option. By doing the comparison, spending more time on studies thus getting better results and obtaining a scholarship is a better one. In conclusion, the statement that it is important for college students to have a part time job should be discarded as it is not a viable alternative of solving a person's financial constraint problems. It is not wise for a student to forgo his studies to support his or her school tuition fees.	These days, fee of university is expensive. Many students are given to an exhibition or it is difficulty that having a part-time job and going to university. So, I agree to important for college students having a part-time job. First, Grow up students assists of parents. Make your pocket money and fee of university for having a part-time job. Naturally, it is difficult that concentrate of major and it is tired to less of sleeping. Immunity is weak, so you should sick but, everybody parent is not rich. So, they have a part-time job. Second, a part-time job is kind of social life. Therefore, they are experience to social life and after their graduate university, it is important to experience social life. Naturally, university life is community life. But, it is different to having part-time job. Last, you having a part-time job are realized value of money. One is non-having a part-time job; the other is having a part-time job. It is different that wastefully of money. Non-having a part-time job does not realize value of money. But, having a part-time job buy something is think about spend the money. It is important for college students to have a part-time job. Therefore, I think I agree to important for college students having a part-time job.

As mentioned in the comparison of speeches, it would be better for a teacher to focus on a few points that they think are the most important for the students. Here we discuss three points: grammatical accuracy, reference to the authority, and flexibility in a claim.

First, regarding grammatical accuracy, language problems are observed in both essays. However, the number of errors in the essay of KOR_004 is smaller, and they hardly influence the intelligibility of the text (e.g., "there have also been … too" ➔ "there have also been …," "this has to take into account …" ➔ "one has to take into account …"). Meanwhile, the essay of KOR_003 includes a great number of serious errors, and they significantly deteriorate the intelligibility of the text. For example, its second sentence ("Many students are given to an exhibition …") would be the least readable for most readers. By pointing out some of these problems, showing how they should be corrected, and explaining the difference between local errors and global errors, a teacher could help the students be more careful and attentive writers. The students would also realise that even a highly rated essay may include a few small errors, which should encourage them.

Second, as regards the reference to the authority, KOR_004 often borrows terms and concepts from economics by mentioning "opportunity cost" and "investment of time." This expands the scope of her discussion and makes her claim more academic and reliable. Meanwhile, KOR_003 discusses only the matters about herself or around her personal life—a family and college life, for instance, which makes her claim sound less persuasive. By analysing the effects of the technical terms adopted in the essays, a teacher can demonstrate how academic writing is different from other types of writing and make the students understand the importance of standing on the shoulders of giants when insisting on something.

Finally, flexibility in a claim is an important factor common to both good speeches and good essays. Most of the writers who are given this topic tend to mention the importance of either money or study (e.g., Students should work part-time to earn money/Students should not work part-time but focus on their studies). However, if a writer chooses one of the two options about a highly controversial topic, their claim may not be supported by readers having different opinions. Therefore, KOR_004 flexibly presents the third option by suggesting to study hard, gain a scholarship, and obtain money. Her claim reconciles the opposition between money and study, and therefore it would satisfy a wider range of readers. Meanwhile, KOR_003's essay seems to include serious confusion in terms of logic. At the end of her essay, she concludes that it is important for college students to work part-time. From such a standpoint, she mentions that it helps the students to be independent and financially "assist" their families, experience society beforehand, and understand the value of money. However, she also insists that working part-time makes it difficult for the students to concentrate on their studies, and it may affect their health. Opposing opinions presented in parallel make it extremely difficult for readers to understand her position. By pointing out such a difference seen in the logical structures of the two essays, a teacher could make the students grasp that when writing a topic essay, it is vital to analyse the topic carefully, establish one's claim flexibly, and present it logically.

As illustrated in the two analyses shown above, a teacher-centred guided text comparison activity can be a good introductory task for novice students. As a next step, a teacher could encourage them to analyse a new set of benchmark outputs by themselves, which greatly helps them be more careful and conscious speakers and writers.

In the sample analyses above, we compared the outputs of Level A and Levels E/F. However, a teacher can choose the levels of the outputs to be compared freely from the six levels (A–F) according to the proficiency of the target students and the needed task difficulty level. Regarding the former, a comparison of Levels A and B may be suitable for advanced students, while a comparison of Levels B, C, and D may suit intermediate students. Then, regarding the latter, a comparison of the outputs of near levels (e.g., Levels A and B) can be naturally more challenging than a comparison of those of far levels (e.g., Levels A and F). Also, when demonstrating the sample analyses, a teacher can add a level guessing task. For example, a teacher presents the students with a pair of the benchmark outputs of Level A and Level C without clarifying each level. The students are then encouraged to discuss which is better and why they think so. Through the scrutiny of each sample with their own eyes and discussion with the others, the students will deepen their understanding of the essence of a good speech/essay.

From a pedagogical viewpoint, such an approach leads to a harmonious combination of a reading skill's teaching and a writing skill's teaching, which is another possibility of DDL (Timmis, 2015, p. 136).

8.4.4 Summary

In this section, we used the assessment data from the ICNALE Global Rating Archives and analysed the aspects of a set of level-specified benchmark samples. Major findings are summarised in Table 8.20.

A series of analyses conducted in this section suggest that leaner benchmark samples identified from the rating dataset can be utilised for various research and teaching purposes.

As mentioned in Section 8.1.1.4, the use of a limited set of ENS outputs as a sole source for LCR/CIA and ELT can be problematic because it does not represent the variety of the actual English language use in the contemporary world, including the spreading ELF use, and it may cause the imposition of ENS centrism or a false identity on learners and teachers. However, excluding any type of ENS references would be unreal and even unnecessary (Gilquin, 2022). Therefore, collecting a sizable amount of performance-based rating data, choosing a reliable set of learner samples representing different quality levels, and using the identified benchmark samples as an additional yardstick for research and teaching matter to us.

Summarising Willis (1999), Timmis (2015) introduces five models with which L2 teachers can present their students: (i) standard British English, (ii) international English (i.e., ELF), (iii) world Englishes, (iv) successful L1 speakers' (i.e., learners') outputs, and (v) native speaker English plus a consciousness-raising task (pp. 190–192). The approach we have demonstrated in this section can be

TABLE 8.20 Summary of the findings: aspects of benchmark samples

Criteria	*Speech*	*Essay*
ENS output quality	Mean ORS: 78.64 Mean Level: A	Mean ORS: 64.66 Mean Level: B
Level A learner outputs	11 samples CHN:3 HKG/KOR/TWN:2 IDN/THA:1	9 samples SIN:3 CHN:2 HKG/IDN/KOR/PHL:1
Learners' overused keywords	Overlapping in the keywords based on learner and ENS yardsticks: 7/10 words	Overlapping in the keywords based on learner and ENS yardsticks: 5/10 words
Learners' Benchmark samples	Level A (THA, KOR, CHN, TWN) Level B (CHN:2, TWN, KOR) ...	Level A (SIN:2, PHL, HKG) Level B (IDN:2, JPN, TWN) ...
Pedagogical application	Teacher-centred learner benchmark text comparison ➔ Student-centred learner benchmark text comparison	

classified as the fourth type. Timmis suggests that it may lead to limited exposure to "different cultures and different language communities," but when using learner outputs as an additional model rather than an alternative model, we could minimise its potential drawback.

Finally, we would like to mention the further possibility of combining learners' output rating data with other learner-related data. Regarding the relationship between learners' proficiency and their output text quality, Durrant et al. (2021) suggest that the validity of inference "from text to proficiency" is not wholly guaranteed. They note, "even if a writer with a specified underlying proficiency creates a piece of writing with particular textual characteristics, it does not thereby follow that any text with those characteristics could only be produced by someone with the specified proficiency" because "any identified linguistic properties of a written text remain themselves the combined result of both the linguistic and the extralinguistic" resources. The same thing also applies, more or less, to the inference from proficiency to text. In this sense, integrating different types of data—output rating, learner proficiency, and other learner-related metadata—rather than focusing only on rating data would have many merits. First, it leads teachers and researchers to see learner outputs from a more careful and balanced viewpoint. Second, it may help neutralise conceptual conflicts existing in the previous studies of language assessment: discrete-point assessment vs. integrative assessment, direct assessment vs. indirect assessment, objective assessment vs. subjective assessment, and group assessment vs. individual assessment (Leclercq & Edmonds, 2014). Third, it is expected to promote data triangulation in LCR (see Chapter 9) and enhance the reliability of the findings from LC. These possibilities need to be further explored in LCR. ICNALE, which includes a variety of text/learner-related data, could contribute to such a new challenge.

9
CONCLUSION

In the previous chapters, we discussed the possibilities of applying the ICNALE data to learner corpus research (LCR) by presenting sample studies focusing on vocabulary, grammar, pragmatics, individual differences, and assessment. A variety of data included in ICNALE would undoubtedly expand the scope of LCR and enable researchers and teachers to examine the aspects of Asian learners' spoken and written L2 English use from a newer and wider perspective than before. In this section, we would like to briefly touch upon six points to be considered when conducting an LC-based study—definition of L2 learners, dynamic systems, a yardstick, triangulation, statistics, and new research topics.

The first point is how to define L2 learners as a target of the study. In the broadest sense, L2 learners refer to any type of people learning L2 in some way. By definition, they may include young children who have just begun to learn L2, secondary school students, college students, business persons, and even near native speakers. However, most of the existing LC, including larger LC such as ICLE and ICNALE, cover only a limited range of learners. Therefore, LC researchers need to be aware that their findings may not be fully generalisable; in other words, they may not apply to the whole of the target learner groups that they like to discuss. Strictly speaking, all they can ascertain from the analyses of ICLE and ICNALE is the features of college–student learners rather than learners in general. In addition, LC researchers need to carefully consider whether they should include highly proficient speakers, especially those who regularly use L2 for professional purposes, as a target of their research. Mauranen (2011), who is one of the influential advocates of the concept of English as a lingua franca (ELF), insists that there should be a divide between learners and users, second language acquisition (SLA) and second language use (SLU), and learner corpora and ELF corpora such as VOICE. According to Mauranen, L2 users are readily distinguished from L2 learners in terms of their

DOI: 10.4324/9781003252528-11

social status (learners use L2 with those sharing the same L1, while users do not), cognition (learners focus on language forms, while users on contents), and interaction (learners accept the norms of L1 English native speakers [ENS], but users co-construct their own norms through negotiations). However, Timmis (2015) casts doubt on such a view by suggesting that "the distinction between a successful user and an advanced learner" is not clear as generally believed (p. 186).

The second point, which also concerns the definition of learners as a research target, is how to respond to the recent research trend prioritising the dynamic changes of individuals rather than the static traits of groups. Regarding this, Hamaker (2012) introduces an interesting data sample about typing speed and typo ratio. When analysing many typists as a single group, we are likely to see a negative correlation because typists with more experience type faster and make fewer mistakes. However, when re-analysing the correlation with each of them, we perhaps find a positive correlation because if a typist tries to type faster, they naturally make more mistakes. Thus, Hamaker suggests that the cross-sectional relationship at the population level does not reflect the relationship at the within-person level. This also applies to LC data. We often discuss the features of learners in general or particular learner groups (e.g., Asian learners in English as a foreign language (EFL) regions, novice learners, L1 Thai learners), but whether a group trend is applicable to each in the group is not necessarily guaranteed. Then, Verspoor et al. (2021) insist that L2 development should be redefined from a perspective of a complex dynamic systems theory (CDST), which is based on the "longitudinal, individual case studies with enough data points in which various subsystems of the linguistic system are plotted and traced." They also note, "[w]hile developmental findings of individual cases cannot be generalised to groups of learners, the results from group studies cannot be individualised, as they cannot reveal the nonlinear and variable paths that individual learners tend to follow." Also, Bulté and Housen (2020) suggest that CDST approach, which is often based on the "longitudinal designs with increased density of data collection" or the mixed-method research designs, enables researchers to discuss (i) L2 development in learners over time, (ii) individual developmental pathways rather than an overall developmental trend, (iii) variation and individual differences as well as non-linear development and variability, and (iv) interrelationships between a variety of related variables, though they carefully add that these merits of CDST do not deny the values of conventional cross-sectional studies. It is true that there hardly exist full-scale longitudinal LC with enough data collection points, but LC users would be encouraged to pay attention not only to cross-sectional data but also to longitudinal data when discussing L2 learners' developments.

The third point is how to choose an appropriate yardstick for a comparative study. Traditionally, many LC researchers have used a relatively narrow range of ENS outputs as a sole reference. Gilquin (2022) reports that more than 80% of the representative LC studies are more or less dependent on ENS data (see Section 4.4.4 and 8.1.1.4). However, this may potentially lead to the strengthening of "[n]ative speaker authority and superior expertise" (Mauranen, 2011). Regarding the narrowness in the range of referential data, recent LC researchers have come to grope for greater diversity in it. The CIA2 model (Granger, 2015), for instance, encourages us to pay sufficient attention to register/dialect variability in reference (see Section 1.3.2). Gilquin (2022) also mentions that LC researchers should note a possible variety in native reference data in terms of the regions (e.g., British or American), literacy levels (e.g., non-expert or expert), and text types (e.g., argumentative essays or others). Then, regarding the dependence on ENS outputs, Gilquin (2022) presents two noteworthy suggestions. One is to use non-native expert outputs (e.g., academic papers) or institutionalised "new Englishes" as an alternative reference. The other is to focus only on one of the two CIA components, that is, a comparison of learners with different L1 backgrounds, with low/high L2 exposure, and at different L2 acquisition stages, or learner outputs produced in different situations (e.g., timed and untimed). When using ICNALE, researchers are also advised to pay due attention to the regional and occupational backgrounds of ENS participants and consider using high-quality learner benchmark samples as an additional yardstick for contrastive interlanguage analysis (CIA). What should be noted here is that using learner samples as a new yardstick does not necessarily mean the complete removal of the ENS references. As Gilquin admits, using "a (corpus-based and explicit) native norm … makes sense in view of (certain) learners' needs and wishes," and it does not necessarily mean that "learner language must be seen as 'deficient' if it differs from native language."

The fourth point is how to promote triangulation in terms of data, theory, and methodology. Regarding data triangulation, LC researchers first need to collect and analyse a greater variety of learner data in terms of data collection method (cross-sectional and longitudinal), production mode (spoken and written), and learner types (gender, proficiency, region, motivation). Then, regarding theoretical and methodological triangulation, LC researchers should be willing to collaborate with other research fields. As a future direction of corpus linguistics (CL), McEnery and Hardie (2012) write:

> [T]he triangulation of corpus methods with other research methodologies will be an important further step in enhancing both the rigour of corpus linguistics and its incorporation into all kinds of research, both linguistic and non-linguistic. To put it another way, the way ahead is methodological pluralism. This kind of methodological triangulation is already happening, to some extent, in the case of corpus methods and the methods of experimental psycholinguistics … But we would argue that it needs to be taken further.
>
> *(p. 227)*

Egbert and Baker (2020) point out eight benefits associated with methodological triangulation: (i) detailed and balanced presentation of the situation, (ii) comprehensive understanding of the issue, (iii) confirmation of research findings, (iv) cross-checking of data to search for (ir)regularities, (v) evidence for the validity of research findings, (vi) demonstration of the reliability of the methods and findings, (vii) robust interpretations, and (viii) collaboration among scholars with different theoretical orientations and/or methodological expertise (pp. 5–6). In addition, collaboration leads to a higher degree of data triangulation. All of these apply not only to CL but also to LCR. Some of the expected fruits of collaboration between LCR and SLA are already showcased in Le Bruyn and Paquot (2021a). What should be added here is the importance of mutual understanding and mutual concession on an equal footing. If LCR and SLA are regarded merely as data providers and data consumers, it might not be called true collaboration. As LCR needs to step further up to SLA, SLA also needs to step further up to LCR because both the two approaches have their own merits, and each has achieved a lot of things so far. As Granger (2021) emphasises, "the field of L2 studies would benefit greatly if SLA researchers were more familiar with the research carried out in LCR, and vice versa."

The fifth point is how to deal with statistics more appropriately in LCR. Paquot and Plonsky (2017) point out that some of the LC studies report only the *p*-values and advise reporting additional information such as effect size (see Section 1.3.3). In addition, LC researchers would need to be careful about the limitation existing in hypothetical testing itself. As explicitly shown in the statement of the American Statistical Association (ASA), *p*-values indicate only the incompatibility of data and model, and they never "measure the probability that the studied hypothesis is true," and as such, "[s]cientific conclusions and business or policy decisions should not be based only on whether a *p*-value passes a specific threshold" (Wasserstein & Lazar, 2016). One of the problems with *p*-values is that they are easily changeable by adopting a different statistic, which leads to the so-called *p*-hacking and data dredging. For example, when the frequencies of a target word in two 100-word essays are 10 and 20, the difference is not significant in the chi-squared test ($X^2 = 3.18$, $p = .075$, Odds ratio= .444), but it becomes significant in the log-likelihood test ($LL = 3.99$, $p = .046$). Considering these cavities, some statisticians go as far as to insist on the ban on hypothetical testing. *Basic and Applied Social Psychology*, one of the influential journals in psychology, is known to have prohibited the contributors from performing any type of null hypothesis significance testing procedure (NHSTP) in their research because "the $p < .05$ bar is too easy to pass and sometimes serves as an excuse for lower quality research." Thus, the journal editor explicitly mentions that "prior to publication, authors will have to remove all vestiges of the NHSTP (*p*-values, *t*-values, *F*-values, statements about "significant" differences or lack thereof, and so on)" (Trafimow & Marks, 2015). Though it is uncertain whether such a trend may reach applied linguistics, it would be better for LC researchers to put more emphasis on descriptive statistics rather than inferential statistics and on exploratory statistical analyses rather than confirmatory analyses.

The last point is how to further widen the research scope. There are several research topics that may not have been fully explored yet in LCR. First, a comparison of learners' L1 and L2 outputs would reveal many interesting facts. Chun et al. (2021) adopt a CIA technique to discuss evaluative stances seen in L1 Vietnamese and L2 English essays written about the same topics and by the same authors. They find out both commonalities and discrepancies between the stances expressed in two language varieties. Second, analysing the output data together with process data seems to be another promising approach. Gilquin (2021) introduces her Process Corpus of English in Education (PROCEED), which includes not only written texts but also keystroke log files and screencast (screen capture) videos. Such corpus helps researchers to analyse how writers use language and construct the texts step by step. Also, if using the eye cameras, smartphone apps, and smartwatch functions, we could collect richer physiological data such as eye movement, body temperature, heart rate, blood pressure, and blood oxygen. Combining these data with LCR would have many merits.

It is true that there exist many issues to be considered and more to be conducted, but I believe that LCR will overcome these challenges and continue developing steadily. It is a pleasure if ICNALE contributes to such further development of LCR and helps LC researchers in the world to pay increasing attention to L2 English learners in Asia.

BIBLIOGRAPHY

Ädel, A. (2008). Involvement features in writing: Do time and interaction trump register awareness? In G. Gilquin, S. Papp, & M. B. Díez-Bedmar (Eds.), *Linking up contrastive and learner corpus research* (pp. 35–53). Brill Rodopi.

Ädel, A. (2015). Variability in learner corpora. In S. Granger, G. Gilquin, & F. Meunier (Eds.), *The Cambridge handbook of learner corpus research* (pp. 401–421). Cambridge University Press.

Adolphs, S., & Carter, R. (2013). *Spoken corpus linguistics: From monomodal to multimodal.* Routledge.

Aijmer, K. (2011). *Well I'm not sure I think...* The use of *well* by non-native speakers. *International Journal of Corpus Linguistics, 16*(2), 231–254.

Alexopoulou, T., Geertzen, J., Korhonen, A., & Meurers, D. (2005). Exploring big educational learner corpora for SLA research: Perspectives on relative clauses. *International Journal of Learner Corpus Research, 1*(1), 96–129.

Altenberg, B. (1997). Exploring the Swedish component of the International Corpus of Learner English. In B. Lewandowska-Tomaszcyk & P. J. Melia (Eds.), *PALC'97: Practical applications in language corpora* (pp. 119–132). Lódz University Press.

Altenberg, B., & Tapper, M. (1998). The use of adverbial connectors in advanced Swedish learners' written English. In S. Granger (Ed.), *Learner English on computer* (pp. 80–93). Longman.

Anthony, L. (2022). *AntConc* (Version 4.0.4). [Computer Software]. Waseda University. www.laurenceanthony.net/software

Babanoğlu, M. P. (2015). A corpus-based study on the use of feelings and emotions vocabulary by male and female EFL learners. *International Journal of Language and Linguistics, 3*(4), 203–209.

Bachman, L. (1990). *Fundamental considerations in language testing.* Oxford University Press.

Bachman, L. F., & Palmer, A. (1996). *Language testing in practice: Designing and developing useful language tests.* Oxford University Press.

Baker, P. (2014). *Using corpora to analyze gender.* Bloomsbury.

Ballesteros Chica, M. G., & Fernández-Cruz, J. (2020). Design and analysis of an annotated gender-based English learner corpus. *Revista International Congress on the Didactics of the English Language, 3*(1), 1–10.

Ballier, N., Canu, S., Petitjean, C., Gasso, G., Balhana, C., Alexopoulou, T., & Gaillat, T. (2020). Machine learning for learner English: A plea for creating learner data challenges. *International Journal of Learner Corpus Research*, *6*(1), 72–103.

Ballier, N., & Martin, P. (2015). Speech annotation of learner corpora. In S. Granger, G. Gilquin, & F. Meunier (Eds.), *The Cambridge handbook of learner corpus research* (pp. 108–134). Cambridge University Press.

Barker, F., Salamoura, A., & Saville, N. (2015). Learner corpora and language testing. In S. Granger, G. Gilquin, & F. Meunier (Eds.), *The Cambridge handbook of learner corpus research* (pp. 311–533). Cambridge University Press.

Barth, D., & Schnell, S. (2022). *Understanding corpus linguistics*. Routledge.

Belz, M., Sauer, S., Lüdeling, A., & Mooshammer, C. (2017). Fluently disfluent? Pauses and repairs of advanced learners and native speakers of German. *International Journal of Learner Corpus Research*, *3*(2), 118–148.

Biber, D. (1988). *Variation across speech and writing*. Cambridge University Press.

Biber, D., Conrad, S., & Reppen, R. (1998). *Corpus linguistics: Investigating language structure and use*. Cambridge University Press.

Biber, D., Reppen, R., Staples, S., & Egbert, J. (2020). Exploring the longitudinal development of grammatical complexity in the disciplinary writing of L1-English university students. *International Journal of Learner Corpus Research*, *6*(1), 38–71.

Bicknell-Holmes, T., & Hoffman, P. S. (2000). Elicit, engage, experience, explore: Discovery learning in library instruction. *Reference Services Review*, *28*(4), 313–322.

Blanchard, D., Tetreault, J., Higgins, D., Cahill, A., & Chodorow, M. (2014). *ETS corpus of non-native written English*. [Corpus]. https://catalog.ldc.upenn.edu/LDC2014T06

Blanchard, M., & Buysse, L. (2021). *Like* in discourse marker combinations in spoken interaction. *International Journal of Corpus Linguistics and Pragmatics*, *5*(4), 463–485.

Blanco Suárez, Z., Gallardo-del-Puerto, F., & Gandón-Chapela, E. (2020). The Primary Education Learners' English Corpus (PELEC): Design and compilation. *Research in Corpus Linguistics*, *8*(1), 147–163.

Bley-Vroman, R. (1983). The comparative fallacy in interlanguage studies: The case of systematicity. *Language Learning*, *33*, 1–17.

Block, D. (2003). *The social turn in second language acquisition*. Georgetown University Press.

Boulton, A. (2010). Data-driven learning: Taking the computer out of the equation. *Language Learning*, *60*(3), 534–572.

Braine, G. (2018). Non-native-speaker English teachers. In C. A. Chapelle (Ed.), *The encyclopedia of applied linguistics* (pp. 1–5). John Wiley & Sons.

Brand, C., & Götz, S. (2011). Fluency versus accuracy in advanced spoken learner language: A multi-method approach. *International Journal of Corpus Linguistics*, *16*(2), 255–275.

Brezina, V. (2018). *Statistics in corpus linguistics: A practical guide*. Cambridge University Press.

Brezina, V., Gablasova, D., & McEnery, T. (2019). Corpus-based approaches to spoken L2 production: Evidence from the Trinity Lancaster Corpus. *International Journal of Learner Corpus Research*, *5*(2), 119–125.

Brown, A. (1995). The effect of rater variables in the development of an occupation-specific language performance test. *Language Testing*, *12*(1), 1–15.

Brown, P., & Levinson, S. C. (1987). *Politeness: Some universals in language usage*. Cambridge University Press.

Bruner, J. S. (1961). The act of discovery. *Harvard Educational Review*, *31*(1), 21–32.

Brunner, M.-L., Diemer, S., & Schmidt, S. (2016). "It's always different when you look something from the inside": Linguistic innovation in a corpus of ELF Skype conversations. *International Journal of Learner Corpus Research*, *2*(2), 323–350.

Bulté, B., & Housen, A. (2020). A critical appraisal of the CDST approach to investigating linguistic complexity in L2 writing development. In G. G. Fogal & M. H. Verspoor (Eds.), *Complex dynamic systems theory and L2 writing development* (pp. 207–238). John Benjamins.

Burnard, L. (2005). Metadata for corpus work. In M. Wynne (Ed.), *Developing linguistic corpora: A guide to good practice* (pp. 30–46). Oxbow Books.

Burstein, J., Chodorow, M., & Leacock, C. (2004). Automated essay evaluation: The Criterion online writing service. *AI Magazine*, *25*(3), 27–36.

Burstein, J., KuKich, K., Wolff, S., Lu, C., Chodorow, M., Braden-Harder, L., & Harris, M. D. (1998). Automated scoring using a hybrid feature identification technique. *Proceedings of the 36th annual meeting of the association for computational linguistics*, 206–210.

Caines, A., & Buttery, P. (2018). The effect of task and topic on opportunity of use in learner corpora. In V. Brezina & L. Flowerdew (Eds.), *Learner corpus research: New perspectives and applications* (pp. 5–27). Bloomsbury Academic.

Callies, M. (2013). Agentivity as a determinant of lexico-grammatical variation in L2 academic writing. *International Journal of Corpus Linguistics*, *18*(3), 357–390.

Callies, M. (2015). Learner corpus methodology. In S. Granger, G. Gilquin, & F. Meunier (Eds.), *The Cambridge handbook of learner corpus research* (pp. 35–55). Cambridge University Press.

Callies, M. (2016). Towards a process-oriented approach to comparing EFL and ESL varieties: A corpus-study of lexical innovations. *International Journal of Learner Corpus Research*, *2*(2), 229–251.

Carlsen, C. (2012). Proficiency level: A fuzzy variable in computer learner corpora. *Applied Linguistics*, *33*(2), 161–183.

Carroll, J. B. (1967). On sampling from a lognormal model of word-frequency distribution. In H. Kučera & W. N. Francis (Eds.), *Computational analysis of present-day American English* (pp. 406–424). Brown University.

Castello, E. (2015). Towards a longitudinal study of metadiscourse in EFL academic writing: Focus on Italian learners' use of *it*-extraposition. In E. Castello, K. Ackerley, & F. Coccetta (Eds.), *Studies in learner corpus linguistics: Research and applications for foreign language teaching and assessment* (pp. 179–197). Peter Lang.

Castello, E., & Gesuato, S. (2019). Holding up one's end of the conversation in spoken English: Lexical backchannels in L2 examination discourse. *International Journal of Learner Corpus Research*, *5*(2), 231–252.

Centre for English Corpus Linguistics (2022, January 10). *Learner corpora around the world.* Université catholique de Louvain.

Cervantes, I. M., & Gablasova, D. (2018). Phrasal verbs in spoken L2 English: The effect of L2 proficiency and L1 background. In V. Brezina & L. Flowerdew (Eds.), *Learner corpus research: New perspectives and applications* (pp. 28–46). Bloomsbury Academic.

Chapelle, C. A., & Plakans, L. (2013). Assessment and testing: Overview. In C. A. Chapelle (Ed.), *The encyclopedia of applied linguistics* (pp. 240–244). Wiley-Blackwell.

Chen, H.-I. (2010). Contrastive learner corpus analysis of epistemic modality and interlanguage pragmatic competence in L2 writing. *Arizona Working Papers in Second Language Acquisition and Teaching*, *17*, 27–51.

Chen, M. (2013). Overuse or underuse: A corpus study of English phrasal verb use by Chinese, British and American university students. *International Journal of Corpus Linguistics*, *18*(3), 418–442.

Chen, M. (2018). Beyond frequencies: Investigating the semantic and stylistic features of phrasal verbs in a three-year longitudinal study corpus by Chinese university students. In V. Brezina & L. Flowerdew (Eds.), *Learner corpus research: New perspectives and applications* (pp. 134–154). Bloomsbury Academic.

Chiang, I. A., Jhangiani, R. S., & Price, P. C. (2015). *Research methods in psychology*. (2nd Canadian ed.). B.C. Open Textbook Collection.

Chitez, M. (2014). *Learner corpus profiles: The case of Romanian learner English*. Peter Lang.

Chuang, F.-Y., & Nesi, H. (2006). An analysis of formal errors in a corpus of L2 English produced by Chinese students. *Corpora, 1*(2), 251–271.

Chung, T.-T., Bui, L.-T., & Crosthwaite, P. (2021). Evaluative stance in Vietnamese and English writing by the same authors: A corpus-informed appraisal study. *Research in Corpus Linguistics, 10*(1), 1–30.

Coates, J. (1986). *Women, men and language*. Longman.

Cook, V. (1997). Monolingual bias in second language acquisition research. *Revista Canaria de Estudios Ingleses, 34*, 35–50.

Corder, S. P. (1967). The significance of learners' errors. *International Review of Applied Linguistics in Language Teaching, 5*(4), 161–170.

Council of Europe. (2001). *Common European framework of reference for languages: Language, teaching, assessment*. Cambridge University Press.

Crossley, S., Salsbury, T., Titak, A., & McNamara, D. (2014). Frequency effects and second language lexical acquisition: Word types, word tokens, and word production. *International Journal of Corpus Linguistics, 19*(3), 301–332.

Crosthwaite, P. (2016). L2 English article use by L1 speakers of article-less languages: A learner corpus study. *International Journal of Learner Corpus Research, 2*(1) 68–100.

Crystal. D. (1995). Redefining stylistic discourse categories. In G. Melchers & B. Warren (Eds.), *Studies in Anglistics* (pp. 35–46). Almqvist & Wiksell International.

Crystal, D. (2003). *English as a lingua franca* (2nd ed.). Cambridge University Press.

Crystal, D., & Quirk, R. (1964). *Systems of prosodic and paralinguistic features in English*. Mouton.

Cunningham, U. (2009). Models and targets for the pronunciation of English in Vietnam and Sweden. *Research in Language*, 7, 113–128.

Czerwionka, L., & Olson, D. J. (2020). Pragmatic development during study abroad: L2 intensifiers in spoken Spanish. *International Journal of Learner Corpus Research, 6*(2), 125–162.

Dagneaux, E., Denness, S., Granger, S., Meunier, F., Neff, J. A., & Thewissen, J. (2008). *Error tagging manual* (Version 1.3). Centre for English Corpus Linguistics.

De Bot, K., Lowie, W., & Verspoor, M. (2005). *Second language acquisition: An advanced resource book*. Routledge.

De Cock, S. (1995). *Louvain corpus of native English conversation (LOCNEC)*. [Corpus]. https://corpora.uclouvain.be/catalog/corpus/locnec

De Cock, S. (2010). Spoken learner corpora and EFL teaching. In M. C. Campoy-Cubillo, B. Bellés-Fortuño, & M. L. Gea-Valor (Eds.), *Corpus-based approaches to English language teaching* (pp. 123–137). Continuum.

Deci, E. L., & Ryan, R. M. (1985). *Intrinsic motivation and self-determination in human behavior*. Berlin Springer Science & Business Media.

DeKeyser, R. M. (2015). Skill acquisition theory. In B. VanPatten & J. Williams (Eds.), *Theories in second language acquisition* (pp. 94–112). Routledge.

Deshors, S. C. (2016). Inside phrasal verb constructions: A co-varying collexeme analysis of verb-particle combinations in EFL and their semantic associations. *International Journal of Learner Corpus Research, 2*(1), 1–30.

Deshors, S. C. (2018). Does the passé composé influence L2 learners' use of English past tenses? A semantic exploration of the present perfect in French-English interlanguage. *International Journal of Learner Corpus Research, 4*(1), 23–53.

Deshors, S. C., Götz, S., & Laporte, S. (2016). Linguistic innovations in EFL and ESL: Rethinking the linguistic creativity of non-native English speakers. *International Journal of Learner Corpus Research*, *2*(2), 131–150.

DiCerbo, K., Lai, E., & Ventura, M. (2020). Assessment design with automated scoring in mind. In D. Yan, A. A. Rupp, & P. W. Foltz (Eds.), *Handbook of automated scoring: Theory into practice* (pp. 29–48). Routledge.

Díez-Bedmar, M. B., & Pérez-Paredes, P. (2020). Noun phrase complexity in young Spanish EFL learners' writing: Complementing syntactic complexity indices with corpus-driven analyses. *International Journal of Corpus Linguistics*, *25*(1), 4–35.

Dörnyei, Z. (2005). *The psychology of the language learner: Individual differences in second language acquisition*. Lawrence Erlbaum.

Dörnyei, Z., & Ottó, I. (1998). Motivation in action: A process model of L2 motivation. *Working Papers in Applied Linguistics*, *4*, 43–69.

Dörnyei, Z., & Skehan, P. (2003). Individual differences in second language learning. In C. J. Doughty & M. H. Long (Eds.), *The handbook of second language acquisition* (pp. 589–630). Wiley.

Dulay, H., & Burt, M. (1973). Should we teach children syntax? *Language Learning*, *23*, 95–123.

Durrant, P. (2014). Corpus frequency and second language learners' knowledge of collocations: A meta-analysis. *International Journal of Corpus Linguistics*, *19*(4), 443–477.

Durrant, P., Brenchley, M., & McCallum, L. (2021). *Understanding development and proficiency in writing*. Cambridge University Press.

Edwards, A., & Lange, R.-J. (2016). In case of innovation: Academic phraseology in the three circles. *International Journal of Learner Corpus Research*, *2*(2), 252–277.

Egbert, J., & Baker, P. (2020). Introduction. In J. Egbert & P. Baker (Eds.), *Using corpus methods to triangulate linguistic analysis* (pp. 1–21). Routledge.

Evanini, K., Heilman, M., Wang, X., & Blanchard, D. (2015). Automated scoring for the TOEFL Junior® comprehensive writing and speaking test. *ETS Research Report*, *15*(09), 1–11.

Firth, J. R. (1957). *Papers in linguistics, 1934–1951*. Oxford University Press.

Flowerdew, J. (2010). Use of signalling nouns across L1 and L2 writer corpora. *International Journal of Corpus Linguistics*, *15*(1), 36–55.

Foltz, P. W., Yan, D., & Rupp, A. A. (2020). The past, present, and future of automated scoring. In D. Yan, A. A. Rupp, & P. W. Foltz (Eds.), *Handbook of automated scoring: Theory into practice* (pp. 1–12). Routledge.

Fries, C. C. (1945). *Teaching and learning English as a foreign language*. The University of Michigan Press.

Friginal, E. (2013). Twenty-five years of Biber's multi-dimensional analysis: Introduction to the special issue and an interview with Douglas Biber. *Corpora*, *8*(2), 137–152.

Friginal, E, (2018). *Corpus linguistics for English teachers: New tools, online resources, and classroom activities*. Routledge.

Fuchs, R., & Werner, V. (2018). The use of stative progressives by school-age learners of English and the importance of the variable context: Myth vs. (corpus) reality. *International Journal of Learner Corpus Research*, *4*(2), 195–224.

Fung, L., & Carter, R. (2007). Discourse markers and spoken English: Native and learner use in pedagogic settings. *Applied Linguistics*, *28*(3), 410–439.

Gablasova, D. (2021). Corpora for second language assessment. In P. Winke & T. Brunfaut (Eds.), *The Routledge handbook of second language acquisition and language testing* (pp. 45–53). Routledge.

Gablasova, D., & Brezina, V. (2018). Disagreement in L2 spoken English: From learner corpus research to corpus-based teaching materials. In V. Brezina & L. Flowerdew (Eds.), *Learner corpus research: New perspectives and applications* (pp. 69–89). Bloomsbury Academic.

Gablasova, D., Brezina, V., & McEnery, T. (2019). The Trinity Lancaster Corpus: Development, description and application. *International Journal of Learner Corpus Research, 5*(2), 126–158.

Gablasova, D., Brezina, V., McEnery, T., & Boyd, E. (2017). Epistemic stance in spoken L2 English: The effect of task and speaker style. *Applied Linguistics, 38*(5), 613–637.

Gabrielatos, C. (2005). Corpora and language teaching: Just a fling or wedding bells. *TESL-EJ, 8*, 1–35.

Gardner. R. C., & Lambert, W. E. (1972). *Attitudes and motivation in second language learning.* Newbury House.

Gardner, R., & MacIntyre, P. (1991). An instrumental motivation in language study: Who says it isn't effective? *Studies in Second Language Acquisition, 13*(1), 57–72.

Garner, J. R. (2016). A phrase-frame approach to investigating phraseology in learner writing across proficiency levels. *International Journal of Learner Corpus Research, 2*(1), 31–67.

Gass, S. M. (1988). Integrating research areas: A framework for second language studies. *Applied Linguistics, 9*(2), 198–217.

Gerckens, C., & Gans, A. (2015). I didn't really *understood what it was about, but it really *made fun: A longitudinal corpus-based study of tense/aspect and high-frequency verbs in learner English. In E. Castello, K. Ackerley, & F. Coccetta (Eds.), *Studies in learner corpus linguistics: Research and applications for foreign language teaching and assessment* (pp. 143–157). Peter Lang.

Gilquin, G. (2000). The integrated contrastive model: Spicing up your data. *Languages in Contrast, 3*(1), 95–123.

Gilquin, G. (2008). Hesitation markers among EFL learners: Pragmatic deficiency or difference? In J. Romero-Trillo (Ed.), *Pragmatics and corpus linguistics: A mutualistic entente* (pp. 119–149). Mouton de Gruyter.

Gilquin, G. (2015). From design to collection of learner corpora. In S. Granger, G. Gilquin, & F. Meunier (Eds.), *The Cambridge handbook of learner corpus research* (pp. 9–34). Cambridge University Press.

Gilquin, G. (2019). Light verb constructions in spoken L2 English: An exploratory cross-sectional study. *International Journal of Learner Corpus Research, 5*(2), 181–206.

Gilquin, G. (2020). Learner corpora. In M. Paquot & S. Th. Gries (Eds.), *A practical handbook of corpus linguistics* (pp. 283–304). Springer.

Gilquin, G. (2021). The Process Corpus of English in Education: Going beyond the written text. *Research in Corpus Linguistics, 10*(1), 31–44.

Gilquin, G. (2022). One norm to rule them all? Corpus-derived norms in learner corpus research and foreign language teaching. *Language Teaching, 55*(1), 87–99.

Gilquin, G., De Cock, S., & Granger, S. (2010). (Eds.) *Louvain international database of spoken English interlanguage.* Press universitaires de Louvain.

Gilquin, G., & Granger, S. (2015). Learner language. In D. Biber & R. Reppen (Eds.), *The Cambridge handbook of English corpus linguistics* (pp. 418–436). Cambridge University Press.

Glaznieks, A., Frey, J.-C., Stopfner, M., Zanasi, L., & Nicolas, L. (2022). Leonide: A longitudinal trilingual corpus of young learners of Italian, German and English. *International Journal of Learner Corpus Research, 8*(1), 97–120.

Götz, S. (2019). Filled pauses across proficiency levels, L1s and learning context variables: A multivariate exploration of the Trinity Lancaster Corpus sample. *International Journal of Learner Corpus Research, 5*(2), 159–180.

Götz, S., & Mukherjee, J. (2019). Investigating the effect of the study abroad variable on learner output: A pseudo-longitudinal study on spoken German learner English. In V. Brezina & L. Flowerdew (Eds.), *Learner corpus research: New perspectives and applications* (pp. 47–65). Bloomsbury Academic.

Granger, S. (1993). International corpus of learner English. In J. Aarts, P. de Haan, & N. Oostdijk (Eds.), *English language corpora: Design, analysis, and exploitation* (pp. 57–71). Rodopi.

Granger, S. (1996). From CA to CIA and back: An integrated contrastive approach to computerized bilingual and learner corpora. In K. Aijmer, B. Altenberg, & M. Johansson (Eds.), *Languages in contrast: Papers from a symposium on text-based cross-linguistic studies* (pp. 37–51).Lund University Press.

Granger, S.(Ed.) (1998). *Learner English on computer.* Longman.

Granger, S. (2002). A bird's eye view of learner corpus research. In S. Granger, J. Hung, & S. Petch-Tyson (Eds.), *Computer learner corpora, second language acquisition and foreign language teaching* (pp. 3–33). Benjamins.

Granger, S. (2003). Error-tagged learner corpora and CALL: A promising synergy. *CALICO Journal, 20*(3), 465–480.

Granger, S. (2005). *Louvain corpus of native English essays (LOCNESS).* [Corpus]. https://corpora.uclouvain.be/catalog/corpus/locness

Granger, S. (2009). The contribution of learner corpora to second language acquisition and foreign language teaching: A critical evaluation. In K. Aijmer (Ed.), *Corpora and language teaching* (pp. 13–32). Benjamins.

Granger, S. (2015). Contrastive interlanguage analysis: A reappraisal. *International Journal of Learner Corpus Research, 1*(1), 7–24.

Granger, S. (2021). Commentary: Have learner corpus research and second language acquisition finally met? In B. Le Bruyn & M. Paquot (Eds.), *Learner corpus research meets second language acquisition* (pp. 243–257). Cambridge University Press.

Granger, S., & Bestgen, Y. (2014). The use of collocations by intermediate vs. advanced non-native writers: A bigram-based study. *International Review of Applied Linguistics in Language Teaching, 52*(3), 229–252.

Granger, S., Dagneaux, E., & Meunier, F. (Eds.) (2002). *International corpus of learner English.* Press universitaires de Louvain.

Granger, S., Dagneaux, E., Meunier, F., & Paquot, M. (Eds.) (2009). *International corpus of learner English* (Version 2). Press universitaires de Louvain.

Granger, S., Dupont, M., Meunier, F., Naets, H., & Paquot, M. (2020). *The international corpus of learner English.* (Version 3). Louvain-la-Neuve: Presses universitaires de Louvain.

Granger, S., Gilquin, G., & Meunier, F. (2015). Introduction: Learner corpus research——Past, present and future. In S. Granger, G. Gilquin, & F. Meunier (Eds.), *The Cambridge handbook of learner corpus research* (pp. 1–4). Cambridge University Press.

Granger, S., & Rayson, P. (1998). Automatic profiling of learner texts. In S. Granger (Ed.), *Learner English on computer* (pp. 119–131). Longman.

Granger, S., Swallow, H., & Thewissen, J. (2022). *The Louvain error tagging manual.* (Version 2.0). Centre for English Corpus Linguistics, Université catholique de Louvain.

Graziano, M., & Gullberg, M. (2013). Gesture production and speech fluency in competent speakers and language learners. *Proceedings of the Tilburg gesture research meeting (TiGeR) 2013*, 1–4.

Grice, P. (1975). Logic and conversation. In P. Cole & J. Morgan (Eds.), *Syntax and semantics. 3: Speech acts* (pp. 41–58). Academic Press.

Gries, S. Th., & Deshors, S. C. (2005). EFL and/vs. ESL? A multi-level regression modeling perspective on bridging the paradigm gap. *International Journal of Learner Corpus Research, 1*(1) 130–159.

Gries, S. Th., & Wulff, S. (2009). Psycholinguistic and corpus-linguistic evidence for L2 constructions. *Annual Review of Cognitive Linguistics*, 7(1), 163–186.

Gries, S. Th., & Wulff, S. (2013). The genitive alternation in Chinese and German ESL learners: Towards a multifactorial notion of context in learner corpus research. *International Journal of Corpus Linguistics, 18*(3), 327–356.

Guiraud, P. (1960). *Problèmes et méthodes de la statistique linguistique*. Presses universitaires de France.

Gut, U. (2012). The LeaP Corpus: A multilingual corpus of spoken learner German and learner English. In T. Schmidt & K. Wörner (Eds.), *Multilingual corpora and multilingual corpus analysis* (pp. 3–23). John Benjamins.

Hamaker, E. L. (2012). Why researchers should think "within-person": A paradigmatic rationale. In M. R. Mehl & T. S. Conner (Eds.), *Handbook of research methods for studying daily life* (pp. 43–61). Guilford.

Hashimoto, K., & Takeuchi, K. (2012). Prototypical design of learner support materials based on the analysis of non-verbal elements in presentation. In T. Watanabe, J. Watada, N. Takahashi, R. J. Howlett, & L. C. Jain (Eds.), *Intelligent interactive multimedia: Systems and services. Proceedings of the 5th international conference on intelligent interactive multimedia systems and services (IIMSS 2012)* (pp. 531–540). Springer.

Hasselgren, A. (1994). Lexical teddy bears and advanced learners: A study into the ways Norwegian students cope with English vocabulary. *International Journal of Applied Linguistics, 4*(2), 237–258.

Hasselgren, A. (2002). Learner corpora and language testing: Smallwords as markers of learner fluency. In S. Granger, J. Hung, & S. Petch-Tyson (Eds.), *Computer learner corpora, second language acquisition and foreign language teaching* (pp. 143–173). Benjamins.

Hendrikx, I., van Goethem, K., & Wulff, S. (2019). Intensifying constructions in French-speaking L2 learners of English and Dutch: Cross-linguistic influence and exposure effects. *International Journal of Learner Corpus Research, 5*(1), 63–103.

Herdan, G. (1960). *Quantitative linguistics*. Butterworth.

Herry-Bénit, N., Lopez, S., Kamiyama, T., & Tennant, J. (2021). The Interphonology of Contemporary English Corpus (IPCE-IPAC). *International Journal of Learner Corpus Research*, 7(2), 275–289.

Higgins, D., Ramineni, C., & Zechner, K. (2015). Learner corpora and automated scoring. In S. Granger, G. Gilquin, & F. Meunie (Eds.), *The Cambridge handbook of learner corpus research* (pp. 587–604). Cambridge University Press.

Higgs, T. V. (1984). *Teaching for proficiency: The organizing principle*. National Textbook Company.

Hijikata-Someya, Y., Ono, M., & Yamanishi, H. (2015). Evaluation by native and non-native English teacher-raters of Japanese students' summaries. *English Language Teaching, 8*(7), 1–12.

Hilton, H. (2009). Annotation and analyses of temporal aspects of spoken fluency. *CALICO Journal, 26*, 644–661.

Hilton, H., Osborne, J., Derive, M-J., Succo, N., O'Donnell, J., Billard, S., & Rutigliano-Daspet, S. (2008). *Corpus PAROLE (Parallèle Oral en Langue Étrangère)*. Laboratoire LLS – Équipe Langages, Université de Savoie.

Holliday, A. (2006). Native-speakerism. *ELT Journal, 60*(4), 385–387.

Hong, H., & Cao, F. (2014). Interactional metadiscourse in young EFL learner writing: A corpus-based study. *International Journal of Corpus Linguistics, 19*(2), 201–224.

Horch, S. (2016). Innovative conversions in South-East Asian Englishes: Reassessing ESL status. *International Journal of Learner Corpus Research, 2*(2), 278–301.

Huang, Y., Murakami, A., Alexopoulou, T., & Korhonen, A. (2018). Dependency parsing of learner English. *International Journal of Corpus Linguistics, 23*(1), 28–54.

Huiping, Z., & Yongbing, L. (2014). A corpus study of most frequently used English verbs by Chinese beginner learners from a conceptual transfer perspective. *International Journal of Corpus Linguistics, 19*(2), 252–279.

Hulstijn, J. H. (2011). Language proficiency in native and nonnative speakers: An agenda for research and suggestions for second-language assessment. *Language Assessment Quarterly, 8*(3), 229–249.

Hyland, K. (2004). *Disciplinary discourses: Social interactions in academic writing*. The University of Michigan Press.

Hyland, K. (2005). *Metadiscourse: Exploring interaction in writing*. Continuum.

Ionin, T., & Díez-Bedmar, M. (2021). Article use in Russian and Spanish learner writing at CEFR B1 and B2 levels: Effects of proficiency, native language, and specificity. In B. Le Bruyn & M. Paquot (Eds.), *Learner corpus research meets second language acquisition* (pp. 10–38). Cambridge University Press.

Ishii, Y., & Kondo, Y. (Eds.) (2020). *Eigo kyoiku ni okeru jido saiten: Genjo to kadai*. Hitsuji Shobo. [Automated scoring in English language education: The current situation and issues].

Ishikawa, S. (2013). The ICNALE and sophisticated contrastive interlanguage analysis of Asian learners of English. *Learner Corpus Studies in Asia and the World, 1*, 91–118.

Ishikawa, S. (2014). Design of the ICNALE Spoken: A new database for multi-modal contrastive interlanguage analysis. *Learner Corpus Studies in Asia and the World, 2*, 63–76.

Ishikawa, S. (2017). Learners' acquisition and use of L2 Japanese vocabulary: Influence of L1 backgrounds and L2 proficiency levels: A learner corpus-based analysis. *Acquisition of Japanese as a Second Language, 20*, 10–27.

Ishikawa, S. (2018a). The ICNALE Edited Essays; A dataset for analysis of L2 English learner essays based on a new integrative viewpoint. *English Corpus Studies, 25*, 117–130.

Ishikawa, S. (2018b). Comparison of three kinds of alternative essay-rating methods to the ESL Composition Profile. *International Journal of Computer-Assisted Language Learning and Teaching, 8*(4), 31–44.

Ishikawa, S. (2019). The ICNALE Spoken Dialogue: A new dataset for the study of Asian learners' performance in L2 English interviews. *English Teaching, 74*(4), 153–177.

Ishikawa, S. (2020a). Gender differences in L2 English persuasion role-plays: A study based on the ICNALE Spoken Dialogue. In Y. Ishikawa (Ed.), *Jienda to eigo kyoiku: Gakusaiteki apurochi* (pp. 130–151). Daigaku Kyoiuku Shuppan. [Gender and English language teaching: An integrative approach].

Ishikawa, S. (2020b). Aim of the ICNALE GRA project: Global collaboration to collect ratings of Asian learners' L2 English essays and speeches from an ELF perspective. *Learner Corpus Studies in Asia and the World, 5*, 121–144.

Ishikawa, S. (2021). *Beshikku kopasu gengogaku*. (2nd ed.). Hitsuji Shobo. [A basic guide to corpus linguistics].

Ishikawa, S. (2022). L2 English learners' gesture use in a picture description task: A study based on the ICNALE Spoken Dialogue module. In J. R. G. Ojeda & R. R. Cecilia (Eds.), *Investigación e innovación en lengua extranjera: Una perspectiva global* (pp. 721–750). Tirant Humanidades.

Ishikawa, S. (Forthcoming). A new yardstick of comparison for contrastive interlanguage analysis: A study on the ICNALE Global Rating Archives. *Proceedings of the 20th AsiaTEFL international conference.*

Ishikawa, Y. (2014). Gender differences in the ICNALE-Spoken Baby: Who uses hesitators and hedges? *Learner Corpus Studies in Asia and the World, 2*, 251–258.

Izumi, E., Uchimoto, K., & Isahara, H. (2003). *Nihonjin 1200 nin no eigo supikingu kopasu.* ALC. [English speaking corpus of 1200 Japanese people].

Jacobs, H. L., Zinkgraf, S. A., Wormuth, D. R., Hartfiel, V. F., & Hughey, J. B. (1981). *Testing ESL composition: A practical approach.* Newbury House.

Jarvis, S., & Hashimoto, B. J. (2021). How operationalizations of word types affect measures of lexical diversity. *International Journal of Learner Corpus Research*, 7(1), 163–194.

Jenkins, J. (2009). English as a lingua franca: Interpretations and attitudes. *World Englishes, 28*(2), 200–207.

Johns, T. (1991). Should you be persuaded: Two samples of data-driven learning materials. *English Language Research Journal, 4*, 1–16.

Johnson, S. (1997). Theorising language and masculinity: A feminist perspective. In S. Johnson & U. H. Meinhof (Eds.), *Language and masculinity* (pp. 47–64). Blackwell.

Johnson, W. (1939). *Language and speech hygiene: An application of general semantics.* Institute of General Semantics.

Jones, C., Byrne, S., & Halenko, N. (2018). *Successful spoken English: Findings from learner corpora.* Routledge.

Jönsson, A., Balan, A., & Hartell, E. (2021). Analytic or holistic? A study about how to increase the agreement in teachers' grading. *Assessment in Education: Principles, Policy & Practice, 28*(3), 212–227.

Kachru, B. B. (1985). Standards, codification and sociolinguistic realism: The English. In R. Quirk & H. G. Widdowson (Eds.), *English in the world: Teaching and learning the language and literature* (pp. 11–30). Cambridge University Press, The British Council.

Kachru, B. B. (1991). Liberation linguistics and the Quirk concern. *English Today*, 7(1), 3–13.

Kachru, B. B. (1992). Teaching world Englishes. In B. B. Kachru (Ed.), *The other tongue: English across cultures* (2nd ed.) (pp. 355–365). University of Illinois Press.

Kasper, G., & Rose, K. R. (2002). *Pragmatic development in a second language.* Blackwell.

Kekki, N., & Ivaska, I. (2022). The use of synonymous adjectives by learners of Finnish as a second language: Applying the MuPDAR(F) approach. *International Journal of Learner Corpus Research, 8*(1), 67–96.

Kendon, A. (2004). *Gesture: Visible action as utterance.* Cambridge University Press.

Kilgarriff, A. (1995). Review of D. Biber (1995), Dimensions of register variation: A cross-linguistic comparison. *Journal of Natural Language Engineering, 1*(4), 611–613.

Kobayashi, Y. (2013). Analyzing developmental patterns of vocabulary used by Japanese EFL learners: A comparison of spoken and written learner corpora. In S. Granger, G. Gilquin, & F. Meunier (Eds.), *Twenty years of learner corpus research: Looking back, moving ahead* (pp. 277–287). Presses universitaires de Louvain.

Kobayashi, Y., & Abe, M. (2016). Automated scoring of L2 spoken English with random forests. *Journal of Pan-Pacific Association of Applied Linguistics, 20*(1), 55–73.

Kobayashi, Y., Tanaka, S., & Tomiura, Y. (2011). Meta danwa hyoshiki o sosei to suru patan ninshiki o mochiita eigo kagaku rombun no shitsu hantei. *IPSJ Symposium Papers, 2011*, 51–58. [Judgment of the quality of English scientific articles based on the pattern recognition technique utilizing meta-discourse markers].

Koch, C., Lange, C., & Leuckert, S. (2016). "This hair-style called as 'duck tail'": The 'intrusive as'-construction in South Asian varieties of English and Learner Englishes. *International Journal of Learner Corpus Research, 2*(2), 151–176.

Kojima, M., & Kaneta, T. (2020). Raityingu hyoka to gengoteki shihyo no kankei: Meta bunseki ni yoru kenkyu seika no togo. In Y. Ishii & Y. Kondo (Eds.), *Eigo kyoiku ni okeru jido saiten: Genjo to kadai* (pp. 33–72). [Relationship between ratings of writing outputs and linguistic indices: Integration of research findings based on the meta-analysis].

Kosmala, L., Candea, M., & Morgenstern, A. (2019). Synchronization of (dis)fluent speech and gesture: A multimodal approach to (dis)fluency. *Proceedings of the 6th gesture and speech in interaction conference* (pp. 56–61).

Krashen, S. (1977). Some issues relating to the monitor model. In H. D. Brown, C. A. Yorio, & R. H. Crymes (Eds.), *On TESOL '77: Teaching and learning English as a second language: Trends in research and practice* (pp. 144–158). TESOL.

Krashen, S. (1982). *Principles and practice in second language acquisition.* Pergamon Press.

Krashen, S. (1985). *The input hypothesis: Issues and implications.* Longman.

Krashen, S., Butler, J., Birnbaum, R., & Robertson, J. (1978). Two studies in language acquisition and language learning. *ITL Review of Applied Linguistics, 39/40*, 73–92.

Kreyer, R., & Schaub, S. (2018). The development of phrasal complexity in German intermediate learners of English. *International Journal of Learner Corpus Research, 4*(1), 82–111.

Kuiken, F., & Vedder, I. (2021). Scoring approaches: Scales/rubrics. In P. Winke & T. Brunfaut (Eds.), *The Routledge handbook of second language acquisition and language testing* (pp. 125–134). Routledge.

Kwon, M. H., Partridge, R. S., & Staples, S. (2018). Building a local learner corpus: Construction of a first-year ESL writing corpus for research, teaching, mentoring, and collaboration. *International Journal of Learner Corpus Research, 4*(1), 112–127.

Kyle, K., Crossley, S. A., & Kim, Y. (2015). Native language identification and writing proficiency. *International Journal of Learner Corpus Research, 1*(2), 187–209.

Lado, R. (1957). *Linguistics across cultures.* The University of Michigan Press.

LaFlair, G. T., Staples, S., & Yan, X. (2020). Connecting corpus linguistics and assessment. In J. Egbert & P. Baker (Eds.), *Using corpus methods to triangulate linguistic analysis* (pp. 109–140). Routledge.

Lakew, A. K., Teshome, S., & Negede, D. (2021). Introducing corpus-informed spoken grammar instruction in EFL classrooms: The Ethiopian experience. *International Journal of Corpus Linguistics and Pragmatics, 5*(4), 487–510.

Lakoff, R. (1975). *Language and woman's place.* Harper & Row.

Lakoff, R. T. (1990). *Talking power: The politics of language in our lives.* Harper Collins.

Lange, C., & Leuckert, S. (2020). *Corpus linguistics for world Englishes.* Routledge.

Larsen-Freeman, D. (2014). Another step to be taken: Rethinking the end point of the interlanguage continuum. In Z. Han & E. Tarone (Eds.), *Interlanguage: Forty years later* (pp. 203–220). John Benjamins.

Larsen-Freeman, D., & Cameron, L. (2008). *Complex systems and applied linguistics.* Oxford University Press.

Larsson, T., Callies, M., Hasselgård, H., Laso, N. J., Van Vuuren, S., Verdaguer, I., & Paquot, M. (2020a). Adverb placement in EFL academic writing: Going beyond syntactic transfer. *International Journal of Corpus Linguistics, 25*(2), 155–184.

Larsson, T., & Kaatari, H. (2019). Extraposition in learner and expert writing: Exploring (in)formality and the impact of register. *International Journal of Learner Corpus Research, 5*(1), 33–62.

Larsson, T., Paquot, M., & Plonsky, L. (2020b). Inter-rater reliability in learner corpus research: Insights from a collaborative study on adverb placement. *International Journal of Learner Corpus Research, 6*(2), 237–251.

Lazaraton, A. (2001). Teaching oral skills. In M. Celce-Murcia (Ed.), *Teaching English as a second or foreign language* (3rd ed.) (pp. 103–115). Heinle Cengage Learning.

Le Bruyn, B., & Paquot, M. (Eds.) (2021a). *Learner corpus research meets second language acquisition.* Cambridge University Press.

Le Bruyn, B., & Paquot, M. (2021b). Learner corpus research and second language acquisition: An attempt at bridging the gap. In B. Le Bruyn & M. Paquot (Eds.), *Learner corpus research meets second language acquisition* (pp. 1–9). Cambridge University Press.

Leclercq, P., & Edmonds, A. (2014). How to assess L2 proficiency: An overview of proficiency assessment research. In P. Leclercq, A. Edmonds, & H. Hilton (Eds.), *Measuring L2 proficiency: Perspectives from SLA* (pp. 3–26). Multilingual Matters.

Lecumberri, M. L. G., Cooke, M., Wester, M., Cooke, M., & Wester, M. (2017). A bi-directional task-based corpus of learners' conversational speech. *International Journal of Learner Corpus Research, 3*(2), 175–195.

Leech, G. (1983). *Principles of pragmatics*. Longman.

Leech, G. (1998). Preface. In S. Granger (Ed.), *Learner English on computer* (pp. xiv–xx). Longman.

Leech, G. (2014). *The pragmatics of politeness*. Oxford University Press.

Leedham, M. (2015). *Chinese students' writing in English: Implications from a corpus-driven study*. Routledge.

Leńko-Szymańska, A. (2012). The role of conventionalized language in the acquisition and use of articles by Polish EFL learners. In Y. Tono, Y. Kawaguchi, & M. Minegishi (Eds.), *Developmental and crosslinguistic perspectives in learner corpus research* (pp. 83–103). John Benjamins.

Leńko-Szymańska, A. (2014). The acquisition of formulaic language by EFL learners: A cross-sectional and cross-linguistic perspective. *International Journal of Corpus Linguistics, 19*(2), 225–251.

Leńko-Szymańska, A. (2015). The English vocabulary profile as a benchmark for assigning levels to learner corpus data. In M. Callies & S. Götz (Eds.), *Learner corpora in language testing and assessment* (pp. 115–140). John Benjamins.

Leow, R. P. (2015). *Explicit learning in the L2 classroom: A student-centered approach*. Routledge.

Leow, R. P., & Suh, B-R. (2022). Theoretical perspectives on L2 writing, written corrective feedback, and language learning in individual writing conditions. In R. M. Manchón & C. Polio (Eds.), *The Routledge handbook of second language acquisition and writing* (pp. 9–21). Routledge.

Lester, N. A. (2019). That's hard: Relativizer use in spontaneous L2 speech. *International Journal of Learner Corpus Research, 5*(1), 1–32.

Leuckert, S. (2018). Adverbial subordination across variety types: A synchronic analysis of the syntax and semantics of since- and while-clauses in ENL, ESL, and EFL. In E. Seoane, C. Acuña-Fariña, & I. Palacios-Martínez (Eds.), *Subordination in English* (pp. 235–262). De Gruyter.

Lin, C-H., & Lin, Y-L. (2019). Grammatical and lexical patterning of *make* in Asian learner writing: A corpus-based study of ICNALE. *3L: The Southeast Asian Journal of English Language Studies, 25*(3), 1–15.

Lindquist, H. (2009). *Corpus linguistics and the description of English*. Edinburgh University Press.

Long, M., & Robinson, P. (1998). Focus on form: Theory, research and practice. In C. Doughty & J. Williams (Eds.), *Focus on form in classroom second language acquisition* (pp. 15–41). Cambridge University Press.

Lorenz, G. (1998). Overstatement in advanced learners' writing: Stylistic aspects of adjective intensification. In S. Granger (Ed.), *Learner English on computer* (pp. 53–66). Longman.

Lowe, R. J., & Pinner, R. (2016). Finding the connections between native-speakerism and authenticity. *Applied Linguistics Review*, 7(1), 27–52.

Lozano, C., & Mendikoetxea, A. (2010). Interface conditions on postverbal subjects: A corpus study of L2 English. *Bilingualism: Language and Cognition, 13*(4), 475–497.

MacIntyre, P. D. (1994). Variables underlying willingness to communicate: A causal analysis. *Communication Research Reports, 11*, 135–142.

MacIntyre, P., Clément, R., Dörnyei, Z., & Noels, K. A. (1998). Conceptualizing willingness to communicate in a L2: A situational model of L2 confidence and affiliation. *Modern Language Journal, 82*(4), 545–562.

Maden-Weinberger, U. (2008). Modality as indicator of L2 proficiency? A corpus-based investigation into advanced German interlanguage. In M. Walter & P. Grommes (Eds.), *Fortgeschrittene Lernervarietäten: Korpuslinguistik und Zweitspracherwerbsforschung* (pp. 141–164). Max Niemeyer Verlag.

Malvern, D., & Richards, B. (2002). Investigating accommodation in language proficiency interviews using a new measure of lexical diversity. *Language Testing, 19*(1), 85–104.

Manchón, R. M., & Polio, C. (2022). L2 writing and language learning. In R. M. Manchón & C. Polio (Eds.), *The Routledge handbook of second language acquisition and writing* (pp. 1–5). Routledge.

Mauranen, A. (2011). Learners and users: Who do we want corpus data from? In F. Meunier, S. De Cock, G. Gilquin, & M. Paquot (Eds.), *A taste for corpora: In honour of Sylviane Granger* (pp. 155–172). John Benjamins.

McEnery, T., & Hardie, A. (2012). *Corpus linguistics: Method, theory and practice*. Cambridge University Press.

McNamara, T. (1996). *Measuring second language performance*. Longman.

Meara, P. (1992/2010). *EFL vocabulary tests*. Swansea Centre for Applied Language Studies, Wales University.

Meara, P., & Milton, J. (2003). *X_Lex, The Swansea Levels Test*. Express.

Meriläinen, L. (2018). The progressive form and its functions in spoken learner English: Tracing the effects of an exposure-rich learning environment. *International Journal of Learner Corpus Research, 4*(2), 164–194.

Meriläinen, L. (2021). The interplay between universal processes and cross-linguistic influence in the light of learner corpus data: Examining shared features of non-native Englishes. In B. Le Bruyn & M. Paquot (Eds.), *Learner corpus research meets second language acquisition* (pp. 67–95). Cambridge University Press.

Meunier, F. (2015a). Developmental patterns in learner corpora. In S. Granger, G. Gilquin, & F. Meunier (Eds.), *The Cambridge handbook of learner corpus research* (pp. 379–400). Cambridge University Press.

Meunier, F. (2015b). Introduction to the LONGDALE project. In E. Castello, K. Ackerley, & F. Coccetta (Eds.), *Studies in learner corpus linguistics. Research and applications for foreign language teaching and assessment* (pp. 123–126). Peter Lang.

Milton, J. (2010). The development of vocabulary breadth across the CEFR levels: A common basis for the elaboration of language syllabuses, curriculum guidelines, examinations, and textbooks across Europe. In I. Bartning, M. Martin, & I. Vedder (Eds.), *Communicative proficiency and linguistic development: Intersections between SLA and language testing research* (pp. 211–232). Eurosla.

Moisl, H. (2020). Cluster analysis. In M. Paquot & S. Th. Gries (Eds.), *A practical handbook of corpus linguistics* (pp. 404–434). Springer.

Möller, V. (2017). *Language acquisition in CLIL and non-CLIL settings: Learner corpus and experimental evidence on passive constructions*. John Benjamins.

Mukherjee, J. (2009). The grammar of conversation in advanced spoken learner English: Learner corpus data and language-pedagogical implications. In K. Aijmer (Ed.), *Corpora and language teaching* (pp. 203–230). John Benjamins.

Murakami, A., & Alexopoulou, T. (2015). L1 influence on the acquisition order of English grammatical morphemes: A learner corpus study. *Studies in Second Language Acquisition, 38*(3), 365–401.

Murphy, B. (2010). *Corpus and sociolinguistics: Investigating age and gender in female talk.* John Benjamins.

Naismith, B., Han, N.-R., & Juffs, A. (2022). The University of Pittsburgh English Language Institute Corpus (PELIC). *International Journal of Learner Corpus Research, 8*(1), 121–138.

Nation, I. S. P., & Beglar, D. (2007). A vocabulary size test. *The Language Teacher, 31*(7), 9–13.

Nesselhauf, N. (2004). Learner corpora: Learner corpora and their potential for language teaching. In J. M. Sinclair (Ed.), *How to use corpora in language teaching* (pp. 125–152). John Benjamins.

Nini, A. (2019). The multi-dimensional analysis tagger. In B. T. Sardinha & M. V. Pinto (Eds.), *Multi-dimensional analysis: Research methods and current issues* (pp. 67–94). Bloomsbury.

O'Barr, W. M., & Atkins, B. K. (1980). 'Women's language' or 'powerless language?' In S. McConnell-Ginet, N. Borker, & R. Thurman (Eds.), *Women and language in literature and society* (pp. 93–110). Praeger.

Ochs, E. (1979). Transcription as theory. In E. Ochs & B. Schieffelin (Eds.), *Developmental pragmatics* (pp. 43–72). Academic Press.

O'Donnell, M. (2015). Using learner corpora to order linguistic structures in terms of apparent difficulty. In E. Castello, K. Ackerley, & F. Coccetta (Eds.), *Studies in learner corpus linguistics: Research and applications for foreign language teaching and assessment* (pp. 71–82). Peter Lang.

O'Donnell, M. B., Römer, U., & Ellis, N. C. (2013). The development of formulaic sequences in first and second language writing: Investigating effects of frequency, association, and native norm. *International Journal of Corpus Linguistics, 18*(1), 83–108.

O'Keeffe, A., & Mark, G. (2017). The English grammar profile of learner competence: Methodology and key findings. *International Journal of Corpus Linguistics, 22*(4), 457–489.

Olshtain, E. (2001). Functional tasks for mastering the mechanics of writing and going just beyond. In M. Celce-Murcia (Ed.), *Teaching English as a second or foreign language* (3rd ed.) (pp. 207–217). Heinle Cengage Learning.

Osborne, J. (2008). Adverb placement in post-intermediate learner English: A contrastive study of learner corpora. In G. Gilquin, S. Papp, & M. B. Díez-Bedmar (Eds.), *Linking up contrastive and learner corpus research* (pp. 127–146). Rodopi.

Osborne, J. (2011). Fluency, complexity and informativeness in native and non-native speech. *International Journal of Corpus Linguistics, 16*(2), 276–298.

Öztürk, Y., & Köse, G. D. (2021). "*Well* (er) *you know* ...": Discourse markers in native and non-native spoken English. *International Journal of Corpus Linguistics and Pragmatics, 5*(2), 223–242.

Palacios-Martínez, I., & Martínez-Insua, A. (2006). Connecting linguistic description and language teaching: Native and learner use of existential there. *International Journal of Applied Linguistics, 16*(2), 213–231.

Paquot, M. (2013). Lexical bundles and L1 transfer effects. *International Journal of Corpus Linguistics, 18*(3), 391–417.

Paquot, M., & Gries, S. Th. (Eds.) (2020). *A practical handbook of corpus linguistics.* Springer.

Paquot, M., Gries, S. Th., Yoder, M. (2020). Measuring lexicogrammar. In P. Winke & T. Brunfaut (Eds.), *The Routledge handbook of second language acquisition and language testing* (pp. 223–232). Routledge.

Paquot, M., Naets, H., & Gries, S. Th. (2021). Using syntactic co-occurrences to trace phraseological complexity development in learner writing: Verb object structures in LONGDALE. In B. Le Bruyn & M. Paquot (Eds.), *Learner corpus research meets second language acquisition* (pp. 122–147). Cambridge University Press.

Paquot, M., & Plonsky, L. (2017). Quantitative research methods and study quality in learner corpus research. *International Journal of Learner Corpus Research, 3*(1), 61–94.

Pennington, M. (2003). The impact of the computer in second language writing. In B. Kroll (Ed.), *Exploring the dynamics of second language writing* (pp. 287–310). Cambridge University Press.

Pérez-Paredes, P., & Díez-Bedmar, M. B. (2019). Certainty adverbs in spoken learner language: The role of tasks and proficiency. *International Journal of Learner Corpus Research, 5*(2), 253–279.

Pérez-Paredes, P., & Sánchez-Tornel, M. (2014). Adverb use and language proficiency in young learners' writing. *International Journal of Corpus Linguistics, 19*(2), 178–200.

Petch-Tyson, S. (1998). Writer/reader visibility in EFL written discourse. In S. Granger (Ed.), *Learner English on computer* (pp. 107–118). Longman.

Pęzik, P. (2015). Using n-gram independence to identify discourse-functional lexical units in spoken learner corpus data. *International Journal of Learner Corpus Research, 1*(2), 242–255.

Phillipson, R. (1992). *Linguistic imperialism.* Oxford University Press.

Phillipson, R. (2018). Linguistic imperialism. In C. A. Chapelle (Ed.), *The encyclopedia of applied linguistics* (pp. 1–7). John Wiley & Sons Ltd.

Picoral, A., Staples, S., & Reppen, R. (2021). Automated annotation of learner English: An evaluation of software tools. *International Journal of Learner Corpus Research*, 7(1), 17–52.

Pitzl-Hagin, M.-L. (2022, October 2). *Introducing VOICE 3.0: ELF perspectives for learner corpus research.* [Featured talk]. The 48th Conference of Japan Association of English Corpus Studies. Online.

Polio, C., & Yoon, H. (2021). Exploring multi-word combinations as measures of linguistic accuracy in second language writing. In B. Le Bruyn & M. Paquot (Eds.), *Learner corpus research meets second language acquisition* (pp. 96–121). Cambridge University Press.

Popper, K. R. (1934/2006). *Logic of scientific discovery*. Routledge.

Prodromou, L. (1998). ELT Journal correspondence. *ELT Journal, 52*(3), 266–267.

Prodromou, L. (2008). *English as a lingua franca: A corpus-based analysis.* Continuum.

Quirk, R. (1990). Language varieties and standard language. *English Today, 6*(1), 3–10.

Rankin, T. (2010). Advanced learner corpus data and grammar teaching: Adverb placement. In M. C. Campoy-Cubillo, B. Bellés-Fortuño, & M. L. Gea-Valor (Eds.), *Corpus-based approaches to English language teaching* (pp. 205–215). Continuum.

Rankin, T. (2015). Learner corpora and grammar. In S. Granger, G. Gilquin, & F. Meunier (Eds.), *The Cambridge handbook of learner corpus research* (pp. 231–254). Cambridge University Press.

Rankin, T. (2017). The distribution of reflexive intensifiers in learner English. *International Journal of Learner Corpus Research, 3*(1), 36–60.

Rankin, T., & Schiftner, B. (2011). Marginal prepositions in learner English: Applying local corpus data. *International Journal of Corpus Linguistics, 16*(3), 412–434.

Rautionaho, P., & Deshors, S. C. (2018). Progressive or not progressive? Modeling the constructional choices of EFL and ESL writers. *International Journal of Learner Corpus Research, 4*(2), 225–252.

Reder, S., Harris, K., & Setzler, K. (2003). The multimedia adult ESL learner corpus. *TESOL Quarterly, 37*(3), 546–557.

Rencher, A. C., & Christensen, W. F. (2012). *Methods of multivariate analysis* (3rd ed.). Wiley.

Ringbom, H. (1998). Vocabulary frequencies in advanced learner English: A cross-linguistic approach. In S. Granger (Ed.), *Learner English on computer* (pp. 41–52). Longman.

Römer, U., & Garner, J. (2019). The development of verb constructions in spoken learner English: Tracing effects of usage and proficiency. *International Journal of Learner Corpus Research, 5*(2), 207–230.

Romero-Trillo, J. (2002). The pragmatic fossilization of discourse markers in non-native speakers of English. *Journal of Pragmatics*, *34*(6), 769–784.

Rosen, A. (2016). The fate of linguistic innovations: Jersey English and French learner English compared. *International Journal of Learner Corpus Research*, *2*(2), 302–322.

Rühlemann, C. (2019). *Corpus linguistics for pragmatics: A guide for research*. Routledge.

Rühlemann, C., & Clancy, B. (2018). Corpus linguistics and pragmatics. In C. Ilie & N. R. Norrick (Eds.), *Pragmatics and its interfaces* (pp. 241–266). John Benjamins.

Schäfer, R. (2020). Mixed-effects regression modeling. In M. Paquot & S. Th. Gries (Eds.), *A practical handbook of corpus linguistics* (pp. 535–561). Springer.

Schanding, B., & Pae, H. K. (2018). Shell noun use in English argumentative essays by native speakers of Japanese, Turkish, and English: Frequency and rate of noun-pattern attraction. *International Journal of Learner Corpus Research*, *4*(1), 54–81.

Schmidt, R. W. (1990). The role of consciousness in second language learning. *Applied Linguistics*, *11*(2), 129–158.

Schneider, G., & Gilquin, G. (2016). Detecting innovations in a parsed corpus of learner English. *International Journal of Learner Corpus Research*, *2*(2), 177–204.

Schweinberger, M. (2020). A corpus-based analysis of differences in the use of *very* for adjective amplification among native speakers and learners of English. *International Journal of Learner Corpus Research*, *6*(2), 163–192.

Scott, M. (2020). *WordSmith Tools*. (Version 8). [Computer software]. Lexical Analysis Software. https://lexically.net/wordsmith/

Sean, W. (2021). *Statistics in corpus linguistics research: A new approach*. Routledge.

Seidlhofer, B. (2005). Key concepts in ELT: English as a lingua franca. *ELT Journal*, *59*(4), 339–341.

Seidlhofer, B. (2012). Corpora and English as a lingua franca. In K. Hyland, M. H. Chau, & M. Handford (Eds), *Corpus applications in applied linguistics* (pp. 135–149). Continuum.

Selinker, L. (1972). Interlanguage. *International Review of Applied Linguistics in Language Teaching*, *10*(3), 209–241.

Selinker, L. (1992). *Rediscovering interlanguage*. Longman.

Selinker, L. (2014). Interlanguage 40 years on. Three themes from here. In Z. Han & E. Tarone (Eds.), *Interlanguage: Forty years later* (pp. 221–246). John Benjamins.

Shatz, I. (2019). How native language and L2 proficiency affect EFL learners' capitalisation abilities: A large-scale corpus study. *Corpora*, *14*(2), 173–202.

Shatz, I. (2020). Refining and modifying the EFCAMDAT: Lessons from creating a new corpus from an existing large-scale English learner language database. *International Journal of Learner Corpus Research*, *6*(2), 220–236.

Shi, L. (2001). Native- and nonnative-speaking EFL teachers' evaluation of Chinese students' English writing. *Language Testing*, *18*(3), 303–325.

Shin, G.-H., & Jung, B. K. (2021). Automatic analysis of passive constructions in Korean: Written production by Mandarin-speaking learners of Korean. *International Journal of Learner Corpus Research*, 7(1), 53–82.

Shrout, P. E., & Fleiss, J. L. (1979). Intraclass correlations: Uses in assessing rater reliability. *Psychological Bulletin*, *86*(2), 420–428.

Signell, K. (2012). Gender-based differences in learner English: A syntax study of Swedish high school students' written production [Unpublished project paper]. Uppsala University. www.diva-portal.org/smash/get/diva2:600750/FULLTEXT01.pdf

Simpson-Vlach, R. C., & Leicher, S. (2006). *The MICASE handbook: A resource for users of the Michigan corpus of academic spoken English*. The University of Michigan Press.

Sinclair, J. (1991). *Corpus, concordance, collocation*. Oxford University Press.

Sinclair, J. (2004). *Trust the text: Language, corpus and discourse*. Routledge.

Smith, G. F., Kyle, K., & Crossley, S. A. (2020). Word lists and the role of academic vocabulary use in high stakes speaking assessments. *International Journal of Learner Corpus Research, 6*(2), 193–219.

Smith, L. B., & Thelen, E. (Eds.) (1993). *A dynamic systems approach to development: Applications.* The MIT Press.

Stormbom, C. (2018). Epicene pronouns in intermediate to advanced EFL writing. *International Journal of Learner Corpus Research, 4*(1), 1–22.

Sulistyaningrum (2018). Typical writing styles among genders: A corpus study in Asian L2 learners' academic writing. *The Asian conference on arts & humanities 2018 official conference proceedings*, 1–12.

Swain, M. (1985). Communicative competence: Some roles of comprehensible input and comprehensible output in its development. In S. Gass & C. Madden (Eds.), *Input in second language acquisition* (pp. 235–253). Newbury House.

Szudarski, P. (2018). *Corpus linguistics for vocabulary*. Routledge.

Tannen, D. (1990). *You just don't understand. Women and men in conversation.* Ballantine Books.

Thomas, M. (1994). Assessment of L2 proficiency in second language acquisition research. *Language Learning, 44*, 307–336.

Thomas, M. (2013). History of the study of second language acquisition. In J. Herschensohn & M. Young-Scholten (Eds.), *The Cambridge handbook of second language acquisition* (pp. 26–45). Cambridge University Press.

Timmis, I. (2013). Spoken language research: The applied linguistic challenge. In B. Tomlinson (Ed.), *Applied linguistics and materials development* (pp. 79–95). Bloomsbury.

Timmis, I. (2015). *Corpus linguistics for ELT: Research and practice.* Routledge.

Tizón-Couto, B. (2014). *Clausal complements in native and learner spoken English: A corpus-based study with LINDSEI and VICOLSE.* Peter Lang.

Tognini-Bonelli, E. (2001). *Corpus linguistics at work.* John Benjamins.

Tono, Y. (2007). *Nihonjin chukosei ichiman nin no eigo kopasu: Chukosei ga kaku eibun no jittai to sono bunseki.* Shogakkan. [A corpus of English essays by 10,000 junior/senior high school students: Features and analysis of students' essays].

Tono, Y. (2012). International corpus of crosslinguistic interlanguage: Project overview and a case study on the acquisition of new verb co-occurrence patterns. In T. Tono, Y. Kawaguchi, & M. Minegishi (Eds.), *Developmental and crosslinguistic perspectives in learner corpus* research (pp. 27–46). John Benjamins.

Tono, Y., & Díez-Bedmar, M. B. (2014). Focus on learner writing at the beginning and intermediate stages: The ICCI corpus. *International Journal of Corpus Linguistics, 19*(2),163–177.

Tottie, G. (2011). *Uh* and *um* as sociolinguistic markers in British English. *International Journal of Corpus Linguistics, 16*(2), 173–197.

Trafimow, D., & Marks, M. (2015). Editorial. *Basic and Applied Social Psychology, 37*(1), 1–2.

Van Rooy, B., & Kruger, H. (2016). The innovative progressive aspect of Black South African English: The role of language proficiency and normative processes. *International Journal of Learner Corpus Research, 2*(2), 205–228.

Van Vuuren, S., & Laskin, L. (2017). Dutch learner English in close-up: A Bayesian corpus analysis of pre-subject adverbials in advanced Dutch EFL writing. *International Journal of Learner Corpus Research, 3*(1), 1–35.

Verspoor, M., Lowie, W., & Wieling, M. (2021). L2 developmental measures from a dynamic perspective. In B. Le Bruyn & M. Paquot (Eds.), *Learner corpus research meets second language acquisition* (pp. 172–190). Cambridge University Press.

Voegeli, V. (2005). Differences in the speech of men and women —— Linguistic construction and performance of gender: The German subtitling of gender-specific English in the documentary *Venus Boyz* [Unpublished Thesis]. Zurich University of Applied Sciences.

VOICE (2021, October 20), Statistics VOICE 2.0 online. www.univie.ac.at/voice/stats/voice20_languages

Vyatkina, N., & Cunningham, D. J. (2015). Learner corpora and pragmatics. In S. Granger, G. Gilquin, & F. Meunier (Eds.), *The Cambridge handbook of learner corpus research* (pp. 281–305). Cambridge University Press.

Wallis, S. (2021). *Statistics in corpus linguistics research*. Routledge.

Wang, Y. (2017). Lexical bundles in spoken academic ELF: Genre and disciplinary variation. *International Journal of Corpus Linguistics*, *22*(2),187–211.

Wasserstein, R. L., & Lazar, N. A. (2016). The ASA statement on *p*-values: Context, process, and purpose. *The American Statistician*, *70*(2), 129–133.

Weigle, S. C. (1994). Effects of training on raters of ESL compositions. *Language Testing*, *11*(2), 197–223.

Weigle, S. C. (2002). *Assessing writing*. Cambridge University Press.

Weisser, M. (2018). *How to do corpus pragmatics on pragmatically annotated data: Speech acts and beyond*. John Benjamins.

Werner, V. (2017). Adversative pragmatic markers in learner language: A cross-sectional perspective. *International Journal of Corpus Linguistics and Pragmatics*, *1*(2), 135–158.

Werner, V., Fuchs, R., & Götz, S. (2021). L1 influence vs. universal mechanisms: An SLA-driven corpus study on temporal expression. In B. Le Bruyn & M. Paquot (Eds.), *Learner corpus research meets second language acquisition* (pp. 39–66). Cambridge University Press.

Whong, M., & Wright, C. (2013). Scope and research methodologies. In J. Herschensohn & M. Young-Scholten (Eds.), *The Cambridge handbook of second language acquisition* (pp. 71–92). Cambridge University Press.

Wilkinson, M. D., Dumontier, M., Aalbersberg, I. J., Appleton, G., Axton, M., Baak, A., Blomberg, N., Boiten, J-W., da Silva Santos, L. B., Bourne, P. E., Bouwman, J., Brookes, A. J., Clark, T., Crosas, M., Dillo, I., Dumon, O., Edmunds, S., Evelo, C. T., Finkers, R.,… Mons, B. (2016). The FAIR guiding principles for scientific data management and stewardship. *Scientific Data*, *3* (160018). https://doi.org/10.1038/sdata.2016.18

Willis, D. (1999, March 28–April 1). *An international grammar of English?* [Conference presentation]. 33rd IATEFL Conference, Edinburgh, UK.

Winter, T., & Le Foll, E. (2022). Testing the pedagogical norm: Comparing *if*-conditionals in EFL textbooks, learner writing and English outside the classroom. *International Journal of Learner Corpus Research*, *8*(1), 31–66.

Wulff, S., & Gries, S. Th. (2021). Exploring individual variation in learner corpus research: Methodological suggestions. In B. Le Bruyn & M. Paquot (Eds.), *Learner corpus research meets second language acquisition* (pp. 191–213). Cambridge University Press.

Xi, X., Higgins, D., Zechner, K., & Williamson, D. M. (2008). Automated scoring of spontaneous speech using SpeechRater SM v1.0. *ETS Research Report*, 8–62.

Xia, D., Ai, H., & Pae, H. K. (2022). "Please let me know": Lexical bundles in business emails by business English learners and working professionals. *International Journal of Learner Corpus Research*, *8*(1), 1–30.

Yan, D., & Bridgeman, B. (2020). Validation of automated scoring systems. In D. Yan, A. A. Rupp, & P. W. Foltz (Eds.), *Handbook of automated scoring: Theory into practice* (pp. 297–318). Routledge.

Yoon, S. (2020). The learner corpora of spoken English: What has been done and what should be done? *Language Research*, *56*(1), 29–51.

Zechner, K., Higgins, D., Xi, X., & Williamson, D. M. (2009). Automatic scoring of non-native spontaneous speech in tests of spoken English. *Speech Communication*, *51*(10), 883–895.

Zhang, J. (2014). A learner corpus study of L2 lexical development of Chinese resultative verb compounds. *Journal of the Chinese Language Teachers Association, 49*(3), 1–24.

Zhao, H., & Shirai, Y. (2018). Arabic learners' acquisition of English past tense morphology: Lexical aspect and phonological saliency. *International Journal of Learner Corpus Research, 4*(2), 253–276.

Zimmerman, D., & West, C. (1975). Sex roles, interruptions and silences in conversation. In B. Thorne & N. Henley (Eds.), *Language and sex: Difference and dominance* (pp. 105–129). Newbury House.

INDEX

Made in the USA
Las Vegas, NV
29 October 2024

86a5a094-9f98-4752-ae79-f656caa42362R01